The Death of James Dean

Warren Newton Beath

Grove Press
New York

This book is dedicated
to Zenna Lee Beath
'There are no accidents'

Published by Grove Press
a division of Wheatland Corporation
920 Broadway
New York, N.Y. 10010

First Grove Press Edition 1986
First Evergreen Edition 1988

Library of Congress Cataloging-in-Publication Data

Beath Warren, 1951-
The death of James Dean.

I. Dean, James, 1931–1955—Death and burial.
2. Moving-picture actors and actresses—United States—Biography. I. Title.
PN2287.D33B4 1986 791.43′028′0924 [B] 86-45520
ISBN 0-394-55758-1
ISBN 0-8021-3143-3 (pbk.)

Manufactured in the United States of America

10 9 8 7 6 5 4 3 2 1

'For what is your life? It is even a vapor, that appeareth for a little time and then vanisheth away.'

The Book of James

'When are you ghouls going to eat?'

Anonymous Hollywood reporter

Acknowledgements

Thanks to the following people: Charles Adams, Albert Call, Roger Cannon, Jack Douglas, Clifford Hord, Phil Hord, Ruth Hord, O. V. Hunter, Kenneth Kendall, Larry F. Minor, Ron Nelson, Maila Nurmi, John W. Stander, Ernie Tripke, and Bill Hickman.

I am also indebted to Marian Terstegge of the Tulare County Library, and the research staffs of the Bakersfield, San Luis Obispo, Salinas, and Pomona libraries. Jim Hines of the San Luis Obispo Coroner's Office was helpful in disclosing file no. 116 containing the accident reports, plus related unpublished documents, concerning the death of James Dean. Friedhelm Baas, Erster Polizeihauptkommissar of Kupferzell, Germany, contributed invaluable information which completed the story of the last years and the death of Rolf Weutherich. Alice Shafer translated the material.

Special thanks to Roger Eastman and Julian Bach, and to Edward Rae Paine and Geraldine Gleffe, my mother, who were very supportive.

The Death of James Dean

Chapter 1

There is a telephone pole in California. It stands by a highway on a grassy plain twenty-eight miles north-east of Paso Robles, which is itself two hundred miles north up the coast from Los Angeles on Highway 101. An aluminium plaque is hammered into the wood with heavy nails. It has become yellowed and rusted with rain and wind. It depicts movie idol James Dean at the wheel of the low-slung and predatory racing car he had nicknamed 'The Little Bastard'. Dean is wearing glasses, his head turned sharply to profile. The picture was taken by his uncle on the day Dean died, 30 September 1955. The wreck was at the intersection to the east.

The intersection as it existed at the time of the accident was obliterated in 1959 when the highway was widened and rechannelled with a safety island. In the early 1970s, mechanical pole lights were added to illuminate the intersection at night. Warning lights were strung overhead to wink an ominous yellow. On the road surface, in the middle of the safety lane, a group of self-styled Dadaist artists from Union City, disguised as surveyors, painted a four-colour portrait of Dean on his birthday in February 1982. He would have been fifty-two years old. The rainy months and the black scrubbing of tyres have left it a mere smoky smudge.

A mile to the west, around a curve in the highway, is the sign CHOLAME. This is the Cholame Valley. That is Cholame Creek. Those are the Cholame Hills. The name has its origin with the long-dead Chumash, the Indians who lived on this land before there was a highway and telephone poles. Past the sign, there is a grove of trees to the left where a school once stood. On the right, set off the highway, is a tiny 10 ft by 7 ft ramshackle U.S. Post Office. The little building has been there since 1935, when it was the quarters for the foreman of the road crew building the highway.

Near the highway is a tree. Snaked around it is a gleaming chromium sculpture as striking and anomalous as a spaceship settled in the desert in a 1950s horror movie. It was built and brought here from Japan in 1977 by a rich Japanese businessman named Seita Ohnishi at a cost of $15,000.

JAMES DEAN
February 8 1931 September 30 1955 p.m. 5:59

There is the symbol of infinity. The mirror surface of the steel reflects the intersection where it happened.

On Saturday, 26 September 1981, Ohnishi returns to his monument from Japan. He has brought his interpreter. The occasion is the advent of the twenty-sixth anniversary of Dean's death. He is met by Roger Cannon of Carmel, the founder of the James Dean Memorial Car Rally. Cannon presents him with a complimentary rally map and route guide. Each year, participating Dean fans retrace the route their hero took from Los Angeles on his last day.

Around 2 p.m., twenty hot-rodders pull up. They are members of Will O'Neil's vintage car club. Led by O'Neil, they, too, caravan every year from Van Nuys on the death route to meet at the cenotaph. The two rallies do not celebrate one another's arrival. The O'Neil club is more car-orientated, and the day is largely an excuse to get out and show off their restored machines. The Dean purists of Roger's rally tend to look down on them.

The 1949 Mercs and 1950 Fords clustered around the monument give it a festive air. Ohnishi has brought some Japanese lanterns, each bearing a letter. Once in place, festooned across the sculpture with coloured bulbs, they spell out JAMES DEAN FOREVER.

Ohnishi, who speaks no English, hands out small cards which read:

A TRIBUTE TO JAMES DEAN

His name was James Byron Dean. He was an actor. He died in an automobile accident just before sunset on September 30, 1955 at the intersection 800 meters east of this tree, which has long been called the 'tree of heaven'. He was only twenty-four years old.

Aside from appearing in several Broadway plays, he starred in just three motion pictures before he died: EAST OF EDEN, REBEL WITHOUT A CAUSE, and GIANT. Only one, EAST OF EDEN, had been released prior to his death. Yet, before he was in his grave, he was already a myth. With the subsequent release of the other two pictures, he became a legend.

It is fitting tribute to his brilliance as an actor that his movies continue to be shown throughout the world even today. Every day somewhere, in a cinema or on television, his image lives on, an inspiration to millions everywhere, young and old alike. His fame is international; his impact, historic. He was the brief, living manifestation of a new era, the persona to which a whole generation pinned its hopes for a better tomorrow. He was more than merely a movie star. He was, and remains, a symbol.

I am only one of many who feel strongly that James Dean should not be forgotten. There are some things, like the hatred that accompanies war, that are best forgotten. There are others, like the love inspired by this young actor, that should be preserved for all time.

Yet this monument is not intended to be merely a tribute to James Dean. It is also meant to be a reaffirmation of the value of all human life. That is why, in accordance with an old Japanese custom, this marker has been placed at the site of the accident that took his life, to serve both as a memorial to the young man I so admired and a reminder to all that life is a precious gift to be preserved at all costs.

. . . I have at long last been able to realize my dream. Having transported this monument across the Pacific Ocean from Japan where it was designed and made, I have had it erected on this spot and dedicated to this day. For me, there is no greater happiness. It is but a small token of the appreciation I feel for all that I have learned from America.

Months earlier, a woman from Shandon, the little town up the road, had approached Ohnishi saying that she owned the hulk of the old tow truck which had hauled the wreck of Dean's sports car from the roadside on the fatal day. Ohnishi had instructed his aide to peel three hundred-dollar bills from a roll and hand them to her. He had restored the truck at a Paso Robles body shop, and on this day it has been hauled on a trailer for display at the monument. Some local people say knowingly that it is the *wrong* truck, including the son of the man who owned and drove it in 1955.

A movie crew is on hand from Hollywood. It is an independent company filming scenes from a script called 'The Junkman'. It is a project which had run out of money, but they have found new backing and the cameras are rolling again. The makers claim that one hundred and fifty cars will be wrecked in the course of the story, which is a thinly plotted celebration of speeding cars and highway destruction. Dean's spirit is pervasive. The shooting locale is the vicinity of his death. Inquest photos have been obtained for inclusion, and the retired patrolman who had actually investigated the accident in 1955 will be interviewed in front of the monument. The première is to be Dean's apotheosis – the God of Fast Driving.

That night they all packed up and went home. It was the most excitement the place had ever seen. It is usually dead quiet.

Lilly Grant has been the postmaster for many years. She works from eight in the morning until two in the afternoon. When the weather is bad, or when she does not feel well, she sleeps at the post office. She has two large scrap-books in which she has taped the newspaper articles about the monument, and also letters and photos and signatures from people who have sought her out with questions. There is no one else to answer them.

Though the violent death of Dean at the wheel is a central ingredient in his myth, not even the locals seem to know exactly what happened that day in 1955. Some say he ran off the road and hit a tree or a pole. None of the Dean biographies which have been published devote more than a sentence or two to the accident itself – and most of this is misinformation. Some say that Dean's head was nearly torn from his body. Many disagree as to where the crash occurred. All give the impression that the accident was pretty much a cut and dried thing, despite the fact that there was an inquest. The only thing that everyone agrees on is that

Dean was speeding. The man who fills your tank at the Chevron station at Cholame will tell you, when asked, *'He came out of those hills like a bat out of hell.'* Yet the few living people who were closest to the events of that day have their doubts.

Though the sign outside the town says, POPULATION 65, no one appears to live in Cholame. 'Trouble is,' Lilly Grant says, 'I don't know where Cholame is. I live in Cholame, but I live fourteen miles from Cholame.' Residents are deemed such only for postal purposes. Mostly ranchers, their homes are scattered throughout the hills outside the city limit.

Besides the post office, there is a restaurant called STELLA'S COUNTRY KITCHEN. It is known for the quail and buffalo meat on its menu. It sells a few posters, T-shirts, and postcards with Dean's face on them. On the way to the lavatory, there is a bulletin board with pictures and an article which tells the story of the wreck. Near the coffee counter are faded xeroxes of the newspaper accounts of Dean's career and death. One article says that he had a premonition of the crash which killed him.

Promotion of the souvenirs is reluctant. The restaurant owner, Ed Randall, is disgusted with the whole Dean business. The visitors to the monument come in and use the lavatory and mess it up, then leave. They do not eat, nor do they buy anything. Randall would like to sell out. Like Lilly, he does not live in the village, though his son sleeps sometimes in the shed at the back.

In 1955 the building was owned by Paul Moreno. It was not a restaurant but a grocery store with two petrol pumps at the front. He operated a garage and towing service in the big tin barn next door. A deputy sheriff, he also had the only ambulance in the area. He ran the big Buick wagon out of the adjoining shed with sliding wood doors. The garage has been closed for many years, its windows broken or boarded. Its trade has been assumed by the new Chevron station a stone's throw down the road, which is run by Ed Randall's brother. A big metal sign, CHOLAME GARAGE, hung for many years over the door with its eyeless light socket where June bugs used to buzz and tick on summer nights. Fallen or removed, it now rusts against the side of the building.

In the south-east corner of the restaurant, the initials P M and the date 1953 can still be seen where Moreno wrote them in wet concrete many years ago. The land itself is now owned by the Hearst Corporation. The garage is empty except for bags of the polished stones from Japan which are stored to replenish those taken from the base of the Dean monument for souvenirs.

Sleepy and tranquil as it appears on the surface, the landscape is prone to strange and violent assaults from above and below. In 1974, the spot was singled out for a meteor shower. There are occasional earthquakes that rattle the windows of the Chevron station and ripple the walls. A geology professor from the California Institute of Technology has predicted a dubious distinction for Cholame: he believes the town will be the epicentre of the ultimate Killer California Earthquake. Kerry Sieh insists that an earthquake of a magnitude of 6.0 on the Richter Scale will hit a thirteen-mile-long segment of the San Andreas fault that winds through the hills. He is convinced this will topple other geological dominoes and set off a greater earthquake – a 7.0 or even an 8.0 – along a sixty-two-mile-long crack in the area. The locals do not worry. They generally believe they are more likely to die on the highway.

Originating at Highway 99, seventeen miles north of Bakersfield in Kern County, Highway 46 stretches west on an almost straight line for nearly a hundred miles through such isolated towns as Wasco and Lost Hills to Paso Robles in San Luis Obispo County. Though the name was shortened to Highway 46 in the 1960s, the street signs in Wasco still read 466. The landscape is flat and arid, more like Kansas or Texas than one's idea of California. Director Alfred Hitchcock used to commute by car on this route from Los Angeles to his home in Scotts Valley near Santa Cruz up the coast. When he filmed his classic *North by Northwest* in 1957, it was to this highway he returned for the famous scene in which Cary Grant is stranded on a dusty roadside and pursued across a barren field by a homicidal cropduster. Except for the dog-leg that jogs around an old section of highway up in the hills that was abandoned by the state in 1959, the road retraces the identical route James Dean drove to his death. And at the Kern County line about five miles east of Cholame, the road suddenly narrows into a little two-lane, just as it was in 1955.

Pockmarked with chuck holes, the crumbling road surface is lipped at the outside edges. There are small dirt shoulders, and no turnouts or passing lanes for motorists. Though the chief of the California Transportation Department's maintenance division claims there is 'no significant correlation between pavement roughness and accident rates', in the five-year period from 1978–81 this ninety-two-mile stretch of Highway 46 has seen 761 traffic accidents resulting in 47 fatalities.

James Dean died in 1955, yet interest in him continues unabated. He is still one of our most popular and beloved stars. As a symbol, he has come to occupy a unique place in our history and culture. Twenty-five years after his death, his name was in lights on Broadway marquees as the central figure of a controversial play. His name is frequently invoked in the lyrics of rock music. In 1983, the 1956 film *Giant* was bought by Kino Productions and released theatrically again solely on the strength of Dean's final appearance in the film. Two documents signed by Dean have been assigned a value of $7,000 by a respected appraiser. Billboards outside Sacramento invite travellers to visit JAMES DEAN'S '49 MERC at the Harrah's Auto Collection in Nevada. A sandwich is named after him in Los Angeles. The nearly three decades intervening since the release of *Rebel Without a Cause*, Dean's primary manifesto, have seen it elevated to firm cult status with disciples who know no equals in ferocity of devotion.

The same weekend which sees the car rallies at Cholame witnesses other annual tributes in Fairmount, Indiana, 2,000 miles away. Cholame and Fairmount are the two poles so magnetic to Dean fans. At the first, he died. At the second, he is buried.

Fairmount is the small Indiana town where Dean was raised by his aunt and uncle from the age of nine through his high school years. He had been born in nearby Marion, to Winton Dean, a dental technician, and Mildred Wilson. When he was a toddler, the family moved to California where Winton worked at the Veterans Hospital at Sawtelle.

When Jimmy was nine, his mother died of breast cancer. He accompanied her body on the train ride to Indiana for burial. He did not return to live with his father in Santa Monica until he graduated from high school.

Marcus and Ortense Winslow became his mother and father. He worshipped Marcus, and he called Ortense 'Mom'. The two-storey farmhouse on the Jonesboro Pike was home. It was to here that his body was returned after his highway death at the age of twenty-four. For many years, at the top of the varnished hardwood staircase, Marcus and Ortense kept Jimmy's room just as he had left it. He laughed noiselessly from a framed portrait on the bureau. His bongos were silent, while his motorcycle gathered dust in the barn of the 180-acre farm.

His grave is visited nearly every day by the awestruck. The tombstone is chipped and cracked by putty knives, hammers, and picks. The letters of his name are chiselled and gouged by the relic hunters.

The impetus for the adulation of James Dean has always come from outside Fairmount. Local participation is grudgingly conceded. The town is of two minds.

On the one hand, there are the Dean boosters. The most conspicuous is Adeline Nall. Now in her seventies, she had been Jimmy's high school drama teacher. With Hugh Caughell, Dean's old biology instructor, she will show one of Jimmy's movies on his birthday, or organize a slide show during Museum Days. She is frequently visited in her home by fans. When Hollywood actor Martin Sheen organized the Fairmount Dean tribute in 1979, Adeline was on the memorial committee. When *Come Back to the Five and Dime, Jimmy Dean, Jimmy Dean* played in New York, Adeline attended on the arm of Dustin Hoffmann.

On the other hand, there is the Fairmount Museum and organizers of Museum Days. Museum Days is held always on the weekend nearest the anniversary of Dean's death, and it sees an influx of Dean fans from the world over. And yet it is not called 'Dean Days'. James Dean is Fairmount's main, if not *only*, tourist attraction. The curious are legion. Yet the Fairmount Museum, supported mainly by subscriptions and donations from Dean fans, when it moved into the spacious and historic old Nixon House on Washington

Street, alloted only a 12 ft by 15 ft cubbyhole to Dean and his memorabilia. It is rumoured that many Dean items were kept for years under a bed in a private home, supposedly because their custodian was afraid they would be stolen if displayed.

Adeline feels she, and Jimmy, are somewhat slighted by the townspeople during Museum Days. It is significant that Adeline lives in *Marion*, not Fairmount.

The restraint cannot be entirely accounted for by Hoosier/Quaker reserve. The probable roots of this unspoken antipathy reach back to Dean's own lifetime. It was bad enough that he had gone to New York to become an actor. But a twice-told tale is that the local American Legion discovered he had registered for the draft as a *homosexual*. His family was decent Grant County bedrock, so talk was hushed out of respect and sympathy for them.

The Indiana townspeople have never been comfortable with the hysteria which followed the death of the home town boy who became a movie star. Perhaps they are not comfortable with themselves. The rabid fans who come to visit are 'crazy as hell'. 'We've seen all kinds of weirdos,' says Don Reeves, of Don and Ted's Standard station. 'While back here, they had to send the police out because some guy in a sleeping bag was laying on the grave. We've been here thirty-three years. For the first five–ten years after he died, it was a madhouse, and they're still coming.' Don should know. 'We've got the only restroom in town, so they line up to pee here. When they had the twenty-fifth anniversary, they were lined up four deep.' Brother Ted glances up from the television set in the station. 'We'd go through a roll of toilet paper every fifteen minutes.'

Yet their money is the same colour as that of sane folks. So plaques outside town advertise Fairmount as the 'home' and 'final resting place' of James Dean, while many local people spit in disgust at the delirium which has never receded, yet never quite become an accepted fact of Fairmount life.

Especially upsetting have been the strange goings on at old Park Cemetery outside the town. The nutty rites, the burning incense, the motley parades tramping about and setting up tripods on the ground in which their forefathers rest cannot sit well with the natives.

Sometime in the night of 14 April 1983, a pick-up truck pulled up next to Dean's unassuming plot in Park Cemetery. When it left, the rust-coloured headstone was gone.

Chapter 2

One day in 1947, when she was twenty-five years old, Maila Nurmi had a vision: she suddenly saw herself as much slimmer, four inches taller, and with the burning eyes and pallid skin of a vampire. She was walking into Ciro's with a blond young man following. The honey-headed boy stepped on her train. She turned her head to look back, and, in a moment, he was gone. The vision evaporated. It would be eight years before she understood the dream.

She had been born in Finland, where her father was a newspaper editor and temperance lecturer. The family had journeyed to America when she was two, settling eventually in Oregon. In spite of a strict religious upbringing, she had come to Los Angeles at the age of seventeen to live with relatives while trying to break into the theatre. She was a striking beauty with a remarkable figure. Maila easily found work as an exotic dancer up and down the west coast. She did cheesecake for Bernard of Hollywood, whose stable also included the young Marilyn Monroe. She travelled to New York to appear in Mike Todd's *Spooky Scandals* – as a dancing vampire. It was there that director Howard Hawks spotted her and was struck by her resemblance to Lauren Bacall. He brought her to Hollywood, but nothing much happened.

In 1954, she was thirty-two years old and married to television writer Dean Reisner. When they went to a costume party, Maila chose to make herself up as a sort of Charles Addams character. She made such a vivid impression on producer Howard Koch Jr that he spent the next months trying to locate her again. When he did, she suddenly found herself on television as the hostess of a late-night horror movie theatre. Vampira had been born.

Men found her incredibly and strangely sensuous – and perhaps the *strangeness* was the most important aspect.

Vampira was the eruption of a repressed childhood truth made flesh: the *bad* ladies in the comics, the evil women with the rocket breasts and red lipstick that wanted to corrupt Steve Canyon, were much sexier than the 'nice' ones.

Vampira was tall, with a 38–17–36 figure. Her raven tresses cascaded over a fantastic alabaster bosom. Her clinging gown was tattered as though she had been running through a graveyard rank with thistles. She materialized late on Saturday nights on Channel 17, slinking slowly through an ice mist and past a candelabra. As her face filled the camera, she threw her head back in a bloodcurdling banshee scream. There had never been a woman quite like her on television. She was a brilliant comedienne who knew no peer in the strange demesne she had staked out.

She reclined languorously on a death's head sofa and described her long fingernails as 'haemorrhage red'. She promoted a hospital plan for suicides called 'Yellow Cross'. She signed 'epitaphs, not autographs'. Instantly the darling of millions, she was much in demand for personal appearances. She glided regally to the dais of a beauty contest and announced to the sponsors that she had been under the impression that Rheingolds Beer was the centrepiece of a Wagnerian funeral.

Her studio cheerfully abetted her in cultivating the image off camera, as well. They provided her with an old open-air Packard to tour in with a chauffeur. She ensconsed herself imperiously in the back seat, staring straight ahead, protected from the sun by a black umbrella. She screamed at stop lights. She made sweeping entrances into the most expensive restaurants, though she could not eat even an olive or her waist cinch would pop and she would throw up.

She began to receive sacks of fan mail, and the Academy of Television Arts and Sciences nominated her 'Most Outstanding Female Personality'. *Life* magazine did a four-page layout on her. She remained a sensitive and warm-hearted woman who befriended stray cats and had an instinctive respect for genius and the spiritual world.

It was in 1954, at the height of her fame, that she met James Dean. At the time, her success far outshone his. He did not even have a car, just a red motorcycle.

Dean's first four months in Hollywood had been lonely. He didn't know anyone. He met a waitress named Connie Yaznovak. He did not love her or even like her, but she was somebody to spend time with. They spent a lot of time together, though he did not mention it in the letters he wrote to his New York girl-friend. Then *East of Eden* was released. It was not a huge hit, but everyone knew that Jimmy Dean was going to be a star.

Maila had first seen him at the Hollywood première of *Sabrina*. They had not been introduced. He had been on a studio 'date' with Terry Moore, arranged by their mutual agent, Dick Clayton. However, she did meet a young man named Jack Simmons, who obviously worshipped her and quickly became her familiar. The next day, they were sitting in Googie's, a popular hangout and coffee shop on Sunset Strip, with bit player Jonathon Haze. Maila was suddenly thrilled to see Dean outside the window. '*Jesus Christ!*' she said to Jonathon, who knew Jimmy. 'That's the only guy in Hollywood that I want to meet!'

Jack did not know Dean, but, because Maila wanted to meet him, he introduced them.

The sparks that flew were not essentially romantic. Maila and Jimmy found one another to be instinctively and intuitively similar, each responding like a sympathetic string to the other's sense of humour, no matter how outrageous. Basically Maila found Jimmy to be a clown, and she loved him for it. Once, Jimmy had run naked and screaming onto the *Eden* set when a male dresser had entered his room. Few saw the humour through their shock. In New York, his outré behaviour had been 'cute'; Hollywood, though, was a strangely moral town of appearance and pretence. There were unwritten codes of restraint and reserve. It was said that he had graduated from method school obnoxiousness to exhibitionism, but really his impulses were merely juvenile. Later, while filming *Giant*, he would walk through the Marfa Hotel lobby with unfurled pastry crullers hanging out of each nostril.

Jimmy, Maila, and Jack became close friends, convening their unofficial Rat Pack at Googie's every midnight for nearly a year. Maila would order scrambled eggs or banana cream pie. Jimmy usually just had coffee. Then they would go to Barney's Beanery, or Tiny Nailor's.

Jack and Jimmy eventually moved in together. Jimmy had had several homosexual roommates. By March 1955, when shooting started on *Rebel Without a Cause,* Jimmy had enough clout with the studio to see that Jack was given the bit part of 'Moose'. Jimmy helped Jack to get his nose fixed, though the nickname 'The Hawk' still stuck.

They were like highschool kids. The three would talk about a new song, or what was on one another's mind. They played, laughing and improvising skits. Jimmy was *fun*. He was always drawing or doodling on paper napkins. Jack Simmons saved a lot of the cartoons.

Maila recognized that Jimmy was starving for adulation and morbidly afraid of rejection. Yet there was a strong and uncompromising quality about him that was basically honest and wholesome. He was openly and unashamedly bisexual at a time when no one else was admitting it. He was attracted to – whomever. The androgynous fluidity of his features drew both men and women. Most of his relationships, though, were with women. He had never been part of the homosexual 'scene', except for a period when he was cravenly on the make with ambition. A New York co-worker had said, 'Jimmy would fuck a snake to get ahead.' Enforced attendance at gay parties with an influential producer had left him with an aversion for the 'set', so bound and constrained by their own codes of behaviour.

Jimmy was an artist first, and a sexual creature second. His thoughts turned to sex only when there was nothing more interesting to do, and there was usually *so much* to do.

Maila soon discovered a disturbing undercurrent of Jimmy's personality. She called it *mortido*, the opposite of *libido*. It was an impulse *towards death*.

Dean had always been fascinated by death. He said he would never live to see thirty. His rooms and apartments had for years been decorated with bullfight memorabilia. The bullfight for Dean epitomized man alone in the arena and *mano a mano* with death.

He had hung on his wall a Robert Capra photo of a soldier at the gasping instant of being struck by a bullet. Underneath, Dean had written the parenthesizing dates of Capra's own birth and death.

Jimmy recorded eerie monologues into his tape machine. More than reflections on death, they were darkly imaginative ramblings about what it must be like to be casketed in a dank grave.

When he returned to Fairmount for a visit, he had young Dennis Stock photograph him in Park Cemetery before a stone that read DEAN – though the Dean was Cal, his grandfather. Then he had posed before another stone that read LIFE. As a boy he had wandered and played here, drawn even then to the death in life. In town, Dean had Stock photograph him in a casket at the local funeral parlour. He produced drawings of himself as a corpse surrounded by candles.

Part of his affection and fascination for Maila was because of her own macabre sense of humour, accoutred as it was with shrouds and skulls, and even a spider named Rollo.

It was strange to her that Jimmy had such a reverence for all life except his own. Soon after she met him, and by way of introduction, he took her to his apartment. He had a noose hanging from the ceiling. He wanted her to read a story by Ray Bradbury. It was about a boy who had hung himself in his garage. He was photographed many times with ropes and nooses. He once hung a noose in the spacious back seat of Jack's Cadillac hearse. He tightened the rope around his neck, to Maila's discomfort. 'That's how I'm going to die,' he said to her. She noticed that his reference to death often involved his poor neck.

The hearse figured in other late-night escapades. Sometimes, in the dark cool hours of early morning, Jack and Maila would get in the hearse and follow Jimmy on his red motorcycle to his apartment. Jimmy would ride on the white centre line, then throw his hands over his head and hula his hips from side to side like a kootchy dancer, his thighs nearly scraping the road. Maila knew that should a car come around a curve on its way down Sunset Plaza, Jimmy would be smashed by both the car *and* the hearse. She would scream for him to stop. He would turn his head back and laugh. Jack would finally pull the hearse over and park it. That was the only way to stop Jimmy – to extinguish the footlights. He would fume because they had closed the show.

She watched him acquire and discard a succession of faster and faster motorcycles and cars in his search for the most refined instrument of the greatest speed.

Maila asked Jimmy why he wanted to die. He just grinned. It seemed to her that he was always playing a sort of Russian roulette. He thought he wanted to die, but he was not sure. He did not want to kill himself, but he wanted to risk his life. She asked whether he wanted to be closer to his mother. He said, 'No.'

It was not so much that Jimmy *wanted* to die, but that there were ways he did *not want* to die. His mother's painful and protracted death from breast cancer had made a ghastly and indelible impression on the sensitive nine-year-old. With her loss it seemed that the underpinnings of the universe were knocked out. No horror was beyond possibility. Jimmy was, in fact, terribly afraid of death. He *recognized it*. He was afraid that death would be painful and terrible. Many people with less imagination were unsettled by the *comfort* Jimmy found in the contemplation of a quick and violent death.

At the same time, the world was unfolding for him. True stardom seemed imminent and inevitable. With Maila he would read his fan mail, laughing without malice. He pretended to be blasé, but she could see that he was really thrilled. He wanted to learn to play the piano. He dabbled in dance and sculpting. He was a serious photographer. He painted. He wanted to direct. He wanted to see Europe. He discovered authors and composers.

But he saddened and tired as the year 1955 progressed. The exertion and strain of the last year and a half had been tremendous. His method in his roles was to generate what he called 'emotional memories' for himself, infusing his characters with his own hurts and painful recollections until they seemed to batten on his own psyche. The effort and toll this took was immense. Sports car racing was one of the few experiences intense enough to prick to life his jaded and numbed sensibilities. The concentration and absorption it required seemed to yank him back from morbid contemplation.

Cracks had begun to show in old friendships from the fatigue of pretence. Things were not the same. Jimmy had *arrived.* Maila had her picture taken with Jimmy at the Bakersfield sports car races, but she had asked Frank Worth, the photographer, to destroy the photos lest Jimmy think she was trying to trade on his success because her own star was on the wane. Jealousy led to misunderstanding and sniping. 'I do not date cartoons,' Jimmy said to Hedda when she linked him romantically with Vampira. Maila sent Jimmy a card in which she invited him to join her – in a grave. The friendship endured, but it was never the same.

The last time Maila saw Jimmy was ten days before his death. He told her that he might have to get in touch with her to help him light the candle. At about 10.40 p.m. on the evening of 29 September, Maila got a call from Jimmy. He said he was at the Villa Capri, his favourite restaurant. They had talked for about ten minutes when he said, 'My dinner is here, I have to go.' It was the last time she ever talked to him.

Hollywood had been shocked and saddened when Robert Francis, the Willie Keith of *The Caine Mutiny*, had been killed on 31 July in a plane crash at Burbank. Dean said, 'I'll be next.'

Chapter 3

On 30 September 1955, James Dean was awakened at 7.20 a.m. by his name being called from downstairs. Nicco Romanos was maitre d' at Dean's favourite restaurant, the Villa Capri. He was also his landlord. A month previously, Dean had rented this log house, which sat odd and anomalous among its sedate neighbours on Sutton Street in Sherman Oaks, for $250 a month, plus utilities.

It had not been easy for Nicco to find a tenant. The house had no bedroom, just a second-floor alcove. There was a seven-foot stone fireplace in the large living room, and a white bearskin rug. An old-fashioned wheel lamp hung from the beamed ceiling. Nicco's large bronzed eagle, wings outstretched and talons bared in a paralyzed shriek, and his collection of guns lent the rough walls an effect which was medieval if not downright eerie.

It seemed to suit Dean fine. He had superimposed his own clutter of bongos, underwear, and dirty dishes. The walls were hung with bullfight posters. Mounted horns adorned one wall. Matadors seemed to fascinate him, and they were frequent subjects of his doodles and idle cartoons. One of his favourite books was Hemingway's *Death in the Afternoon*.

In one corner he had his two tape machines, an Ekotape and a V-M. He had several cameras, including an 8 mm zoom Bolex. He was proud of his stereo set. The speakers were stacked almost to the ceiling, with two large horns suspended from the beams. His favourite music was Bartok, the Hungarian composer whose greatest works were produced in the last five years of his life in the triumph of a great spirit over a body wasted by leukaemia. The moody *Concerto for Orchestra* was the inspiration for the weirdly beautiful planetarium theme music in *Rebel Without a Cause*. Dean played his records so loud that they rattled the phoney

Oscar, stolen by Maila and Jack Simmons from the set of *A Star Is Born*, which graced the top of the television.

Nicco dropped by sometimes to make coffee, clean up, and check on the condition of his property, calling, 'Hallo, Jeemie,' from the floor below. When Dean was rested, he delighted in showing visitors how he ascended to his bedroom loft by a wooden ladder. But it was a pain in the groggy mornings. He staggered to the balcony, threw one leg over the railing, and jumped. He didn't say 'Good morning.' He never spoke until he had had some coffee. He sat blearily at the bottom steps in his pyjama bottoms, beating on his bongos.

He missed Marcus, his little Siamese cat, rubbing against his feet. A gift from Elizabeth Taylor, Dean had named the cat after his own Indiana uncle, the man who had largely raised him. The night before he had dropped Marcus off at the apartment of actress Janette Miller, with these instructions scribbled on the back of an envelope:

1 teaspoon white Karo
1 big can evaporated milk
Equal part boiled water or distilled water
1 egg yolk
Mix and chill
Don't feed him meat or formula cold
1 drop vitamin solution per day
Take Marcus to Dr Cooper for shots next week

Jimmy had told her he was leaving town in the morning. He was entered in the airport races at Salinas, three hundred miles to the north, with a holiday to follow in San Francisco. Then he had jumped back in his sports car, and she went back to *The Boy With the Green Hair*, which was playing on the television.

The car was new. He had had it barely two weeks. He had wanted to loosen it up and to familiarize himself with its handling. So the evening before, with car friend Bill Hickman, he had started out north on Highway 101 to open her up on the coast highway near Santa Barbara. They had turned around when the fog began to roll in. A highway patrol car had given chase, but the Spyder easily outran it.

The rest of the evening they had spent 'practising'. With Hickman as his mentor in the seat next to him, they refined the racer's repertoire of shifts and cornerings and accelerations which he would use in Sunday's airport meet. They roared up and down the canyon between Sherman Oaks and Los Angeles, with intermission for a late dinner at the Villa Capri near eleven o'clock. It was 3 a.m. when Dean returned home, exhausted, for a few hours' sleep.

He lit the first cigarette of the day, a Chesterfield. He could still taste on his tongue the last one from the night before. He looked older than his twenty-four years, for his age had been advanced cosmetically. Just the week before he had completed the last 'banquet' scenes of *Giant* at the Statler Hilton, portraying a man twice his actual age. The make-up department had shaved his hairline archly at the temples to recede it and it had not yet grown back. But the black bags under Dean's eyes were his own. In just sixteen short months in Hollywood, he had completed three intense and depleting film performances. There was Cal Trask in *East of Eden*, Jim Stark in *Rebel Without a Cause*, and Jett Rink in *Giant*. There had also been several video plays. What leisure time there had been had not been used for rest. The electrifying realization that *this was his year* and that *it was happening to him* was like neon in his veins, and in his days and nights he wore out and ran through circles of friends who could not keep up with his nearly demented graveyard shifts and dawn patrols.

He threw on faded denims and a white T-shirt, then grabbed his overnight bag. At a quarter to eight he stepped out of the front door. There, on the trailer hooked to the ball hitch of his Ford station wagon, was the Spyder.

His first sports car had been a Porsche, a production model Speedster. But he had wanted to run *real* race cars with larger bore engines, in the 1,100–1,500 cc class. In this year of 1955, the Porsche 550 Spyder owned that division. It had won the major European races and Dean had seen it come in first in the F Division at the meets at which he had participated.

A tubular framed two-seater with an air-cooled rear engine, it was dependable and had tremendous staying power on the track. The only real drawback was high pivot swing axles which aggravated weight transfer during cornering, with resultant vicious oversteer.

Originally, Dean had been impressed with the Bristol. Then Competition Motors on Vine Street, owned by Johnnie von Neumann and a gathering spot for rich car enthusiasts, had received a new Spyder. Dean's close friend Lew Bracker had been sold on the car. Rolf Weutherich, a German mechanic who was a respected race track familiar, wanted Dean to take a look at it. One spin around the block, and Dean was, as he described himself, 'a gone cat'.

He paid $7,000 for it. It was the most expensive thing he had ever bought in his life, and his very first big accoutrement of success. It was an obsessive gesture for a man who never bought anyone coffee. When he paid for his own off someone else's bill he never coughed up the tax, much less a tip.

The car was silver, the racing colour of the Stuttgart Crest. Its lines were primordial, low-slung, and rapacious as a manta ray. On Tuesday, Dean had driven it to George Barris's customizing shop in Compton for some finishing touches. The number 130 was painted on the doors and the hoods, and the two words 'Little Bastard' were painted in red across the rear cowling. It was a private joke. That was Bill Hickman's name for Dean. Hickman, almost two heads taller, was 'Big Bastard'.

Dean slid behind the wheel of the Ford and drove to Hickman's home to pick him up. Maila had no use for Bill. She thought he looked like a killer – which was prescient, as he would two decades later carve a niche for himself as a 'hit man' in such films as *Bullitt* and *The Seven Ups*. She might have been a little jealous. Bill was teaching Jimmy how to drive a racing car, and that meant that they might spend as much as thirty to forty hours a week together.

Outgoing and unaffected, Bill was oblivious of such crosscurrents of competition among Jimmy's friends. A basset-faced 'man's man', Bill was thirty-five years old and a service veteran. He had been born into the film industry. His father had been a director, and his uncle a character actor. Bill himself had made his first screen appearance in 1927. A bit player and stunt man, his biggest part had been that of Clark Gable's mechanic in the 1949 racing epic *To*

Please a Lady. There was not much Bill did not know about cars, or how to handle them. Jimmy looked up to him, and was glad Bill had accepted his plea to accompany him to his first race in the Spyder.

They drove down Sunset Boulevard and made a right turn on Vine. At 1219 North Vine, they pulled into the rear of Competition Motors. Rolf Weutherich was waiting for them.

The darkly handsome twenty-eight-year-old helped them roll the Porsche off the trailer and into the garage. Born Rudolph Karl Weutherich in Heilbronn, Germany, he was the son of a locksmith. He had flown as a Luftwaffe pilot in the last days of the war, when a desperate Hitler had conscripted even boys in their mid-teens. Rolf loved cars, and he was a brilliant mechanic. He had entered the Porsche firm as its forty-second employee on 1 November 1950. Later, he had been assigned to work as service mechanic at Competition Motors in Hollywood to help keep the temperamental cars purring for rich but impatient Americans.

The American market was a rich one, and the Porsche firm was aware that a high-performance sports car could be sold more readily in the United States than in Europe. They had even renamed the car, known in Europe simply as '550', because their American agents had said that a catchy name would help make the car familiar and ingratiate it with its new public. It became the 'Spyder', a name as old as the days of horse and buggy, when it referred to a sporty carriage of English or Irish make. Italian sports car makers used the term to denote an open two-seater in series production. The Porsche firm narrowed the designation to include only a car specially built for racing and equipped with a four camshaft engine.

The Spyders were delicate instruments requiring the finest tuning. Weutherich had experience as racing car mechanic at major European competitions. It was at a California track that he had first met James Dean. The friendship had proceeded despite Rolf's meagre English.

Dean paced the floor as Weutherich worked. 'Can I help?' he asked. 'No,' said Rolf thickly. 'You'll only complicate things.' Dean had been just as impatient as a teenager, when he would take his first motorcycle into Marvin Carter's Bicycle Shop near the Winslow farmhouse for some minor adjustment. If Marvin couldn't get to him right away, he would pout and pace, creating an atmosphere of palpable tension in which the other man would drop what he was doing to work on the bike just to get rid of the kid. Weutherich was intense and single-minded. He ignored Dean, who grinned and picked up a newspaper.

The Spyder owed its success mainly to the 'type 547' engine, the revolutionary design which elevated Porsche to world status as car builders. The brainchild of Professor Ernest Fuhrmann, it had been developed in secrecy. During practice for the German Grand Prix in 1953, a new car was seen which even *sounded* different. The Porsche men would not open its bonnet or allow the engine to be photographed. Ferry Porsche himself conferred in undertones with the drivers and mechanics. The secret was an air-cooled flat-4 with four overhead cams, two dual throat carburettors, a roller-bearing crankshaft, and dry sump lubrication. The valve gear consisted of nine shafts, fourteen bevel gears, and two spin gears. The designer described it as 'thermally symmetrical' – the engine could expand and contract with temperature changes without requiring adjustment of valve gears.

The drawback was the complexity of the engine. It took an expert 547 mechanic 120 hours to assemble one, and 8–15 hours just to set the timing. Its sophistication was intimidating. Dean had purchased the car conditionally – Rolf would have to accompany him to every race in which he participated. Competition, eager to sell the car, complied.

At a quarter to ten, Sanford Roth came through the door. In his late thirties, 'Sandy' was an ex-ad man who had become a popular photographer. His studies of Picasso and Einstein had lent his reputation an 'intellectual' polish which impressed Dean immeasurably. They had met when Roth had been assigned to photograph the *Giant* cast. Now, Jimmy was often a guest of Sanford and his wife, Beulah, in their home.

Dean was fascinated with photography and with being photographed. A serious student of his own features and expressions, it was a rare day that he was not photographed, even if it was only a picture he himself took in a mirror. Since coming to Hollywood there was no period when he did not have a semiofficial photographic Boswell who specialized in studying him in a variety of moods and poses. The *variety* was important. Dean, with strange compulsion, was driven to compile a document of himself, a photographic record of his interests, moods, and personality. Beginning with Dennis Stock, who was eighteen years old when Dean brought him to Fairmount to capture the young actor against the familiar backdrops of his boyhood past, and continuing with Roy Schatt in New York, and now Sandy Roth, each photographer had come to occupy an important place in his life. To be Dean's photographer, one had to be sympathetic, fascinated with James Dean's face and persona, and find no pose or 'scene' too self-indulgent, hokey, ridiculous, or macabre. Stock had been a little awed by Dean and was intimidated into photographing Dean in a casket. Roth, older, more established and secure, was less comfortable with himself as he humoured Dean and photographed him with a noose. In return, Dean granted fame and a sure market for the pictures.

Now, Roth was wrapping up a photo essay on Dean for *Collier's*. The shots he would take at the races and San Francisco would be the capstone of his article. Roth and Bill would drive Dean's 1955 Ford wagon to Salinas.

Jimmy had decided to drive the Spyder on the inland route to the races. The engine needed the mileage, and he would feel more confident at the race with more driving time in the new car. In addition it was a beautiful day. It was not normal practice, but little that Jimmy did was. There was no arguing with him. It was unspoken, but friend, photographer, and mechanic knew that Jimmy was the star, and Jimmy had the money. It was his show.

At ten a.m., Winton Dean, Jimmy's father, arrived. With him was his father's younger brother, Charles Nolan Dean. Charles Nolan was visiting from Indiana with Marcus and Ortense Winslow. Jimmy greeted them excitedly, then the air became subdued.

Jimmy did not get along well with his father. The obvious root of their mutual unease would be Jimmy's sense of abandonment by his father because of his early consignment back to Indiana after the death of his mother when he was nine years old. Perhaps he had felt unwanted because

Winton had not immediately married his mother, Mildred, upon learning she was pregnant. Jimmy had been born five months after the brief ceremony before a Grant County justice of the peace. But time would have smoothed these hurts were it not for something his son found unsatisfying in Winton himself. The man kept himself at a distance that could never be broached, and he maintained a reserve from which he could never be drawn to confront and answer the unspoken accusations.

Yet they were close in a strange way. Like many fathers and sons who cannot talk, they had learned to communicate *without* talking. College friends, visiting the Dean household, hearing Jimmy ask Winton for the car and being answered with a muttered evasion, would be amazed when Jimmy would smile knowingly, *'He'll do it.'*

Dean wanted to take his uncle for a ride in the Spyder. 'Take Winton,' Charles Nolan said, begging off. Jimmy knew better than to ask. 'No, you go ahead,' Winton said. Charles Nolan relented, letting Jimmy drive him two or three times around the block. They returned the car to the garage for Rolf to finish adjusting the engine.

By noon, Weutherich was wiping the grease from his hands. He fixed a safety belt to the driver's seat, but not on the passenger side. Dean would be driving alone in the race. Weutherich ran off to change his clothes. Jimmy, his friends, and his father and uncle, walked the half block to the Hollywood Ranch Market for doughnuts and coffee. They returned to Competition half an hour later.

Winton and Charles sat in the station wagon on the street to talk with Jimmy a while longer. Charles would be leaving that same day to continue his holiday in Mexico, while Ortense and Marcus would be returning to Indiana. It was about 1 p.m. when Weutherich returned, wearing light blue slacks and a red checkered sports shirt. Charles threw an arm around Jimmy. 'Be careful,' he said. 'You're riding in a *bomb.*'

Jimmy giggled. 'That's my *baby!*'

At about 1.30 p.m., Roth wanted to take a picture of Dean and Weutherich in the Spyder. Jimmy grabbed Rolf's hand and raised their arms over their heads in a sign of anticipated victory. Dean clipped a pair of sunglasses over his prescription lenses and tossed his red jacket behind the seat. The safety belt remained unfastened.

The caravan drove down Cahuenga to the freeway, Roth photographing Dean and the Porsche through the window, then through the windscreen as the racer drew ahead. They stopped at a petrol station off Ventura. Jimmy filled the tank himself. They travelled Sepulveda to the Ridge Route, the twisting Highway 99 that led through the mountains to the north.

The trip was starting out leisurely. Hickman, in the Ford, sometimes even led the Porsche. Dean had given Rolf a pair of sunglasses, but the German had forgotten them. Weutherich leaned back, eyes closed, listening to the thrum of the engine.

Dean would not let him rest. Jimmy smoked one cigarette after another. Weutherich lit them for him, hunkered low under the dash so that the wind would not rip the flame away. 'What's the rev number?' Jimmy asked. 'How's the oil temp?'

It was shortly after three o'clock when they stopped at Tips, a diner near the top of the ridge outside Newhall. Dean ordered a glass of milk. He wanted Weutherich to have something. Rolf decided on an ice cream soda. The mechanic cautioned him not to try and go too fast in the upcoming race. The Spyder was a big jump from the Speedster. 'Don't try to win,' he said. 'Drive for the experience.' Dean told him to give the signals as the Spyder went around the track.

Jimmy pulled a ring from his finger. It was an inexpensive band with a Pan American Airlines crest. He gave it to Weutherich, who tried to put it on. But his hands were too big; it only fitted his little finger.

Sandy and Bill were coming through the door. They ordered sandwiches. Bill cautioned Rolf not to let Jimmy drive too fast. 'No, no, no,' the German said, 'that is all settled.' Rolf quickly became a poor fourth in their conversation.

As they were leaving, a waitress stopped Weutherich. 'Was that Jimmy Dean?' she asked. He nodded, and she ran to tell her friends.

The wagon and the sports car headed north on Highway 99. They crossed the line into Kern County. The brown hills levelled onto flat, dusty plains broken only by an occasional field of cotton, or the clustered tanks of an oil refinery. Hollywood was being left far behind. Except for the other racers he might meet on the road or at the checkpoints, no one else Jimmy Dean would meet on this day would recognize his face. The name would be vaguely familiar only because it was the same as that of a country and western singer.

California highway patrolman Otie V. Hunter was working the 2 p.m. to 6 p.m. shift, policing State 99 in southern Kern County. He was on Wheeler Ridge, cruising south toward the county line. He passed Mettler station, which consisted of the Ranch House Cafe. Ahead was the Grapevine, the last stretch of mountain highway descending steeply and clearly visible in the shimmering air. It was nearly 3.30 p.m.

As soon as he saw the silvery little car coming down the slope he knew it was speeding. The highway was two lanes in either direction. The sports car passed in the northbound lane. Hunter glanced in the rear mirror and whipped the patrol car across the gravelly median to take up pursuit. He saw that the little car was not travelling alone. There was a Ford station wagon with a trailer following closely at the same speed. Hunter glanced at his speedometer. He clocked them at around 70 m.p.h. across the flat plain. The speed limit was 55.

Hunter pulled out and passed the wagon. Then he slipped between the racer and the Ford, snapping on the flashing overhead lights. He tapped on his horn to get their attention, motioning for the men in the wagon to pull over as well. The Porsche responded immediately.

Great, thought Dean. The papers would love this if they picked it up. He had just finished filming a highway safety spot in which he had been interviewed by Gig Young.

'Jimmy,' Gig had asked, 'we probably have a great many young people watching our show tonight, and for their benefit, I'd like your opinion about fast driving on the highway. Do you think it's a good idea?'

Dean had muttered uneasily, 'I used to fly about quite a bit, you know, took a lot of unnecessary chances on the highways. Then I started racing, and, uh, now I drive on the highways, and, uh, *extra cautious* – no one knows what they're doing, and half the time you don't know what this guy's going to do, or that one – I don't have the urge to speed on the highway. People say racing is dangerous, but I'll take my chances on the track any day, than on the highway.'

Young had seemed relieved. Dean's slightly ridiculing manner at the beginning of the dialogue had intimidated him. He had not been sure Dean was going to co-operate. There was one last question. Gig asked, 'Do you have any special advice for the young people who drive?'

Dean had turned at the door. 'Take it easy driving. The life you save, *may be mine*.'

He was aware that his recklessness in cars and on motorcycles was already legendary. The great actor Alec Guinness had told Dean he was going to break his neck in the new Spyder. But Dean curbed his bad-boy road antics around the seasoned race drivers who were his heroes. The mere fact that you liked to speed did not qualify you to race competitively in closed events, as had Dean. The first mistake you made on the course, no matter where, was duly recorded by an official and relayed to the start-finish line. If the mistake merited it, the driver would be black-flagged and sidelined until he explained his action. He might then be allowed to continue, or he could be suspended for several races. Dean was qualified, though the opinions of his driving varied. Some thought him reckless, some thought him over-cautious. Hickman was sure Dean was going to be a great driver. In any case he had completed or run in several races, and was entered and accepted to race at Salinas.

Hunter had walked up to the racer. The officer was 6 ft 2 in. tall. Jimmy was looking at his knees.

Hunter asked Dean for his licence, then told him he was being cited for excess speed. He had been doing 65 m.p.h. in a 55 m.p.h. zone. When he asked Dean his place of business, the response, 'Warner Brothers,' made no impression. The young man did not look remarkable. He could have been an electrician or stage hand. The handsome young Hunter looked more like a movie star than Dean.

Jimmy said that he was on his way to the races at Salinas, and that the car had only three hundred miles on it. He was driving it to loosen the engine up. 'It won't run right under eighty,' he told Hunter.

Hunter handed him the ticket in reply. Jimmy wrote 'James Dean' and handed it back. Hunter was curious about the car. They talked for a minute. Dean was pleasant. Hunter cautioned him to slow down, then walked back to cite Hickman in the Ford. Bill's ticket was for 65 m.p.h. too, but he was 20 miles in excess of the speed limit. The statute specified 45 m.p.h. for vehicles towing trailers.

Hunter walked back to his Oldsmobile patrol car. The Spyder and the wagon pulled into traffic and continued north. Officer Hunter headed back south.

Fifteen minutes later, the Spyder drove up the broad palm-lined boulevard of Union Street under the large arch reading BAKERSFIELD. The air was warm. At Stan's Coffee Shop on the 1900 block, full-course dinners were $1.35 and upwards. Dean and Weutherich stopped for several lights, nonchalant despite the curious stares of the locals. Though Bakersfield was a racing town, the 550 was not a car normally seen on the street. The red sobriquet 'The Little Bastard' on the rear hood was not calculated to make it inconspicuous. It was a 'screw you' sort of car.

On their way out of town, they saw that *20,000 Leagues Under the Sea* was playing with *Wyoming Renegades* at a local drive-in. *East of Eden* was scheduled to start next Tuesday, when the shows changed. They crossed the Kern River and followed the railway tracks on their right.

A few minutes later, near the Shafter turnoff, Dean saw a large hangar off to his left, and some old U.S. Air Corps barracks. It was Minter Field, where he had raced in a meet previously.

That earlier meet had been a disaster. He had driven a hundred miles to the race, even bringing some friends to cheer him on, only to blow a fuel pump. Jack Douglas, a comedy writer for Jack Paar, had been there that day to compete. He found Dean's reaction strange. The boy had been reduced almost to tears, though it was not his fault.

When Dean had come to Minter Field, however, it was with glorious results. It had been 1 May, almost five months before. In fact it was the last time he had raced on a course. Squalls and cloudbursts had made the track muddy and treacherous. Turn number three had been especially dangerous. Soaked with rain, the bales that channelled and buffered that corner had become hard and heavy. The outer edge was spongy turf. Instead of sliding into a safe spin-out, drivers who oversteered would trip and roll.

Three cars crashed on the curve that day. Jack McAfee had been leading in his race when he lost his Ferrari on the turn. He escaped with bruises. Arizona driver Jack Drummond was not as lucky. He had been killed when his car flipped.

Jimmy had been entered in the San Luis Trophy Race, a six-lap event for 750–1,500 cc cars. He had placed third with his white Speedster, after Playan in an M.G. Special and J P Kunstle in a Panhard. It had been a wonderful moment.

The meet had been held during the filming of *Rebel.* Right afterwards he had started work on *Giant* for George Stevens. His contract had forbidden him to race for the duration of filming. 'What if you break a leg?' Stevens had asked Dean. Jimmy smiled. 'You mean, what if I break my neck?' He had complied, but as soon as his major scenes were wrapped up it became obvious where his mind had been all the time. He had just signed a $100,000 a year contract with the studio, and the first thing he did was to buy his dream car and enter the next race.

The lesson of that blustery March day at the Shafter Airport had not been lost on Jimmy. The big 25-lap event had been won by Johnnie von Neumann – in a 550 Spyder. This weekend, Dean would be racing against von Neumann himself. He would also be running against Kunstle, who had edged him out of second place. But this time, Dean would be in the Spyder.

Seventeen miles north of Bakersfield, Dean turned west on to Highway 466 at Famosa, a little diner where truckers and patrolmen congregated under a few tall palms. The road narrowed and was straight as a rifle shot. Dean came upon Jack Douglas, towing his Jaguar on a trailer. Jimmy honked his horn, roared around him, and soon disappeared in the distance.

The land was flat and dry. Outside the little town of Wasco the country became even more desolate. Black oil pumps seesawed on both sides of the highway. Tumbleweeds were caught and heaped against the thorny barbed wire that often lined the shoulder. Dean opened the Spyder up, the speedometer needle climbing past 100 m.p.h.

The highway was not deserted. There were quite a few cars. In Jimmy's own lane were the race-bound weekenders towing their sports cars. In the eastbound lane were Paso Robles area families en route to Friday night's big high school football game between the Drillers and the Bearcats. Dean zipped in and out of his lane as he passed the slower cars, which included nearly everything on the road. Bill and Sandy fell far behind.

It was after five o'clock when Dean saw several large, grey cedar trees looming up on the horizon. He slowed. It was Blackwell's Corners, a little petrol station and grocery store at the crossroads of Highway 33 and 466. Jimmy caught sight of Lance Reventlow's 300 S.L. Mercedes parked under the weathered RICHFIELD petrol sign. He braked the Spyder suddenly and swung in beside the other sports car.

Reventlow was the baby-faced twenty-one-year-old son of Woolworth heiress Barbara Hutton. Lance was also racing this weekend, and was travelling with fellow driver Bruce Kessler. Dean jumped out to find them, while Rolf stretched his legs and watched Highway 466 to flag down Hickman in the wagon.

Jimmy was laughing with Lance and Bruce, bragging that he had got the Spyder up to 130 m.p.h. Weutherich spotted the Ford and signalled it over. Sandy bought a bag of apples and offered one to Dean. Jimmy crunched into it, leaning against the weathered side of the station. He had bought a Coke. His face was sunburned around his glasses.

'How do you like the Spyder now?' Sandy asked.

Dean said, 'I want to keep this car for a long time – a real long time.'

Bill wanted to talk to him. He looked seriously into his eyes. 'Be careful of the cars turning in front of you,' he said. 'The Spyder's hard to see, and it's getting near dark.'

Jimmy took the cigarette from Bill's mouth and hot boxed it, his eyes laughing.

'Don't worry, Big Bastard,' he said.

A young man was admiring the Spyder. Jimmy asked him

if he wanted to race. The kid shook his head. Dean finished his Coke.

They decided to stop for dinner in Paso Robles, almost sixty miles up the road. It would be after six o'clock. Then they would head north on Highway 101, the highway that would take them the last hundred miles north up the Salinas Valley, the locale of *East of Eden*. The silver Spyder slid out onto the road that shot across the broad and blistered plains.

John W. Stander was driving his wife and teenaged daughter to the football game in Bakersfield. He heard a high-pitched whine that grew into a roar, and then something passed him in a blur. The other car had seemed almost invisible. It was 'mousey' coloured in the softening light of the sun setting behind the hills at their back.

There was a gradual curve, and Dean and Weutherich could see the highway rising ahead of them for miles up to the distant rolling hills. They crossed the line from Kern into San Luis Obispo County. Jimmy followed the narrow ribbon through the hills, shifting down to trace the tight meanderings of the curves of Polonio Pass.

Chapter 4

Donald Gene Turnupseed, at twenty-three years of age, was a year younger than James Dean. He had been born in Porterville, California, a small rural town snuggled against hot and rocky foothills in the eastern Central Valley.

His father, Harley, had been born in Florida and came to California in 1924 by way of Wichita Falls, Texas, where he had learned to install automatic telephone exchanges. He first settled in the Imperial Valley, and then moved to Tulare, about sixty miles north of Bakersfield, where he had an aunt and uncle. He got a job doing repair and service for Jim Murdock at Murdock's Electric. He found a sweetheart. He married Ruth Bunch in September 1929, almost a year before the Indiana marriage of Winton Dean and Mildred Wilson. After nine years at Murdock's, Harley and Ruth moved to Porterville. They had been married four years when Donald was born.

There followed a move to nearby Visalia, then back to Tulare, where Harley worked at the Harry Crow Hardware Store on South J Street. He bought the owner out in 1947. Two years later, he incorporated. Ruth still worked as a career nurse.

Young Donald helped out at the shop. In 1952, at the age of twenty, he enlisted in the navy. He served most of his time on a hospital ship in Korean waters. In New York, James Dean was experiencing the first flush of success and recognition in the theatre for his portrayal of a seductive homosexual boy in *The Immoralist*. In April 1955, Don had completed his hitch and was discharged. Dean was in Hollywood, filming *Rebel Without a Cause*.

Don planned to continue his education, for the qualifications required for an electrical contractor's licence were rigorous. He was going to follow his father into the family business. He enrolled as a freshman at the California

Polytechnic Institute – known as Cal Poly – in San Luis Obispo, about a hundred miles to the south and near the coast. He would be going to school on the G.I. Bill, majoring in electrical engineering. By September, when Jimmy Dean was finishing the shooting on *Giant*, Don was attending his first classes.

To make the long drives back and forth from the college to home, Don had a 1950 Ford Tudor. It was a nice car. It was painted a two-tone black and white. He endured some joking about its resemblance to a police car. It had been jazzed up a little: fender skirts and other post-factory customizing had been added to make it look like the more expensive Crestliner, the top of Ford's line.

Around 4.30 p.m. on the Friday afternoon of 30 September, Don packed a few things and got into his car. He was heading home to Tulare for the weekend. It had been two weeks since he had seen his family, or had a home-cooked meal. He headed north out of town and up Highway 101 to Paso Robles. There he crossed the concrete bridge over the Salinas River and headed east on Highway 466. The road swept over the many dips in the undulating hilly landscape.

It was a little after 5.30 p.m. when he slowed to pass through the little town of Shandon. He picked up speed on the outskirts. Dry arroyos cracked through the hills and the highway levelled and straightened. The sun was to his left. A sign told him Cholame was up ahead.

Chapter 5

James Dean and Rolf Weutherich followed Highway 466 around the steep hillsides as the white guardrails whizzed past. Just over the top of the mountains, the road straightened into a series of hillocks that rose and fell dizzily before dropping a hundred feet in a mile straight as a plumb shot across the grassy plain of the Cholame Valley. Dean shifted into fourth gear. The dropping sun flared in their eyes directly to the west. From the rollercoaster tops of the last two knolls they could see Highway 41 like a line drawn with a ruler across the dry windswept expanse from the north-east to cut into Highway 466 at the bottom of the valley a mile and a half distant. It was an exciting sight, the sudden unfurling of the open road. The air from the coast was suddenly cooler. Dean pressed the accelerator and the 547 engine roared and vibrated through their spines.

Three miles to the south-west on Highway 466, Tom Frederick, a twenty-eight-year-old beekeeper from Shandon, and his brother-in-law, Don Dooley, were nearing Cholame. They were dressed casually and were en route to that evening's high school football game in Bakersfield. The Paso Robles Bearcats, for whom they were rooting, were having a championship season, and local fervour was running high. The Bakersfield Drillers would make it a grudge match; the Bearcats had dealt them one of their only three losses the previous season. Tom's brother, Paul, and his wife, were following in their car. The men laughed and chatted with the women in the back seat. Up on the left was Moreno's CHOLAME GARAGE with its sides of corrugated sheet metal, and the little country grocery store with two petrol pumps at the front. Across from the tiny post office was a grove of tall trees sheltering the little elementary school. A blink, and the 'town' was in the rear-view mirror.

The two-tone 1950 Ford Tudor with whitewalls which had come up behind now pulled out across the white line and began to overtake them. Its driver, a lean, clean-cut-looking kid, seemed in no particular hurry, passing them at about 60 m.p.h. Frederick and Dooley watched the rear of the tub as it pulled away. They were nearing the north-easterly curve which anticipated the 'Y' intersection of Highways 466 and 41. They knew they were more than eighty miles from Bakersfield, but the game wouldn't start till eight o'clock. It would be dark pretty soon.

A mile ahead and travelling the same direction, an east-bound Pontiac had passed the 'Y' intersection and was starting up Antelope Grade. Behind the wheel was a fifty-year-old farmer, Clifford Hord. His young boy and girl were in the back seat, and, beside him, his wife Ruth was knitting a black lace shawl for their daughter. Her forehead was pinched in concentration on the intricate fine point in her lap. They were also on their way to the football stadium in Bakersfield to cheer on the Bearcats. Since leaving their house outside Paso Robles, they had passed forty or fifty wagons or trucks towing sports cars to Sunday's Salinas airport race.

The road was rising slightly. They had travelled it many times and prepared their stomachs for the dips, the two little knolls where the narrow highway dropped, rose, and sank again to rise on a hill. Hord was cruising steadily at 60 m.p.h. There was a car behind him, and another coming toward him in the westbound lane. The Pontiac was almost to the four trees, two on each side, which stood like sentries at the top of the first little rise.

In the westbound lane, a Pasadena accountant named John Robert White was driving towards Paso Robles. A silver sports car had appeared in his rear-view mirror. The blond driver gunned its engine, which whined angrily, suddenly louder in his open window as it began to pass him at high speed.

Clifford Hord couldn't believe his eyes. A shiny little car had appeared at the top of the hill, had vanished for an instant behind the car ahead of it, and now had lurched abruptly in a sideways manoeuvre into their lane. 'Look at this sonovabitch!' Cliff spat. Ruth and the children glanced up at the same time. Hord saw that the little car wasn't going to make it around the other car in time – there wasn't room. It was coming straight at them. He jerked the steering wheel and the Pontiac rocked in the bumps and pot-holes of the roadside; he was afraid to hit the brakes in the loose gravel of the dirt shoulder. For less than a second, the three cars passed abreast, the Spyder in the middle with its left wheels clear off the road, spitting gravel at the Pontiac. Hord swung back onto the surfaced highway and felt a rush of anger. Another second, and they would have crashed head on. The road was now banked steeply on both sides. He glanced in the mirror; the blond driver and his dark companion had their heads turned, looking back.

The sports car's speed had seemed terrific. The Hords had just returned from Bonneville Flats where they had watched the fastest machines in the world challenge the land speed record. Clifford had seen some clock out at 130 m.p.h. It seemed the little car had been going at least that fast. The anger hit again, then relief. 'I'm glad Phil wasn't right behind us,' he said. Their oldest son and three of his friends were also on the road to the football game, but they had left a little later.

Ruth's hands were trembling and she could not pick up her knitting. She had been sure it was *the end.* When she closed her eyes she saw again the thing that had shocked and frightened her: the two boys in the car had been grinning from ear to ear as they watched the Pontiac veer off the road. She would never forget that smile and the blond hair snapping in the wind.

John Robert White sensed trouble. He saw eastbound traffic approaching the intersection in the distance and it seemed to him the sports car was going far too fast to stop if any of those cars turned off in front of it.

The Ford was coming up on the intersection. It was a marking place for motorists driving from the coast to the Central Valley. It was the point where the highway split and

Highway 41 veered off leftward. The student had driven through many times. Now, home was just an hour away.

He passed the little Parkfield Road and there was the highway sign on his right with an arrow pointing straight ahead, BAKERSFIELD 84, and an arrow to his left, HANFORD 64. The junction was known locally as the 'Y'. It was a typical rural intersection, but it was more dangerous than most. It was unlighted and it was heavily travelled. Most traffic inland from the Central Valley to the coast passed through its narrow conduit. Highway 466 was a popular route from the Los Angeles area to Monterey and San Francisco. The only STOP sign was at the line where westbound Highway 41 traffic was supposed to pause before entering the stream of Highway 466. There were phone poles on both sides of the road. Taut barbed wire was strung on metal stakes to keep in the Jack Ranch cattle which mooed and swatted lazily out on the flat, dung-spotted plain. The dry scar of a wash in a natural depression passed under the highway and spread out on both sides in baked mud pocked with hoof prints. There had been several fatal collisions at the intersection in the past.

There was no left turn lane. The Ford began to head across the white line toward the Highway 41 turnoff. He was not yet at the intersection. He eased the car leftward.

He was straddling the white line when he slammed on the brake pedal suddenly. The rear wheels locked and the Ford slid for thirty screaming feet. The screaming stopped and it crossed further into the other lane. The brakes froze again.

John Robert White watched in horror as the Spyder swerved suddenly. Its brake lights did not flash.

James Dean's leg went rigid to the floorboard in a convulsive reflex. His face contorted as he wrenched the wheel. The bullet-nose grillwork of the Ford was as huge as a drive-in screen.

The student jerked the wheel hard to the right. A sledgehammer crash threw him into the windscreen where he saw an arm fly up over his hood, fist upraised to protect someone's head, and then, crazily, he was looking down into the seat of a small sportscar before it vanished.

Frederick, Dooley, and their wives saw the big car and the little car hit with a bang. The Ford and Spyder were suddenly compressed together. Rolf's hands flew up and his head smashed into the dash. Then the left front fender of the Ford came away and the Spyder flew up.

White saw it smash into the ground two or three times in horrible cartwheels. Frederick, fifty yards away, slammed on his brakes to avoid the Ford, which had slid on in the westbound lane, past the intersection, smearing skid marks until the exploded left front whitewall tyre slipped off the rim and the naked wheel caught the highway. The rear end pivoted and came to rest.

The Spyder landed with a thud next to a phone pole, scooping dirt that flew up to land in fresh clots on the crushed aluminium skin. Frederick pulled off onto the shoulder opposite the Porsche. He got out, and Dooley followed him. There was silence. Another car pulled over in the westbound lane. John Robert White paused, then sped up the road to find a phone. Tom looked both ways and walked across the highway toward the Spyder.

The student was stunned. The steering wheel was in his chest. He was looking through a split and cracked windscreen. His nose began to hurt. It was gashed and bleeding. There was tremendous pain in his left shoulder. His knees shook. He became aware that the broadside of his car was exposed to oncoming traffic.

Tom Frederick saw an injured man on the ground six feet from the driver's side of the Porsche. The man had dark hair, and he was moving. There was another man still in the car. Tom didn't look closely after the first glance. He saw blood and limp arms that were twisted and bent the wrong way.

The driver of the Ford was stepping gingerly out of his car. He was rubbing his left shoulder, stretching and working the left arm in tentative circular motions, but he seemed to be okay. Tom flagged down another car which had slowed and sent it west up the highway to Moreno's garage. Paul Frederick had pulled up. He slid between the Porsche and the barbed wire fence, kneeling by the head of the most seriously hurt of the young men. He didn't want to turn or lift the blond man in the white T-shirt. He was obviously grievously injured. Paul placed his sunglasses under the man's nose. There was no breath to fog the lens.

Another eastbound car had pulled off the highway. In it

was a woman named Coombes, and her daughter. They, too, had been on their way to the football game. Mrs Coombes was a nurse. She got out and hurried to the flattened wreck of the sportscar. She recognized quickly that the boy in the car had a broken neck. She pressed a forefinger to one of the wrists that dangled on limp arms over the door. There was a faint pulse.

The ashen student told Tom, 'I couldn't see him.' Tom felt awkward. 'I couldn't see him, either,' he said. Someone said that a boy was dead or dying in the car. Don would not go near. His arm throbbed in waves of pain.

Seventeen-year-old Phil Hord had been following about two miles behind his family's Pontiac. His pal Richard Bradford was with him, and two other high school buddies. They came around the curve and saw the other cars pulled off the highway. Phil slowed. There was a Ford turned around blocking the other lane. Car parts were strung along the pavement. Dust still drifted up from the shoulder and out into the field. A clump of people stood confusedly around a smashed car. Phil parked. The boys walked across the road.

The little car had landed facing west, the direction it had been headed. A man in a red T-shirt lay on the ground near its left side. Close by was a black racing seat that had been ripped loose. A couple of yards further was the white fender which had been torn from the Ford. Something was wrong with the man. He was raised up on his stiff arms in a push-up position. He stared ahead, terrified and wide-eyed, but he did not see the people walking around him. He saw nothing, or else what his horrified eyes saw no one else could see.

The Spyder had come to rest right side up fifteen feet off the highway. The bonnet had sprung open and the boot gaped wide, exposing the hot engine. The left front tyre had burst on the rim. The left side was mashed like a swatted insect; the right was almost undamaged. The impact had squeezed the car like a triangulated accordion; the bent and twisted steering wheel had been pushed over to the passenger side.

A man was still in the car, his white T-shirt torn and streaked with blood. Dean had been lifted from his seat and thrown backwards. His right hip rested on the cowl. He lay on his back, limp arms outstretched. His head hung sickeningly over the passenger door at almost a right angle. Phil recognized Mrs Coombes, and he heard her say that the man was dying.

The boys walked toward the Ford. Its engine block was broken and the motor was pushed up almost to the seat.

Phil told Richard he ought to take a picture. The camera was in the car. It was a good camera, too. The boys argued back and forth. Richard said that the camera was school property, and so was the film. It was for taking pictures of the football game for journalism class. He was afraid he would get into trouble.

Cars were pulling over, or picking their way cautiously past the broken Ford. Someone held up a hand to slow the oncoming westbound cars, then directed them through the other lane and around. John Robert White had returned. There was a siren. Heads turned. Around the curve from the west came flashing top lights. As it drew closer, Phil saw that it was the ambulance.

It was one minute to six o'clock. California highway patrolman Ernie Tripke was just coming on duty in Paso Robles when he received the call. A navy veteran, he had joined the C.H.P. in 1948 at the age of twenty-five. His original assignment had been east Los Angeles before he was transferred to Paso Robles. The accident was in his beat, which extended to the county line. He sped east out of town on Highway 466.

Patrolman Ron Nelson also heard the call. The tall, handsome young ex-machinist was a friend of Ernie's and worked the same shift. It sounded like a bad one. He hit the siren and headed out to the intersection to lend a hand.

The two-tone Buick ambulance was pulling up opposite the Porsche in the westbound lane. Two hundred and fifty pound Paul Moreno jumped out, followed by his assistant, Collier 'Buster' Davison. They were an odd pair: Moreno was huge, neckless, and bullet-headed under a crewcut, his thick forearms hairy and muscular, while Buster was bony and rail-thin. Moreno, forty-one years old, owned the garage and grocery store at Cholame. He was also a deputy sheriff. All ambulance attendants in the county were deputized.

They quickly opened the right-hand rear door of the ambulance and removed two gurneys from their racks. They left one on the highway and carried the other as they ran to check the injured. The two boys on the north side of the road were hurt badly. Moreno had only the most basic emergency medical training, but he believed the boy in the car was dying.

Ernie Tripke pulled up in his patrol car, siren wailing. It was twenty minutes past six. Ron Nelson arrived moments later. He saw that Ernie had his hands full with the injured. Ron set out flares and began to identify witnesses to find out what had happened.

Moreno had a problem. Dean was pinned in the wreckage of the Porsche. His foot was entangled in the clutch and brake. One of his trouser legs was ripped away as from a blast.

Jack Douglas was coming down the slope. Had he recognized the mangled metal as Jimmy's Porsche, he would have stopped. But he didn't look very closely. It was bad for morale to inspect car crashes when you were on your way to a road race. He drove on.

Sanford Roth and Bill Hickman, in Jimmy's Ford wagon, were coming up to the intersection. To Roth, it looked like a road block ahead. He saw the 1950 Ford and the ambulance and police cars. His heart started to pound in his chest with a premonition. He found the little Porsche off to the side. It looked like a crumpled pack of cigarettes. Hickman numbly pulled the wagon over, then jumped out and ran to the sportscar. Roth followed. Jimmy wouldn't make it, he saw. His head had been thrown back too far. Bill held Jimmy in his big arms, terrified as he yelled to him, trying to get the attention of the unfocused eyes.

The student saw the wagon pull up, trailer in tow. He heard Roth tell the patrolman that the man in the wreckage was Jimmy Dean. He had been on his way to the races in Salinas. The only Jimmy Dean Tripke had ever heard of was the country and western singer.

Roth took a picture of Dean in the car, then another. Bill Hickman, desperate with his helplessness to stop the life ebbing from his friend, saw the camera and was flushed with rage. *'You son of a bitch!'* he roared, *'Help me, come here, help me!'* Jimmy seemed to stir suddenly, almost as if he were going to say something. There was a small convulsive stiffening, and a rasping sigh from the lips. It was the air leaving Jimmy's lungs. His head fell over. Hickman knew he had just seen his friend die, but he could not believe it.

Moreno worked Dean's foot loose. With Davison's help, he lifted the limp body onto the gurney and covered him with a blanket. They strapped him in. Roth snapped another picture as the two men hurried the stretcher to the yawning ambulance door, Davison in the lead at the head, his wattled neck twisted to see where he was going.

Tom Jespersen had pulled up. He wore jeans and a black T-shirt. His mother had owned the store in Cholame before she had sold it to Moreno. Jespersen stood and watched, his thumbs hooked in the pockets of his jeans. There was nothing else to do.

Moreno and Davison returned with the gurney, moving quickly to lift Weutherich. Roth, twenty feet away, snapped another picture, catching the bizarre tableau: the broken Rolf, the intent ambulance attendants, and the stunned driver of the Ford, his thumbs hooked in the pockets of his jeans.

Rolf was strapped in, then hurried across the highway to be slid into the ambulance next to Dean. Buster crawled into the back and Moreno slid behind the wheel. The Buick turned sharply in the road, siren screaming, and they headed west to Paso Robles and the nearest hospital, War Memorial, twenty-eight miles away. Sandy and Bill jumped back in the Ford wagon and sped after them. Dusk was falling quickly.

Officer Nelson was taking a statement from Frederick and Dooley. Then the young beekeeper stood by as the student confirmed that he had been the driver of the Ford. With the removal of the injured, the centre of interest had subtly and instantly shifted.

'What happened?' Nelson asked.

Tripke stood close to the student, but he could smell no liquor on the young man's breath.

'I was going to turn. When I got to the intersection, I started to slow down. Just before I made my turn, I looked straight down 466 but didn't see the car. I was already in my turn when I heard the tyres and saw him. I tried to miss him, but I couldn't.

'How fast were you going?'

'About 55 miles per hour.'

The student showed them his driver's licence and gave his Tulare address. While the officers talked to John White the student heard the accountant say that the sports car had passed him up the road at quite a bit of speed.

The ambulance raced around the curve and past the old cemetery. It hardly slowed in the town of Shandon. The road rose and fell steeply under tall eucalyptus trees as they raced out of town over the old bridge at Cholame Creek.

Five miles out of town, past the Bitterwater Valley Road, Highway 466 became winding and narrow. They were at the bottom of a hill when Moreno saw a car coming toward him up ahead. It slowed for the flashing lights. But it braked too fast for a car following closely behind it, which suddenly swerved in front of the ambulance to avoid a rear end collision. It sideswiped the Buick with a crunching jolt that threw Davison against the ambulance tanks at the head of the gurneys.

The lurching impact had roused the vaguely conscious Rolf Weutherich. His mouth was filled with blood. He thought of Jimmy. He couldn't see him. His clouded mind could not tell if there were curtains, or if he was himself strapped in, or whether he was so broken that his body would not respond when he tried to look around. Then he saw Jimmy, broken and bloody, his face covered by the mask of a respirator.

Moreno stopped at the top of the hill, jumping down to inspect the damage. The left side was creased. Roth and Hickman caught up as Moreno jumped back in to speed off again.

At the bottom of a hill, a shaken young Herlong woman, thirty-one-year-old Carrie Golden, who had been driving the car which had braked suddenly, and twenty-three-year-old Llewelyn Hiatt of Paso Robles, who had hit the ambulance, waited at the roadside. They were afraid to leave. A police car responding to the wreck quickly pulled over near them.

It was dark as the speeding ambulance crossed the bridge over the Salinas River and raced up the winding turns of 15th Street to the bluffs where War Memorial Hospital overlooked the town sprawled on the rolling hills.

Moreno halted the ambulance at the emergency entrance. The harrowing drive had taken twenty minutes. Hickman pulled up right behind them in the wagon.

Dr Bossert was the physician on duty. He had a Vine Street practice with Dr Thompson. Alerted by radio, he had been waiting. Moreno and Davison quickly removed Weutherich and slid the gurney to the ready hands of the attendants. Rolf was rushed inside. 'You better check the fellow in the ambulance first,' Moreno told Bossert. Roth and Hickman stood near as the doctor climbed into the back.

Bossert saw that the man had a broken neck. There was a slight grating noise when he moved the head. The face was bruised and scratched, with several large cuts. The skin was white from loss of blood. The man's chest was covered with cuts and bruises; certainly there were internal injuries. The forearms were broken in several places, and one leg was fractured. Dr Bossert decided the man had died instantly, or very shortly after the crash. Roth and Hickman heard Bossert declare James Dean dead. Hickman could not believe it. He was in shock.

Moreno closed the doors of his ambulance and drove more slowly back down the hill to the Kuehl Funeral Home on Spring Street. Roth looked for a phone. Before the ambulance arrived at the mortuary, the body of Jimmy Dean was rolled for the money in its pockets.

Clifford Hord and his family had parked at a hamburger stand at a little spot in the road called Lost Hills, forty miles east of the intersection where the Ford and Spyder had collided. They were already eating when Phil roared into the parking lot, honking the horn. The boys spilled out of the car and ran in excitedly to tell what they had seen.

Maila and Jack Simmons had been in her house on Larrabee Avenue in Hollywood. As always, the curtains were drawn. At about 5.45 p.m., an unearthly light had infused her living room. Jack said, 'It's creepy in here, let's go out.' Maila found the light mesmerizing in its eerie beauty, but they left.

Fifteen minutes later, she returned. Tony Perkins had stopped by, and he was with her.

On one occasion, Jimmy had come to visit when she was not at home. He had climbed through her window to leave a strange calling card. He had taken one of his 8 by 10-inch publicity photos and cut out the eyes, nose, and an ear, then pinned the mutilated picture on the wall so she would know who had dropped by. It had amused her, and she had left it up.

Now, her phone rang. It was Randy at the Villa Capri. He told her the news. She told him he must be joking. At that moment, one of the pins that was holding Jimmy's partial face to the wall came loose. The picture swung back and forth like a pendulum.

A studio policeman at Warner Brothers in Hollywood was summoned to a night phone line. It was the operator at War Memorial Hospital in Paso Robles. She told him that James Dean was dead. The cop called Henry Ginsberg, the producer of *Giant*, who quickly called Dean's agent, Dick Clayton. Clayton called Jane Deacy, Dean's New York agent, who was in town and staying at the Marmont. Clayton and Deacy headed to Winton Dean's house. They hoped he wouldn't hear it on the radio.

Stewart Stern also received a call from Ginsberg, who cried, 'The boy is dead! The boy is dead!' Unintentionally and unconsciously, he had paraphrased one of Jimmy's lines from Stern's script of *Rebel Without a Cause*: *'Mom, dad, a boy was killed tonight!'* Stern wandered hollowly out onto Sunset Boulevard. Young actors and actresses had clustered on the pavement in front of Googie's. Some were dazed. Many had tears in their eyes.

Ernie Tripke had received a call on his radio about the near-disastrous collision of the ambulance about thirteen miles up the road. He sped off to report to the scene. He talked to the young man and woman at the roadside. He took their names, but did not cite anyone. He headed on to the hospital in Paso Robles.

Ron Nelson had taken his flash camera from the patrol car. He photographed the Ford and the Porsche, capturing enough foreground to show the point of impact and the skids. Boot heels crunched on gravel as men walked around in the harsh, stark light of car headlamps. Other patrol cars had responded and were parked on the roadside.

Moreno had returned with his big tow truck. The westbound lane had to be cleared first. He recommended to the student that the Ford be towed to his garage up the road. The young man numbly assented. He stood back as the tow truck returned for the Porsche. It was too badly wrecked to be towed. Moreno had to work a chain underneath and lifted the whole car. Some of the local press had arrived, and a photographer took a picture of the racer as Moreno prepared to haul it slowly away. The photo would show the undamaged side.

Nelson sketched the skid marks and measured them with a tape. He had learned that Dean was dead. There would be an investigation by the Highway Patrol which would be turned over to the District Attorney's office. The D.A. reviewed the evidence on fatal collisions for the possibility of legal action.

The student's nose had stopped bleeding, but it still hurt. He didn't know what he was supposed to do, now. The patrolman was evidently through with him. He didn't know how he was to get back to Tulare. He asked an officer. The patrolman told him he could 'probably catch a ride home'. He began walking up Highway 41 in the cool dark toward Tulare almost fifty miles away.

His work done and the scene cleared, Nelson made note of the time when he got back into his car. It was five minutes to nine. He headed toward Paso Robles to rejoin Ernie, who had gone to the undertakers'.

The student walked on in the night, turning to extend his thumb when a headlight approached. It was almost ten o'clock before he flagged down a lift. It was eleven before he was dropped off at the Tulare hospital to find a doctor who would examine his nose and the painful bruises.

The Hord family had heard on their car radio that the young man killed earlier in the evening had been a movie actor named James Dean. They passed through the intersection again late that night, on their tired way home. Particles of glass on the road surface sparkled in their headlights and there were white sulphurous blotches where the flares had been set. Phil had never seen *East of Eden*, but he knew he would see a James Dean movie as soon as one came to town.

The Bakersfield Drillers had beaten the Paso Robles Bearcats 13–12.

Chapter 6

It was past midnight when the car carrying John Stander and his family crossed the Salinas River into Paso Robles, the tyres making a hollow thrum on the concrete bridge. They were tired as they drove up Spring Street. Stander's house was next to Kuehl's, the town's only undertakers', where he was employed as a mortician and assistant to Martin Kuehl. The mortuary stood on the corner, an imperturbably solid two-storey gothic house of cheerful red brick with a turret and spire. Before he had even pulled into his drive, Stander noticed something strange. The lights were on at the mortuary. He saw his sleepy family into the house, then went next door.

Martin Kuehl was glad to see him. They had received an accident victim earlier in the evening. The deceased had been a movie star of some sort. Neither man had ever heard of a Jimmy Dean – except for the country singer. Kuehl had never seen anything like it – the phone had not stopped ringing. It had begun even before Moreno's ambulance had pulled into the back of the house.

Stander was aware of a tall man in slacks and sports shirt. Bill Hickman was distraught and chain smoking. He had seen death before. He had been in the services, and he had seen his father die. But now he had just lost a wonderful friend. He couldn't believe he was dead. After Kuehl had cleaned Jimmy up, he had let Hickman come in and see him. Jimmy had not been smashed up that badly. There were several deep cuts, and the forehead was pushed in. He seemed so small. The almost total loss of blood had sharpened the definition of bones and blue veins underneath the sunken skin. Bill kept seeing him in his arms at the wreck, and hearing that last gasping breath. He wouldn't sleep for five or six nights. Jimmy had been a great guy. Hickman couldn't believe it.

Hickman was furious too. The undertaker had given him Jimmy's wallet. There was no money in it. The ambulance men had rolled him. It made Hickman sick. Now he would not leave the horribly exposed and defenceless body of his pal. Big Bastard would stay close.

Kuehl was glad Hickman was there. He was his only source of information about the next of kin of the young man whose death certificate would describe him as a 'transient' in this county.

The bright electric lights of the embalming room were in violent contrast to the soft pastel yellow lamps of the plush and dim front parlour. Kuehl prepared to process the body. There were no cold storage facilities at the mortuary.

Outside, the cars driving by on Spring Street slowed as they passed the undertakers'. The news of the accident had been broadcast quickly and spread throughout the county. Cars pulled up to screeching halts at hamburger stands and the news was shouted. Some young people heard it as they came out of the late show at the Fox Theater up the street. The neon of the marquee flickered and died, but the usual Friday night restless tension had been jolted with a new surge of excitement. *Something was finally happening in Paso Robles*. But what to do about it? The cars drove slowly around the block and past Kuehl's. Some turned their radios up, some turned them down. All wondered which room he was in, and how he looked.

In the ammoniac air of the embalming room, among the gleaming surgical knives and needles and the chromium tubing, Kuehl and Stander were occupied with the technical problems James Dean presented to them. Kuehl moved the head slightly and there was the crepitation of the broken neck which Bossert had observed. There was the possibility of a fracture at the base of the skull. The left side of the face was damaged much more than the right, and had obviously absorbed the brunt of the collision. Small particles of glass were embedded in the flesh. Kuehl figured they were from the windscreen. The upper and lower jaws were broken in several places. The bones of both arms were splintered by the action of being caught in the rolling car. The legs seemed okay. There were many cuts.

The accident was the obvious cause of death, so there

would be no need of an autopsy. Officer Tripke of the highway patrol had stopped by at eight o'clock to inspect the injuries as part of his investigation. He had requested a blood sample to test and determine whether Dean had been drinking. Kuehl had poked and probed. There was hardly any blood left in the body. The arterial system was intact, though, so embalming would be possible.

Stander was inured to the physical aspects of death, but the phone calls made his spine crawl. Already it seemed that the death of this boy had ripped the mask from a face of humanity he had never seen. He did not like it. It made him uncomfortable. There was a call from southern California, with party noises in the background. The man had been drunk and pushy. There were calls from New York, London, and even one from South America, a voice accusatory and hysterical, shrilling, 'He's not dead! I know he's alive!'

The undertakers worked for three hours through the deep darkness of the early morning. The left side of the face would be set in the soft cushions of the casket, and so hidden. The relatively undamaged right side would be displayed. Barely a month previously, Edna Ferber had remarked to Jimmy, 'You have a profile like John Barrymore's – but your racing will soon take care of that.' Devastated at his death, she would regret the remark. But when Stander and Kuehl had finished the profile was unblurred and intact.

On Saturday morning a shaken Winton Dean arrived in Paso Robles escorted by the chief of security from Warner Brothers. He met Hickman at Kuehl's where he quietly asked the undertakers to be careful that none of his son's effects were left behind to fall into anyone's hands. He selected a casket, and handed over the suit he had brought for Jimmy to be dressed in. The torn and bloodied clothing was destroyed.

That same Saturday morning in Tulare, a hundred miles to the north-east, the phone rang in a little house in Academy Street. The student came to the phone to find himself talking to a reporter from the local paper.

'I looked, but I didn't see him coming,' he said. The man driving behind the Ford hadn't seen the Porsche, either.

And the student said he had heard a man who had been driving behind Dean say that the Porsche had passed him up the road 'going at quite a bit of speed'. He told the reporter that a station wagon pulling a trailer had stopped right after the crash. Dean had been on his way to the races at Salinas.

He said that the highway patrol had not offered him any help in getting home to the next county. It had been five hours before he had received any treatment for his own injuries. The interview appeared that night as a related story under the headline TULAREAN, ACTOR IN WRECK.

Actress Mercedes McCambridge, who had become close to Jimmy during the Texas location shooting of *Giant*, had decided to celebrate the completion of filming with a driving holiday to San Francisco. She and her husband Fletcher had reserved the Fairmont's finest room over the bay. They set out on Friday and spent the night at the home of friends in Terra Bella, northwest of Bakersfield. Saturday night they decided to spend in Pebble Beach, and they picked the quickest route to the coast – Highway 466. The flat and barren plains between Lost Hills and Paso Robles reminded her of Marfa and the *Giant* locale.

Fletcher noticed they were low on fuel and told her to watch for a petrol station. They went around a curve and pulled up to the pumps in front of Moreno's store. A thickset and fleshy girl, who was evidently the proprietor of the pumps, came up to the car. Fletcher filled the tanks, and Mercedes wandered into the cubbyhole of an office to get some Cokes from the machine. Outside, over the rustling of the leaves in the tall tree that shaded the windows, she heard the girl telling Fletcher, 'We have Jimmy Dean's sports car in the garage.' Fletcher knew that Dean was racing in the area that weekend and figured the car had broken down and was laid up for repairs.

From outside, he heard Mercedes gasp. 'Oh my God!' She had probably seen Jimmy coming out of the lavatory and was greeting him, surely a pleasant surprise. But another lumpy girl had appeared at the counter and pointed out the Spyder. Mercedes had shrieked when she saw the crushed aluminium and the blood. 'They said they'd never seen a body so limp and broken,' the woman said. Mercedes felt instant contempt for her through the shock and hurt, but she had to ask what had happened. The girl told her it was a local boy's fault. He had turned in front of the sports car. Everyone knew it was a dangerous turnoff.

They were stunned as they drove on to Paso Robles, where they found the Kuehl Funeral Home. Mercedes knew he was in there. She wanted to do something, but there were so many cars parked in front. Fletcher numbly circled the block a few times in indecisive tribute, then headed back to the highway and San Francisco. Two days later, Mercedes broke out in a fever and Fletcher flew her home to Saint John's Hospital.

At about a quarter to two that afternoon, Ernie Tripke returned to the intersection to confirm measurements and take some daytime photographs of the skid marks. The accident had occurred on his beat, and he was chiefly responsible for the investigation. He parked the patrol car on the south shoulder. The point of impact was marked by a shiny scuff on the highway, near the small curve of a slight skid made by the Spyder as it impacted the larger car.

While Paul Moreno prowled around the north side of the road where the Porsche had landed, Tripke photographed the two sets of tyre burns that showed the Ford's path to collision. He brought out his long tape and made notations on his clipboard.

At around 5.30 p.m., he walked east on the highway a little distance before he turned to take a last photograph of Highway 466 looking west to the intersection and beyond as the sun was sinking behind the brown and dappled Cholame Hills.

At the Sunday morning service at the First Christian Church in Marfa, Texas, the Reverend Earl Zetsche asked his congregation to remember in their prayers a young man who had visited their town and come upon an accident on Highway 90. The driver had lain injured in a ditch. The Samaritan had stopped another car and sped it up the road for an ambulance, in the meantime shielding the victim's face from the sun with his cowboy hat. The next Sunday, the minister had led his flock in a prayer of thanks for the outsider's kindness, which helped save a life. On this day he asked them to remember that young man again, himself dead at the age of twenty-four in a car wreck in California.

Also on Sunday morning, 2 October, 8,000 fans crowded the Salinas Municipal Airport to watch 160 drivers compete in nine races. They had paid $1.50 at the gate, and they got their money's worth. There were numerous spin-outs and fender scrapes, but no injuries. The race was Le Mans style. At the starting gun, the drivers ran to their cars, fastened their seat belts, revved their engines, and roared and jostled for position on the track.

Louis Brero took the big car event, but the fastest time of the day was turned in by Sterling Edwards, who had won the trophy at the May Bakersfield meet in which Dean had run. Edwards's Ferrari Monza burned up the back stretch at 128 m.p.h. In the under 1,500 cc event in which Dean had been entered, J P Kunstle, who five months earlier had edged Dean out of second place, came in first under the checkered flag. On this day he drove a 550 Porsche Spyder. Ray Ginther finished right behind him at the wheel of Johnnie von Neumann's Spyder, the car which von Neumann had placed first in his division at Bakersfield. Lance Reventlow made a good showing in his race. Jack Douglas didn't place at all.

Brero and Kunstle accepted their trophies at a victory dinner that night. The awards were presented by the Salad Bowl Queen, and the president of the local Optimist Club spoke briefly.

On Monday morning, a death certificate was signed by John Stander in his capacity as deputy coroner. It stated that 24-year-old James Byron Dean, actor, never married, had met his death on 30 September 1955 at 5.45 p.m., one mile east of Cholame at the junction of Highways 466 and 41 in San Luis Obispo County. Chief cause of death was a broken neck, with numerous other fractures and internal injuries.

Meanwhile, patrolman Ernie Tripke met with assistant

district attorney Harry Murphy in San Luis Obispo. He submitted his report of the investigation into the accident.

That afternoon's edition of the *Paso Robles Daily Press*, which was not printed on weekends, carried the accident on its front page with large photographs of the two cars and a smaller picture of Dean in a sweater from *East of Eden*. The article described the collision as 'one of the most terrific crashes of two cars in the county's record', and said that Dean was one of two 'speed-loving young men' who had been killed that weekend.

Across the country, in Indiana, Marcus and Ortense Winslow pulled into the drive of their farmhouse after their long drive from California. Friends met them with the shattering news. They were soon on the phone to Winton in Santa Monica.

Winton had first wanted to send his son's body to Grant Memorial Park, in Marion, Indiana, for burial next to his mother Mildred. But he talked to Marcus and Ortense, and it was decided to commit Jimmy to the ground in Park Cemetery so close to the Jonesboro house where his aunt and uncle had raised him outside Fairmount.

That night, *Rebel Without a Cause* opened across the country. Indifferently scripted by Stewart Stern and charactered with types, it was nevertheless a haunting and powerful film. It had much in common with *High Noon*. The story unfolded and ended within a timeframe of twenty-four hours. With a Warner Color palette of eerie blues and smouldering reds, director Nicholas Ray and James Dean painted one boy's passage into manhood in one day and one night. With an assortment of incisive sketches and quirky details, Dean pulled tremendous life and truth from himself to create the quintessential First American Teenager. It was a performance both charming and magnetic. The intensity and reality of his observation drew his audience wholly into yearning participation in an apocalyptic juvenile fantasy: the complete and violent reversal of adolescent torment and confusion into a triumph over love, the need for approval, the fear of homosexuality, the police, and Mum and Dad. Leonard Rosenmann's weirdly moving theme music perfectly underscored Dean's moods and the sense of a cool and magical night in which life was full of infinite possibilities and anything might happen. He would use the same score two years later in *Bombers B–52*, to no effect.

Dean's death three days earlier imbued the film with a deeper significance and more personal symbolism. New motifs appeared like ghosts on the screen. The chickie-run scene was a preview from the past of Dean's imminent real death at the wheel. His anguished cry, *'A boy was killed!'* thrilled audiences with its precognition. The film had an unexpected new counterpoint.

The film also completed a rite of passage for James Dean: he was a screen personality of the first magnitude, with a face forty feet high which was a land and geography unto itself, incredibly absorbing, enchanting, and seductive. He was a real movie star. Perhaps he was the last one.

On Tuesday morning, John Stander loaded the casket with Dean's body into the black hearse and began the long drive down the coastal Highway 101. His destination was the Los Angeles Airport.

He stopped in Santa Barbara for petrol. Young people appeared and gathered silently and at a distance. They had seen the hearse and casket on the highway and recognized the significance of the Paso Robles placards on the funeral vehicle. James Dean was on his way home.

The young people were awkward. Stander was sympathetic. He knew that they wanted to do something, but that they didn't know what it was they wanted to do. He removed the Kuehl Funeral Home placards from the windows before he got back on the highway.

He met Winton Dean at the airport. Security was tight as he signed the body over to airport officials.

There was a new development in Paso Robles that morning. Sheriff-coroner Paul E. Merrick made an announcement: he was ordering an inquest into the death of James Dean. The hearing was to be held in the Paso Robles City Council Chamber at 10 a.m. the next Tuesday. The *Daily Press* covered the story on its front page. It reported that it was assumed witnesses would include John White of Los Angeles, and Tom Frederick and Don Dooley of Shandon.

The article said that Dean had a 'reputation for fast driving'. It mentioned that he was on his way to a race, and that he had been ticketed an hour earlier in Bakersfield for speeding. It attributed to highway patrol officers the statement that Dean must have averaged 75 m.p.h. between the ticketing and the scene of the crash. Several Paso Robles football fans had been 'forced to leave the highway' by Dean's 'wildly speeding' car. The Spyder was described as 'careening' at the time of the wreck.

At 10.17 p.m. that night, a Hunt Funeral Home hearse met the plane returning the body to Indiana at the Indianapolis Airport. James Dean was taken to Vernon Hunt's where, the *Fairmount News* reported, 'Friends may call.' It had been at Hunt's, on his last trip home in March, that his friend Dennis Stock had photographed him as he posed in a casket, flashing the victory sign, scratching his tousled hair quizzically, or crossing his arms in a semblance of nonchalant death.

Rolf Weutherich was in great pain in his room at War Memorial Hospital in Paso Robles. His jaw was broken and his left femur crushed. In a haze from painkillers, he found himself the object of great attention. Held immobile in traction splints, taking nourishment intravenously and through straws, one of the first interviews he had had to endure was with a representative of Porsche. He was concerned for Rolf, and he was also concerned with his firm's liability for the German mechanic's injuries. He was also keenly aware of the unwanted publicity the 550 Spyder might now garner as a result of the much-publicized death of this movie star at its wheel. Johnnie von Neumann had had No. 130 brought to Los Angeles – under a tarpaulin.

The hospital tried to screen his calls and visitors. One who came to see him was more insistent than most, if more pleasant. Betty Shaw* was an attractive young blonde of about twenty-five years. She was an acquaintance of Jimmy's and a friend of Maila's. She had worked as a police recording secretary and was fascinated by detective work.

* not her real name

Instantly intrigued by the death of Dean in the little town so far from Hollywood, she had driven up earlier in the week.

She questioned Rolf, who obliged in thick English made more impenetrable by the appliances holding his fractured jaw in place. He told her that he had been conscious when placed in the ambulance. He had felt that Jimmy was still alive at that time. The drive had been a nightmare. There had been confusion and terror at not being able to move. When he had fully come to himself in the hospital, he had found that the Pan Am flight ring Jimmy had given him was now gone from his finger. It had come off in the wreck – or in the ambulance.

On Wednesday, 5 October, at quarter past two in the afternoon, Rolf was visited by five men and a woman. Sheriff Merrick, assistant district attorney Harry Murphy, coroner's assistant Albert Call, and patrolman Ernie Tripke arranged themselves around the bed. A local minister and respected figure in the German community, Reverend M J Galle of the First Mennonite Church, had been brought along because he was fluent in Rolf's native tongue. Judith Rooney was present to record the deposition. Due to his injuries, the mechanic would be unable to testify at the inquest.

Murphy asked the questions. Rolf, through the interpreter, said that it was 1.50 p.m. when they left Los Angeles on the 30th. He remembered Jimmy getting the ticket near Bakersfield. After they had turned left onto Highway 466, he thought they had travelled at a speed of '65–60–65 on the open road, not any more'. The interpreter was having trouble understanding Rolf – it seemed he was saying something about having a different speedometer on his side. 'He said something about revolutions per minute,' interjected Tripke, who knew some German. 'That is a tachometer.'

Murphy asked, 'At any time, this side of Bakersfield, was the speed more than 65?'

'Yes,' the interpreter said after consulting Rolf, 'it is apparent that they had driven faster than 65, but not at the accident.'

'Not at the accident, but sometimes on the road, they were going faster?'

'Yes.'

Just before the crash, Rolf remembered the car was in fourth gear. He didn't know whether Jimmy might have changed gears at the last moment.

Murphy asked Rolf whether he had slept at all during the drive. The factory representative of the Porsche company had said that Rolf had told him that he had been dozing just before the wreck. Rolf said he was awake all the time. Galle said, 'He just – from the time of the impact and what folowed, he doesn't know a thing.'

Rolf estimated the speed of the Spyder at the time of the collision as 65 m.p.h. He could not say whether the car had slowed to that speed, or whether they had been going any faster during the five minutes before the accident – it seemed to Rolf they had held steady at 65 m.p.h.

Murphy said, 'Ask him if he remembers, within the five minutes immediately preceding the accident, if he remembers seeing a car have to go off the road to avoid him, that is, a car coming toward him?'

'There was a car, a car met him,' Galle replied, 'but it didn't have to go off the highway on account of him.'

Rolf said that he hadn't been on Highway 466 before, but he thought Dean had.

Murphy asked whether Dean was wearing glasses just before the accident. 'Yes . . . he had on dark glasses to protect against the sun.'

'Ask him how long before the actual accident that he saw the other car?'

'He couldn't tell.'

'Was he looking ahead on the road before the accident?'

'Yes.'

'Did Dean say anything just before the accident?'

'Nothing – he can't recall.'

'Did he make any sound at all, did he yell or scream?'

Rolf remembered nothing like that.

'Did he have any time to estimate the speed of the other car?' Murphy asked Galle.

'No, he can't.'

'Does he remember Dean doing anything, either putting on the brakes or turning the wheel some way in any attempt to avoid the accident?'

'It is a bit dark to him, but it seems to him that he tried to get by on the right side.'

'That is, he turned the wheel?'

'Yes, he turned the wheel.'

'Does he remember the brakes, does he remember being thrown forward by Dean putting on the brakes before the impact?'

'No.'

'Were there safety belts in the car?'

'Yes.'

'But they didn't have them on?'

Tripke translated, 'Just one for Jimmy.'

But the belt hadn't been fastened.

Rolf recalled the stop at Blackwell's. Jimmy had a Coca Cola and an apple. He didn't think they'd been stopped longer than a quarter of an hour.

Sheriff-coroner Merrick asked, 'The position of the sun, what was the position of the sun at the time?'

'Directly in the eyes, shone directly into their eyes. He doesn't know for sure whether the sun was shining at the time of the impact, but before that, it was directly into the eyes, but he doesn't recall whether the sun was shining in their eyes then or was behind something just at the impact.'

'Now at the time – how long prior to the impact does he remember seeing this other car? Ask him if he remembers that car on the road or at the turn.'

'It went very, he says very fast – went very, very fast.'

'In other words then – '

'It seemed as though the car was going the other way, but it went so fast – '

Murphy said, 'He means the accident happened so fast?'

'The accident happened so fast.'

'He doesn't remember?'

'He doesn't remember that at all.'

Merrick asked, 'In other words, he really wasn't conscious of the automobile until the time of the impact?'

'Yes, that is it.'

The sheriff had one last question. 'Is there anything of your own knowledge that might aid or assist us that you would like to add? Anything that wasn't asked you, or any information you would like to supply to us?'

Rolf Weutherich knew nothing more.

The next morning, Thursday, he was transferred by Garges ambulance to the Glendale Sanitarium and Hospital. He was out of danger.

Betty Shaw stayed in town several more days, talking with policemen and reading what reports she could access through her charm. When she returned to Los Angeles, it would be to tell people that something was not right. Anything she said, though, was taken with a grain of salt. It was known that Betty had a fetish, and her real absorption was with men in uniform.

A sheriff's deputy came to the door of the farmhouse of Clifford and Ruth Hord. He handed them a subpoena. Though the highway patrol hadn't interviewed them, the story had reached the sheriff's office about their encounter with Dean so near to his death. Merrick wanted them to testify at the inquest. The officer was accompanied by Lew Bracker of Los Angeles. He was the young cousin of Leonard Rosenmann, and he had been a sports car friend of Jimmy's. He was also an insurance agent. He had obtained Dean's signature on a $100,000 life insurance policy the day before the accident. He had also written the Competition Motors Pacific Indemnity Policy which would have to pay off on Rolf's injuries. 'If you think my name isn't mud,' he told the Hords. Now, he was in the area to investigate the accident for his report.

Shortly after Jimmy's death, his house on Sutton Street was burgled. Stolen were his tape recorder, his bongos, and the drawing he had made of himself lying in state with candles. His 16 mm camera was also missing. It had contained film of a sequence he had improvised with Maila and Jack. They had come over one night after a party and he had used the wall bed as a prop. All Maila had left of him were some napkins with his doodlings which she had saved from the nights at Googie's.

Maila had been fighting with A.B.C. They had wanted her to relinquish the Vampira copyright to them. She refused. Her contract was annulled. A party to celebrate her freedom had been planned for 8 October. Jack and Jimmy were to be there. Instead, Jimmy was buried that day.

It was a Saturday. The service was at 2 p.m. in the Back Creek Friend's Church where Ortense was organist. It was the largest funeral in the history of Fairmount, with 3,000 people in attendance. Pastor Xen Harvey delivered the eulogy, 'James Dean: A Play in Three Acts', concluding, 'And God is directing the production.' The service was conducted by Reverend James de Weerd, an old mentor of Jimmy's, who drew upon the *Book of James*: 'Whereas ye know not what shall be on the morrow. For what is your life? It is even a vapor, that appeareth for a little time and then vanisheth away.'

Elizabeth Taylor and Edna Ferber sent flowers. Warner Brothers sent a wreath. Henry Ginsberg and a studio publicity man were there. But except for Jack Simmons, hardly anyone of Dean's Hollywood friends or co-workers attended. Mourners followed the hearse up the road to Park Cemetery. The Winslows and Winton looked stricken. Jimmy's pallbearers were high school friends and fellow members of his basketball squad.

Adeline Nall, Dean's high school drama teacher, who had once accompanied him to Colorado for the finals of a dramatic contest in which he had competed with a reading of Dickens' 'The Madman', was not at the funeral. Inspired by her star pupil's success, she had left her teaching job and gone to New York, where she worked as a clerk in a hotel while trying to get her foot in the theatrical door. Dean had helped by introducing her to his agent, Jane Deacy. But it was an impossible relationship, with subtle crosscurrents, for there were two women and only one boy. But Adeline still had hopes that Jimmy would open doors for her. Now those hopes were buried near the cornfields on the banks of Back Creek in the small town which she had tried to escape.

Winton flew home the next day. Guards patrolled the grave for two weeks.

Chapter 7

Thirty-seven-year-old Peter Andre, of Andre and Andre, was a war hero and a past director of the Chamber of Commerce. He was also vice-chairman of the Republican Central Committee, and an ex-deputy city attorney for the city of San Luis Obispo. Trim and tan from skiing, golfing, and riding, his prominence and familiarity with the local legal machinery made him an excellent choice to represent the student and his insurance company.

The inquest was called by the Sheriff-Coroner to determine who had died, how he had died, and whether that death was occasioned by the *criminal act* of another. It was not a criminal proceeding, or a jury trial, though it could precede one. The evidence would be heard by twelve jurors, who would render a verdict. If the jury found the other driver responsible for the accident by a criminal act, the district attorney could prosecute him for vehicular manslaughter.

One real comfort the attorney did offer his client was that he would not have to testify under the Fifth Amendment. He would not have to say anything.

On the morning of the inquest, the student appeared at the council chambers in San Luis Obispo, the county seat, with his lawyer and his parents. There was a crowd of spectators, composed of the merely curious, friends and relatives of the witnesses, and fans of James Dean from Hollywood. The little room was far too small. Rather than exclude them, the sheriff adjourned the proceeding to the old U.S.O. building nearby at 10th and Park Streets.

The inquest would be conducted by the sheriff-coroner himself. Paul Merrick had taken office on 3 January the same year. A dapper little man who resembled a pudgy Dagwood Bumstead, in his first ten minutes as sheriff he had fired ten members of the old department. He said it was a 'house-cleaning'. He had run on a strong law-and-order platform. Ready for anything, he had come to the inquest accompanied by two deputy sheriffs.

The district attorney was also present. Fifty-eight-year-old Herbert Catherwood Grundell was a leonine ex-merchant marine who had come to office in the same election as Merrick. He had managed the Pacific Coast Railroad for ten years. Twice married, he held one of the first ham radio licences issued in California. He would interject and oversee the questioning of witnesses.

The jurors, nine men and three women, were all from the Paso Robles–Shandon area and had been drawn from a list supplied to the coroner by the county clerk's office. Their eligibility had been determined after questioning by the coroner and the district attorney. All had visited the crash site, walking around and examining the skid marks.

At 10.15 a.m. they were sworn in. Paul Moreno was the first witness. Under Deputy District Attorney Harry Murphy's questioning, he described receiving the call on 30 September, and what he had found when he arrived at the accident scene.

Murphy asked, 'Anything on the road would either have to be outlined or blend into the colour of those mountains, is that correct?'

'That is correct,' Moreno replied.

Murphy asked about Dean's car.

'What kind of car was this – I forget the name of it – ?'

Moreno helped him. 'Porsche.'

'What colour was this *Porsche* car?'

'Silver grey or something. It blended in with the horizon, and background and the mountains pretty well.' He said he had never seen one of those cars intact, but he knew they were low to the ground. Murphy elicited the testimony that the car 'had no top'.

The deputy D.A. picked up six 8 by 10-inch black and white photos. He handed number three to Moreno. It was a picture Tripke had taken on 1 October. It looked east to the intersection and showed the last set of skid marks and the point of impact. Beyond, the highway rose up steeply at the two knolls. Donald felt fear. He remembered the man taking photographs of Dean in the car. But it was only a photo of the highway.

Murphy was saying, 'It shows the mountains that you have described and the road becomes delineated or merged into the scenery.'

It was hardly a question. Moreno did not understand. 'That is right,' he said quickly. Murphy did not pursue it. He offered the photos in evidence and handed them to the jurors.

Murphy introduced and then read the deposition of Dr Bossert. It described the arrival of the ambulance and the injuries to a body 'said to be, by his friends, James Dean'. Merrick had also been present at the interview with the doctor at his Vine Street office the previous Wednesday.

Murphy had asked, 'Doctor, there were no signs of any glasses or anything on Mr Dean at the time you examined him, were there?'

'He was not wearing glasses at the time I saw him.'

'Was there any evidence that any glasses might have been on him?'

The doctor answered, 'I didn't examine his eyes closely, but he had numerous cuts about the face, and bruises about his face. If he had been wearing glasses, they could have easily been knocked off.'

Murphy had kept at it. 'These cuts he had about his face, could they have come from the glasses being broken in the accident?'

'Well, there were several large cuts which I am sure didn't come from that, they must have come from other sources. It is difficult to tell whether they came from glasses.'

'I realize you couldn't say positively they came from anything.'

'That is open to conjecture completely.'

The doctor had apologized for being late.

Murphy introduced a letter from Sanford Roth and read it into the record. Roth said he had been present at the doctor's examination and confirmed that the body pronounced dead was that of his friend, James Dean. The letter had been notarized by Lewis Bracker, Jimmy's racing buddy who had sold him the $100,000 policy on his life.

Patrolman Ernie Tripke was next called to the stand. He

had brought a large diagram, and Murphy asked him to pin it up on the blackboard near the witness's chair. It was not exact, Tripke said, but a substantial depiction of the accident scene. He began to explain. Grundell interjected and told him to slow down – he was talking too fast for the court reporter. 'We're trying to make a record here.'

A box representing the Ford, with one corner flattened to show the smashed fender, had been drawn across the westbound lane. A smaller bullet shape, near the phone pole on the north shoulder, represented the Porsche.

Murphy asked him about the other markings on the diagram.

'Starting from the west, practically straddling the centre line of Highway 466, are a set of skid marks thirty-nine feet in length . . . and for a distance of thirty-three feet in the westbound lane of Highway 466, there are no skid marks; however, the skids again start in the westbound lane, the second skids being twenty-two feet in length. These are entirely in the westbound lane of Highway 466 to a point which we determine as the point of impact of the two cars.'

Murphy asked how he had determined the point of impact.

'From the skid marks, it took a sharp turn to the right and there are gouges in the pavement and tyre burns.'

The point of impact was deep in the westbound lane, Dean's lane, where he had had the right of way. But the assistant D.A. did not pause.

'Was there anything else in the area – was there glass from the cars or dirt?'

'The whole general area had dirt and glass.'

Murphy persisted. Some reporters were mystified.

'Was there more in that area than any other?'

'Well, actually, there was more dirt beyond that area than there was right in that particular spot.'

A little later, Murphy asked, 'Now you saw the Porsche that night?'

'Yes, sir.'

'What colour was it?'

'It was a silvery grey colour.'

'Could you determine by looking at that time how high it was when whole, before the accident?'

'Oh, approximately three feet in height, it was very low – built very low to the ground.'

' – By the way,' Murphy said, 'you said you were out there the next day . . . how late were you out there the night of the next day?'

'I was out there from – probably 1.45 until after six o'clock.'

'You were out there around 5.30 the next afternoon?'

'Yes.'

'You saw the amount of sunlight there was present at that time?'

'Yes, sir. At 5.30 the sun had gone down behind the hills, but it was not dark yet. There was no sun in anyone's eyes at that time. It had not gotten dark yet, at 5.45 there was still light, but it was getting dusky, and at six it was getting dark.'

'Now, considering the colour of the car, the height of the car, the time of day and the amount of sunlight, do you have any opinion as to how hard or difficult or easy it would be to see this car coming up the highway?'

'Well, it would blend in pretty well with the highway colour and the horizon, it being silvery grey. There were some red stripes on the rear of the Porsche, but they couldn't be seen from the front of it.'

'You examined this car? I notice there was quite a bit of damage done to it – this picture.'

'Yes, there was.'

'Would you say that this car was made of material that is ordinarily found in cars that normally use the highway?'

'No, this car appeared to be made of aluminium and possibly some magnesium and it was very light.'

'And would you say it would be very easily damaged?'

'Yes, aluminium crushes quite easily upon contact with anything.'

'In your examination of the Porsche, did you determine what type of drive it had, was it right- or left-hand?'

'Left-hand drive.'

Grundell asked the officer whether he had talked to Donald Turnupseed at the scene, and whether there had been alcohol on his breath. Tripke said he had talked to him and detected no alcohol. The officer said he had left the scene to respond to the call about the sideswipe to the ambulance.

Murphy asked, 'And when did you next see Mr Dean or his effects?'

'I saw Mr Dean approximately about eight o'clock that evening.'

'Did you then examine the effects of Mr Dean?'

'Not too much, no, sir. He was at the mortuary and Mr Kuehl had gone through the effects.'

'And did you remove anything from Mr Dean's effects?'

'No, sir.'

'Did anyone remove his driver's licence?'

'Apparently. Mr Hickman gave me Mr Dean's licence at the hospital.'

'Do you have that?'

'No, sir, I don't. It was turned in with the accident report.'

'Is it here?'

'I don't have it.'

'Was it an ordinary licence?'

'Ordinary, except that it had a restriction, it required corrective lenses.'

'Mr Dean required corrective lenses to drive the car?'

'Yes, sir.'

'Did you see any physical evidence of glasses?'

'There was a piece of glasses, the part that attaches over the ear, but whether it was Mr Dean's, I don't know, I couldn't say.'

Sheriff Merrick asked whether he had the ear piece.

'No, sir, I do not.'

'Do you know where it is?'

'No, sir.'

The jury had no questions. Murphy detained Tripke for another moment. 'Just one thing about this diagram. Looking at it here, I notice these skid marks, and I notice there is a blank spot of thirty-three feet, and then skid marks of twenty-two feet. Now, it it your testimony that you found these skid marks on the scene; you did not testify, did you, that those skid marks were skid marks of any particular car that was involved in this accident?'

'No, sir, they could have been made by another car.'

'In other words, the first skid marks could have been

made by another car and only the second by the cars involved – or the car involved at the accident, or either of them may have been made by the car involved.'

'Well, that is possible. However, the second set of skid marks tie in perfectly with the point of impact.'

'In your opinion, what would you say would be the normal place to turn, if you are on this highway going to Fresno?'

'Well, when one reaches the intersection.'

'Was it a gradual turn?'

'Yes, I believe so.'

Murphy asked, shortly, 'Is there anything in your diagram that might be a little misleading?'

'These skid marks,' Tripke replied, referring to the first set of tyre burns.

There were several questions about the diagram from the jury, and then the court recessed at 11.10 a.m.

At 11.30 a.m. Thomas Frederick was called to the stand. He said he did not know how fast the Ford had been going as it approached the intersection, but he eventually ventured his best estimate of '40 miles an hour or 45.'

The testimony quickly took an unexpected turn. Frederick testified that the man in the red T-shirt, Rolf Weutherich, had been driving the sports car. James Dean, in a white shirt, *had been the passenger.*

Murphy tried to straighten it out. 'Now, you said that when you saw this car approximately thirty feet – when you first saw the car, there was approximately thirty feet between you?'

'That is right.'

'You remember the one in the red T-shirt being on the left side of the car as it came toward you?'

'Not until after they hit, I didn't pay any attention before the accident.'

'You say you remember the man in the red T-shirt when you saw the car in motion?'

'Yes.'

'He was on the left side?'

'Yes.'

'That is the left side as the car came toward you?'

'Yes, sir.'

The district attorney broke in. 'That would be on the right side?'

Frederick was getting mixed up. 'Wait a minute here – ' he said, 'he was on the left side of the car, closest to us. The way he put it there – '

Murphy cut him off. It was getting out of hand. 'Well, the point is, if he was on the left side of the car as it was coming toward you. Is that what your testimony is?'

'He was on my right, but the left side of the car.'

'Your right as the car was coming toward you?'

'That is right.'

'How do you remember that – what makes you remember the one with the red T-shirt being on the left?'

'I seen him with his hands up in the air, and seen he had a red T-shirt on.'

'When was that?'

'Right after they had the accident.'

'Was he coming up out of the car?'

'He could have been raised off the seat a little, but he was still in sitting position.'

The district attorney suggested he draw a picture on the blackboard. Frederick thought he could show more clearly with one of the inquest pictures. He said he had first seen the Porsche roughly opposite the highway signs just past the intersection.

'I saw them just before they hit, and they were coming down here and the Ford made its turn and started to straighten up and they had their collision right there.'

'You were about fifty yards back when they hit, and you say that the time you saw this man in the red T-shirt was after the collision?'

Frederick said, 'They were coming out this side, right here, and I saw him with his hands up – on my right, the car's left side – of the Porsche.'

'You say you saw the car coming toward you – was it heading toward the telephone pole?'

'That is right.'

'And the man closest to you or farthest away?'

'Closest.'

'The one with the red T-shirt?'

'The closest.'

Grundell interrupted, speaking to the jury. 'Are you clear on where the men were sitting? If you are – '

A juror said, 'I am not clear on it. That would mean he was in the driver's seat, the one with the red T-shirt.'

Grundell said, 'Have the witness draw the car.'

'I am no artist,' Frederick protested.

'It is a very simple matter. Just draw a little box . . . now make three lines for the highway there.'

Frederick drew a box for his own car, and one for the Porsche. Grundell gently instructed him to place an 'X' in the Porsche box to show the position of the man in the red shirt, Rolf Weutherich, prior to the collision. Frederick drew the 'X' in the driver's seat.

Frederick was still sketching.

Murphy said, 'You don't have to draw the Ford.' He was anxious to be on a different line of questioning. He asked, 'Did you see the driver of the Ford after the accident?'

'Yes.'

'Did he identify himself to you?'

'No, sir, he never said his name, but I knew who he was – I saw him get out of the Ford.'

'You saw him get out of the Ford. Was there anybody else in the Ford?'

'No, sir.'

'Did you talk to this gentleman?'

'Yes, sir.'

'Was anyone with you when you talked to him?'

'Yes, sir – I don't know – there was right within hearing distance, I just talked to him, I didn't pay any attention to whether anybody was around or not.'

'And you had conversation then, you and he?'

'That is right. Well, when I heard him say anything about the accident, he was telling the policeman about that.'

'In other words, you had no conversation with him about it?'

'I talked to him, yes.'

'I want his conversation with you, not what you heard him tell the policeman. What did he tell you about the accident?'

'Well, he couldn't see it – couldn't see the Porsche.'

'Did he say anything else?'

'He said he looked up at the road sign just beyond that, and started to make his turn.'

Frederick believed the accident occurred at about 5.30 p.m. Murphy asked whether he remembered where the sun had been at that time.

'It was behind the hills,' he replied, 'but it was still shining up on top of the hills, on the east side – at the scene of the accident, the sun wasn't shining at all.'

Murphy asked, 'Did you see any glasses in the area – in the area or around the car?'

'No.'

Merrick asked, 'Did you look for any?'

'No, I didn't look for any.'

Then Murphy turned to the college student. He directed him to stand. The young man obeyed and Frederick identified him as the man who had stepped out of the Ford after the crash in which James Dean had been killed. Don took his seat again next to his parents and Mr Andre.

Patrolman O V Hunter was sworn in. He testified that he had been requested to measure the distance between where he had cited Dean near Mettler station, and the collision at Highways 41 and 466. It was 107 and eight-tenths miles. He walked to the chalkboard and drew what would have been Dean's route.

Hunter produced Dean's copy of the summons. It had been found on his body and mailed back to the Bakersfield highway patrol headquarters. There was a tear in the centre. It was entered in evidence as Exhibit 10.

A juror asked, 'What time had expired between the accident and the time they left you?'

'Approximately an hour and a half,' said Hunter, 'but they made a stop at Blackwell's Corner by Bakersfield, and they were stopped for ten or fifteen minutes.'

Sheriff Merrick had a question about the glasses. 'Upon examination of Mr Dean's driver's licence, did you notice that corrective lenses were required?'

'I don't remember,' replied Hunter. 'Unless he was in violation, I wouldn't put it on the citation. If it says he has to wear glasses and he has them on, there is nothing put on the citation.'

'Would you notice that he did when you were looking at the licence?'

'Yes, I always look.'

'You saw that glasses were required?'

'If it was on there, I guess I did.'

'You cannot say that he was wearing glasses?'

'If he hadn't been I'd have added that in the citation because that is a violation in itself.'

'But at the time you cannot say whether or not he was wearing glasses?'

'No, I can't.'

Hunter was excused. Murphy read the deposition of Rolf Weutherich into the record. Clifford Hord was called to the stand.

Hord always used his hands when he talked, and he was trying to show what had happened when he had encountered James Dean's Porsche just before the accident. 'Maybe you better use the blackboard,' Murphy suggested.

'I was beyond that intersection here –' Hord said, 'and this car come down and I was going up and this car came up above and just come all the way across, he come clear off the road on the side and pushed me clear off.'

Murphy later said, 'In other words, the car came clear across and on the opposite shoulder?' He wanted Hord to estimate the speed of the Porsche.

'It was terrific,' Hord replied, 'I'd say it was well over a hundred miles an hour or better. It was very terrific.'

There was snickering from some of the Hollywood spectators. Hord's ears burned. Hord was drawing some of the resentment onto himself.

Hord estimated that the near collision happened three or four hundred yards east of the intersection. 'Just beyond the trees?' Murphy asked. Hord said, '. . . There is a bank, I couldn't have got off *there*. It was about the trees.' Had the accident happened just beyond the trees, Dean would have smashed into *him*.

A juror asked whether he had noticed the colour of the clothes of the occupants of the Porsche. 'Just seen there was two guys in there.' That was all he had time to see.

Clifford Hord heard booing as he left the stand. He was angered, and hurt. He had only been trying to tell the truth and do his part as a citizen. It was not fair.

Patrolman Ron Nelson gave testimony. He had trouble remembering the funny-sounding name of the man who had identified himself as the driver of the Ford. 'I can't think of his name right now – Turnupseed.'

He repeated the statement he had taken from Donald at the scene. 'He stated he was going to turn, he had been travelling approximately 55 miles to 60 miles an hour, and as he approached this intersection where the signs point to Hanford and Fresno, he started to slow down, it was his intention to turn left. He said just before he made his turn, he looked straight down U.S. 466 and for some unknown reason, he did not see the other car until he was already in his turn and he heard, he said he heard the squeal of tyres and saw the car, and tried to turn to the right to avoid it, but was unable to.'

For some unknown reason – there was a nuance there, an insinuation of disbelief. The officer seemed so unsympathetic. Don remembered how he had had to hitch a ride back to Tulare. It had all been such a nightmare. A boy was dead, his own car wrecked, and his future suddenly so uncertain. Sometimes Donald felt a strange alienation from all this – the photos, the diagrams, the testimony, everything was so unreal. He wanted it all to be over and was glad when Merrick announced there would be no break for lunch. They would continue right on through. There were no more witnesses.

The sheriff asked, 'If there is anyone present that has anything that may aid or assist us in this inquisition, will you please come forward.'

He was startled when a spectator cried, 'I seen some glasses near the Porsche!'

It was Donald Dooley, Tom Frederick's brother-in-law who had been with him and also witnessed the accident. He was called to the stand.

'Well,' he said, 'we parked and walked toward the Porsche. I seen some yellow glasses lying in the pavement. They looked like they were made out of plastic.'

Murphy asked, 'Were they glasses or goggles?'

'Well, more or less goggles, they cover the whole eyes.'

'I see,' said Murphy.

Dooley said he had seen the Porsche before the Ford had started to make its turn. He could not estimate its speed, or tell whether it had slowed.

Murphy asked, 'Did you see Mr Turnupseed's car just before the accident?' He directed Dooley to the highway patrol diagram. 'You heard the officer refer to these sets of skid marks, did you not?' He pointed to the two sets of burns in the same arc as the Ford's path to point of impact. 'Did you see the Ford, that is the car that Mr Turnupseed was in, throw on its brakes as to leave skid marks?'

'Well, I didn't hear or see anything except the two cars come together.'

'You didn't hear any squeal of tyres?'

'I didn't hear anything.'

'Did you see the Ford either swerve or slide in this area where the marks are?'

'I seen him slow down, and instead of making his turn, try to turn out.'

In a moment, a juror asked Dooley whether he knew which man had been wearing the red T-shirt.

'The man in the white shirt was sitting on the left side coming toward us.'

Later, he was asked, 'Was he driving the car?'

'Well, if it was a left-hand drive, he wasn't the driver.'

The district attorney asked whether he had noticed whether the Porsche was a left- or right-hand drive.

'Well, it looked like the steering wheel was on the left, and it was bent clear over to the right-hand side.'

'And the man in the white T-shirt was not the driver?'

'I don't know,' Dooley now said.

Many of the spectators sympathized with the perplexed juror who asked, 'How are we supposed to know who had a white T-shirt and who had a red one on?'

The district attorney said resignedly, 'You know as much as we do on it.' He continued, 'This court is interested first in, who is the deceased person, and how he came to his death. It is not really material who had a white T-shirt on. What we want to find out is who this person was, and how he came to his death, whether there was negligence on the part of Mr Turnupseed, or whether there wasn't. I made an observation from the testimony given by Mr Hunter, and the time elapsed from the place where this man was stopped, and the fact that they made a stop, was one hour and a quarter, and that divided into 107.8, that would give you between 85 and 90 miles an hour for the distance and measurement.'

At 12.30 p.m. the jury was left to deliberate. There was not much discussion. They were all in agreement that Dean had seemed to be going pretty fast. It took only twenty minutes, much of it spent filling out the form. The verdict was returned and read by foreman D H Orcutt.

'We find no indication that James Dean met death through any criminal act of another, and that he died of a fractured neck and other injuries received.'

The quick return of the verdict seemed further vindication. The student walked up to Clifford Hord and asked again how fast he thought Dean had been driving when he ran the Pontiac off the road.

'100, 140 miles an hour,' Cliff said.

The student told him that he had stopped, then started to pull out, but the other car was coming so fast that he didn't have the time to go ahead, or back.

Everyone went to lunch. The actual proceeding and deliberation had taken only two hours and fifteen minutes.

A bulletin was printed on the front page of the *Paso Robles Daily Press*. But the big story was 'Parade to Top Old Timer's Day'.

'Man, woman, boy, and girl were poised in Paso Robles today for the biggest community event in the history of the town and the surrounding country – the celebration of the Silver Anniversary of Pioneer's Day, tomorrow, the traditional October 12th date.'

Weather was expected to be fair and warm. Perfect. The parade would start at 10 a.m. led by Parade Marshal Fred Blackburn, the descendant of one of Paso Robles' early settlers. Behind him would ride the Pioneer's Day Queen and her attendants, the Pioneer Belles – Verna and Velva Lichti, twin sisters from Templeton.

Chapter 8

Troy McHenry was born in Australia and came to the United States when he was fifteen. A brilliant and ambitious young man, he studied medicine. By the age of thirty-two he was chief of staff of Doctors Hospital in Los Angeles. He married physician Amanda Marshall. In 1956, he was forty-five years old and a prominent Beverly Hills orthopaedic surgeon with all the appurtenances of great success. He was a sportsman. He had sailed to Hawaii in Trans-Pacific Yacht races. When he fell in love with sports car racing, he bought himself a sleek little Porsche Spyder which he hoped would carry him to victory.

On Sunday, 21 October, he was entered in the Pomona road races at the Los Angeles County fairgrounds. Amanda stayed at home, but a crowd of 30,000 was on hand to watch the finale of the two-day event. He was fifteen minutes into the hour-long semi-main race for modified sports cars under 1,500 cc when the Spyder spun out of control and smashed into a tree. McHenry was dead in the wreckage. He had been scheduled the following week to assume the presidency of the American College of Osteopathic Surgeons at their annual convention in Detroit.

The back swing arms which held the rear end of his Porsche had been bought from Dr William F. Eschrich, a racing friend and fellow surgeon from whom he had also bought a Spyder transmission, though he hadn't installed it. The parts had been cannibalized from the wreckage of No. 130, 'The Little Bastard', in which James Dean had been killed thirteen months earlier.

Eschrich had purchased the major components, including the 547 engine, for $1,000 from car customizer and entrepreneur George Barris, who had bought the remains for $2,500 from Winton Dean. Neither doctor had been superstitious. 'Not a bit,' said Eschrich the day following McHenry's death. He said he had raced seven or eight times in his Spyder powered with Dean's engine and he had never been involved in an accident – until Sunday. A wheel had flown off his car, but he had brought it under control and walked away without a scratch. Bob Miller, a Pomona policeman, was not as lucky. The flying wheel had struck him in the face and shoulder, sending him to the hospital for X-rays.

Two months later, in December, the aluminium shell of Dean's Spyder had been welded into a nearly solid glob by Barris and was on display at the 1956 International Motor Sports Show in Hollywood. Anticipating charges of bad taste and cruel exploitation, Barris exhibited the car with a large placard sermonizing on the wages of speed. It was a magnetic exhibit. Occasionally one of the awed would reach out to pluck a piece of silver metal skin as a souvenir.

James Dean's was the brightest star in Hollywood. He was young, he was hot, he was sexy, and he was dead. A year after the funeral, his studio was receiving eight thousand letters a week addressed to him. No living star had as much fan mail. The most grizzled critics, appalled by the corona of hysteria, were not immune to Dean's on-screen charm. In February of 1956, the Academy of Motion Picture Arts and Sciences nominated him as Best Actor for his performance in *East of Eden*. If he won, it would be the first posthumous Oscar.

There were television specials. Steve Allen (a *real* star) came to Fairmount to interview the Winslows for his programme. There were numerous replays of the video dramas in which Dean had appeared. His face haunted the newsstands. Magazines were vomited forth in the pan flash of a new phenomenon, the 'one shotters' – special magazines hurried into print to capitalize on one subject of special interest. He was voted number one in *Photoplay*'s actor popularity poll. His grandparents were flown to Hollywood to accept the award. Two book publishers, impressed by magazine sales of over two million, were climbing onto a bandwagon which *Time* magazine said 'looks disconcertingly like a hearse'.

A television station featured a Dean tribute and received this letter from a fan club member: 'Everyone who joins the club is so happy. They write the club to tell how good it makes them feel inside, how it brings inner peace. We can't accomplish anything by it but his faith is spreading. It is just wonderful meeting people who love Jimmy so much and want to keep him alive in their hearts always.'

Journalist Herbert Mitgang reported a sixteen-year-old girl's story: 'I started out following Jimmy's career when I was fourteen – I was only a kid then. My girl-friend and I would come to New York to see the T.V. stars. We'd go to the Cromwell Drugstore in the R.C.A. Building where the actors would be sitting before the shows. We'd go up and get their autographs. My girl-friend and I noticed Jimmy. He looked so nice. He was so sweet. He smiled at us. I never thought of him as a grownup, more as a friend, like us, but a boy. *He would talk to us even though we weren't anybody.*

'I don't like to talk about his accident. My girl-friends and I were planning to come to see him when he came to New York. We wanted to see if he would recognize us because we were kids then, but we're big now. This other girl-friend of mine, she can't speak a month after the accident, she can't concentrate in school. There's this other girl-friend who hasn't done anything and hardly eats or sleeps since Jimmy died. She dates an older man.

'Jimmy dated a lot of girls but he wasn't serious about any of them. Except Pierre Ann-jelly. She jilted Jimmy. I hate her. A girl-friend of mine found out where she was staying in New York. My girl-friend tripped her in the lobby for what she did to Jimmy.

'I hate all boys compared to Jimmy. I keep looking for him in other boys . . . when you were with Jimmy you knew he was listening to you when you spoke. He was conscious you were there.

'I don't like to talk about the accident. I don't think he was going as fast as the papers say. Maybe he wasn't the one who was driving, I heard it was someone who was with him.'

Dorothy Dix, a lonely hearts columnist, received a plea: 'I am fifteen and in love. The problem is that I love the late James Dean . . . I don't know what to do.' Miss Dix's nostrum for necrophilia was, 'Time heals all wounds.' Pining fans who wandered forlornly in a vague search at

Griffith Planetarium, one of the hallowed sites of Jimmy's career, sometimes encountered a weepy Natalie Wood. Passing weeks brought no surcease of fascination. A German girl committed suicide, unable to accept a loss that seemed intensely personal.

The inevitable expression of the upheaval of posthumous emotion was the rumour that James Dean was still alive. 'Dear Jimmy,' a fan wrote, 'I know you are not dead.' A magazine appeared, *Jimmy Dean Returns!* (Read his own words from the beyond!) A paperback book, *I, James Dean*, told Jimmy's story in the first person, even describing his last moments as he saw the Ford, a looming 'hulk of death' in which his own dead mother beckoned him. Some claimed to know where he was. The story grew that he was disfigured and hiding in the Cholame area, or swathed in bandages in a curtained room of an institution while doctors repaired his face for his return to the lost hearts of his fans. Quotes from the late James Dean were found to support the idea that this adulation was what he had sought, what he would have wanted. 'If a man can bridge the gap between life and death, I mean, if he can live on after he's dead, then maybe he was a great man.'

Some of Dean's friends were appalled. Maila reacted in a distinctive way. She dressed a boy in bandages from head to foot, twisted his hair, gave him horn-rimmed glasses, jeans, a red jacket, and boots, and had him limp into Googie's. *Jimmy would die*, she thought. She won a 'Bad Apple' for bad taste. Many of his friends were young, and death was so new.

'Tribute songs' haunted the airwaves. The main metaphor was astral. Their subliminal consolation was that Dean had died, but survived on another plane. Rudy Vallee had crooned after Valentino's passing 'There's a new star in heaven tonight.' Listening to one of the Dean dirges, the impulse was almost irresistible to peer up into the heavens in recollection of the voice of the narrator in the laserium in *Rebel Without a Cause*: 'People will . . . notice a star, increasingly bright and increasingly near.'

Typical lyrics were:

A star went out, one lonely night,
He was so young, he was so bright,
So clean,
And his name . . . was . . . Dean.

Other songs included two versions of 'Farewell My Jamie Boy', and 'The Ballad of James Dean' which sang the body destructive – 'Faster, faster, something made him keep going faster' – and was distinguished by a strange effect, the punctuating bang on a kettledrum at the fatal moment to signify the fly-swatting palm of fate. The Three Jays spoke for all fans when they warbled stridently, 'I'm in love . . . With the memory of you.'

Warner Brothers hardly discouraged the hysteria, but they did not participate. It had caught them off balance and they were not comfortable with it. The yet-to-be-released *Giant* promised to be a smash on the weight of Dean's appearance alone. Excitement was intense. George Stevens, editing the thousands of feet of film, received letters threatening his life if he excised a single frame of Dean from the picture. *Giant* was to be his epitaph in WarnerColor, his farewell and final statement.

Through it all, Dean lay silent and still in his Indiana grave bedecked by colourful petals. The Fairmount florist shop was almost entirely subsidized by the tributes ordered from all over the country and the world. A young high school girl sent money for flowers and was thrilled to receive a photo of her bouquet against the headstone from Marcus Winslow. A few years later she, too, would rocket from anonymity to international stardom and early death as Jean Seberg. It was not unusual for five hundred people to visit the grave in a day.

A month after the funeral, relieved of her television commitments, Maila had taken a train across country to stand at the plot in Park Cemetery. The cornfield behind the graveyard seemed to her a beautiful and poignant symbol. The playground of Jimmy's boyhood had become his eternal resting place. She felt a happiness for him.

'Few knew him well, none knew him long.' Dean had been shy. Roth had noticed that Dean would sometimes wait for hours in his car across the street from a friend's house, waiting for present company to leave. He was secretive. He would carry on phone conversations in a low murmur, hand cupped around the receiver, and never say the name of the person to whom he was speaking. No hint was given whether he was speaking to a man or a woman. He loved to mystify. Roy Schatt, his New York photographer friend, had asked him why he had a cigarette over one ear. Dean answered that he would light it 'as soon as I'm finished with this one, man. But it's really there for you to ask about.'

He was drawn magnetically to the strange and bizarre. For four days he was nearly inseparable from the young, one-legged girl leader of a gang of male thieves which burgled the homes of movie stars after learning from the social column of the *Hollywood Reporter* that the lord or lady of the manor would be in Palm Springs for the weekend. They obtained addresses from the Thalian's mailing list. She prided herself on her ability to hop naked from the kitchen with a cup of hot cocoa for one of her boys and reach the bedroom without spilling a drop (or scalding herself). But first, he would have to rub her stump. She lived with seven stump-rubbers, including Frank Christie, who would become a small-time hood on screen and off until his unsolved murder twenty-five years later. It was with her that Dean visited the studio of sculptor Kenneth Kendall, who dubbed her 'Lady Dreadful'. She told him that Jimmy was going to be the greatest actor in the world. When Dean shortly tired of her, he remarked to Maila, 'Now why did I do that?' He said he had planned to trip her.

One day in 1954, Dean was driving around in the San Fernando Valley when he saw a brand-new Mercury Montclair in the parking lot of a hamburger stand. As he often did, he pulled in beside it and got out to admire the car. The owner was a man just out of the services and in town visiting an aunt. They talked cars. Dean was fascinated, too, that the man worked as a highway patrol dispatcher in Bakersfield, a hundred miles to the north. Dean sat in the Montclair, and they talked a while longer. Charles Adams was driving away down the road before he realized that the vaguely familiar 'Jimmy' he had just met was *James Dean*, the new movie actor.

Late at night as he worked the graveyard shift at the Bakersfield highway patrol office, Adams received occasional phone calls from Dean. 'If you hadn't answered, I was going to hang up,' Dean said once. He found Adams bright, articulate, and artistic. A thirty-six-year-old family man, Adams was also more mature, a generous and sympathetic long-distance listener far removed from the world of Hollywood and the studios. He seemed indifferent to Dean's status. It appealed to Dean's quirky sense of humour to have as a friend a man who worked for the highway patrol. The monologues often rambled. Dean sometimes seemed depressed.

Adams was saddened when he heard of Dean's death. He knew about it only what he had read. Suddenly, anyone who had ever known Dean began to receive the most desperate pleas for some token of him. 'If he touched a wall, send me a scrap of the wallpaper', begged one letter to Jim Backus. Patrolman Otie Hunter started to receive mail and phone calls from fans and journalists about two weeks after the accident. Hunter was polite, helpful, and basically disinterested.

Vaguely curious, he wrote to the Sacramento headquarters for a copy of the ticket which Hunter had issued to Dean. When he received it, it was accompanied by a note that the family had requested that copies should not be distributed. Adams wrote to Marcus and Ortense Winslow in Indiana and learned that the family had an interest in the circumstances of the accident. He was soon in touch with Jimmy's father and stepmother. He visited their home in Santa Monica. He felt a little trepidation. The movie magazines had portrayed Winton as a cold, authoritarian man who had neglected the boy after the death of his mother and starved him of affection and approval all his life. The implication was that a barren father–son relationship was behind Jimmy's anguish and self-destruction, and that there was much of the autobiographical in Jimmy's portrayals of prodigal sons in *Eden* and *Rebel*. Instead, Adams found much of Jimmy in Winton's shy and retiring nature.

Winton and Ethel, on their part, found Adams to be an earnest and sympathetic young man. Frustrated by an unresponsive bureaucracy, they soon confided that they had unanswered questions about the accident and inquest. Winton said that he had not been informed of the date of the proceeding in Paso Robles, and so had been unable to attend. Adams was professional and tactful. He told them he would look into the circumstances of the death of their boy.

Winton insisted there should be no publicity. He and Ethel had much compassion for the young man who had been driving the car which had hit Jimmy. They were well acquainted with the glare of rabid and hysterical attention which focused on anyone who had fallen within the orbit of Jimmy's life or death and they appreciated more than anyone what the young man would have to live with. Adams assured them that the results of his inquiry would be theirs alone.

Relaxed, the couple gave Adams a tour of their home and showed him some of Jimmy's possessions, such as the ceiling-high rack of stereo speakers from his Sutton Street 'cabin', which now graced their home. Their pride was obvious as they displayed some of Jimmy's paintings and drawings. Adams, who had inherited artistic ability from his mother's side of the family, was struck by the power of Dean's talent.

Driving home over the Ridge Route to Bakersfield, Adams's imagination was fired and life was suddenly charged with excitement.

Winton and Ethel called him at work. Ethel usually did the talking.

As a first step, Adams wrote to San Luis Obispo County Sheriff Paul Merrick requesting a copy of the inquest transcript. He received a cool reply above the sheriff-coroner's signature informing that the inquest transcript was available – but the cost for duplicating it was $65.00. That was a lot of money to Adams. He knew the inquest was a matter of public record. He made the two-hour drive to San Luis Obispo and talked the county clerk into letting him bring his Remington typewriter into their office. Hammering away at eighty words per minute, he copied the sixty-six double-spaced pages.

Adams read the transcript again and again. His time as a highway patrol dispatcher in Kern County had given him an insider's view of the law enforcement community. He was a pretty thorough cynic.

Adams' interest in the inquest became obsessive. He began to work on his investigation on evenings and during weekends. He was married with two children, a boy and girl who were curious about this thing that stirred such intensity in their father.

He made many trips to the intersection of Highway 466 and 41. In February of 1956, the month that would have seen Jimmy's twenty-fifth birthday, Adams inspected the scene with a Patrolman friend from the Bakersfield headquarters. The skidmarks from the Ford's tires were still visible in the highway, as was the gouge in the pavement which marked the point of impact; the men painted a circle with a cross in the center to mark the spot. His friend took photos of the crash site. Adams, in shirt sleeves and with a folder of notes in his hand, stood on the road shoulder for scale.

There was still debris from the cars in the grassy field north of the highway. Adams touched the wood of the phone pole next to which the Spyder had come to rest. There were no scratches or paint on the wood.

The Spyder had not crashed into the pole or fence. Nothing had impeded its trajectory. Jimmy's race car had wound up forty-five feet away from the crash point. The Ford had been found thirty-nine feet up the road from impact. It was hard to believe that the Porsche, at less than *half* the weight of the Ford, would travel only six feet further than the Ford after impaction if it had hit at a speed of even 55 miles per hour. Adams had been an ambulance driver, and he had worked accidents with the Bakersfield patrolmen in his spare time. He had seen enough wrecks to know that a car of the Spyder's light construction would have been *rolled into a ball* at the speed claimed at the inquest. Paul Moreno had given him a negative from which he had obtained a photo of the Spyder at the garage. It was wrecked, but basically intact and in one piece. Though the front and rear hoods were sprung, they were still attached. The right side was unmarred. What made the damage look so dramatic was the crumpling and shredding of the light aluminium skin – which could easily have occured in a collision at low speed.

Had White, or Hord, been mistaken about the speed of the

Porsche? Adams believed so. There was the way the Spyder looked. It was a damned *race car*. An insolently low slung silver bullet, it appeared to be speeding when it was parked. The average guy, driving the speed limit and being passed by such a car, had the indignant reaction, 'Look at that Sonofabitch going 150 miles per hour!' To see such a car passing in the *opposite* direction would heighten the impression of speed.

Adams' couldn't get the accident out of his mind. He was always thinking of inches and seconds and testimony. Something new occured to him everyday. He began to set it all down on paper. He had always been a writer; his family had claimed that at the age of nine he was writing letters like a bank president.

The report was for Jimmy's family. He often started to work on it as soon as he got home from his job, and he would stay up until 2 a.m. pecking away at the typewriter in the other room, wreathed in cigarette smoke as he organized conclusions and test results and fired off more letters of inquiry. With unnerving concentration he began to create two large diagrams which were detailed schemas of the crash to scale. He took the photographs his friend had made and inked in the Ford's skid marks to show its path across the highway. On another photo of the vacant road, he even drew in the two cars as they must have looked approaching each other.

It was 1957 before he finished. The investigation had taken fourteen months. He had wanted to ease the minds of Jimmy's loved ones in California and Indiana by answering the questions that haunted them. Since the family had not been privy to the inquest proceeding, he included the text in his report, but with significant statements typed in red for cross reference with his own comments. He described his report as "purely technical", but he could not suppress a basic humanity. Opposite Doctor Bossert's graphic description of the fatal injuries was Adams' comment that here was proof that death was instantaneous and Jimmy had not suffered.

What had happened that day at the intersection of 41 and 466? Adams believed the Ford had nearly come to a stop by the time of impact. With his friend, he had conducted numerous skid mark tests in a 1950 Ford. They had tried to duplicate the tire burns at the crash site and then measured them against the standard Highway Patrol graph which converted length and density into an estimate of the speed required to produce such markings. The highest speed was 45 miles per hour, and 30 was the lowest; in both cases, the car had come to nearly a dead halt by the termination of the skids. Frederick must have over-estimated the speed at which the Ford had been travelling at impact. Adams knew that people in intense experiences, such as witnessing a car wreck, had the tendency to exaggerate estimates of speed.

The other driver had said he had heard the Spyder's tires just before they hit. The Porsche had left no skid marks. Adams wondered if he hadn't instead heard the squeal of his own reflexively applied brakes. He didn't know, as the man would not talk to him.

Adams completed the large blueprints of the accident. The Patrolmen who had responded to the accident saw it and found it difficult to believe he had not been there. It was a draftsman's conception of the approach to the intersection, the impact, and the paths of the cars to their point of rest. The measurements were painstaking. The Porsche had landed eighteen inches from the pole. He had even shown Dean's body in the Spyder, arms flailed. Adams carefully signed and dated the diagram. It portrayed graphically and dramatically one thing which neither the inquest testimony nor the Highway Patrol sketch had brought forth: the point of impact six feet from the 'Stop' line on Highway 41 was *not* in the westbound lane of 466, but just to the north. Jimmy had headed right, leaving his lane in an evasive action that now looked more poignant because it demonstrated his recognition of the imminent crash.

Adams believed that Jimmy had come off the grade and seen the erratic movement of the Ford crossing indecisively into his lane. He had slowed the Spyder by lifting his foot from the gas, or applying some brake pressure. Adams believed Jimmy had slowed to about 40 miles per hour by the time they hit, and he had tried to get out of the way.

There was a startling speculation in Adams' report: he believed it an even 50-50 chance that James Dean had not even been driving the Spyder.

He had travelled to the little town of Shandon south of Cholame on Highway 466 in search of inquest witnesses Tom Frederick and Don Dooley. Tom had moved to Palmdale, but Adams located his brother Paul who had been following Tom the afternoon of the wreck. The memory of the inquest was still a sore one with the family. Tom's handling by the Assistant D.A. had been unfair, and he would never be convinced that the man in the white shirt had not been the passenger rather than the driver. They had tried to put words in his mouth and make him change his testimony.

Adams studied the photographs of the wrecked cars. He understood physics and the bizarre things which concussion and velocity can do at car wrecks. The impact to the Ford had been at a point on the left front. No other part had been damaged. The damage to the Porsche had also been to the left front at a point. The force of impact and reaction were not dispersed, but focused on a line. The effect could have been to catapult the driver neatly out of the cockpit as the reaction drove the passenger, legs rigidly tensed, into the other side. There was only a slight hump on the floorboard separating the two seats. The ensuing compression could have slammed Jimmy to the other side and snapped him back, accounting for his broken neck and the foot entangled in the clutch and brake.

The Winslows in Indiana had expressed to Adams their belief that what had happened was God's will. In the last paragraph, he said the report was for the enlightenment and peace of mind of the family alone. He made three copies of the text and diagrams. He sent one set to the newly founded James Dean Memorial Foundation in Fairmount. Adams kept a copy for himself. The last he had bound in vellum and mounted in a leather folio with the name embossed WINTON DEAN. It was his gift to Jimmy's father, the result of all his work.

Adams never asked for nor received remuneration for the report. He did once ask Winton for one of Jimmy's little drawings. Winton told him it was still too early. Maybe, later.

Modern Screen magazine was interested in the report. Adams talked with them at their offices in Hollywood. He

The house in Fairmount where James Dean grew up, as it looks today. (Author's collection)

Main street of Fairmount. (Author's collection)

Jimmy Dean's many faces.

On the set of *Rebel Without A Cause*.

As Dean was finishing *Rebel Without A Cause,* he and Elizabeth Taylor began working on *Giant*.

Dean with his racing trophies. (Author's collection)

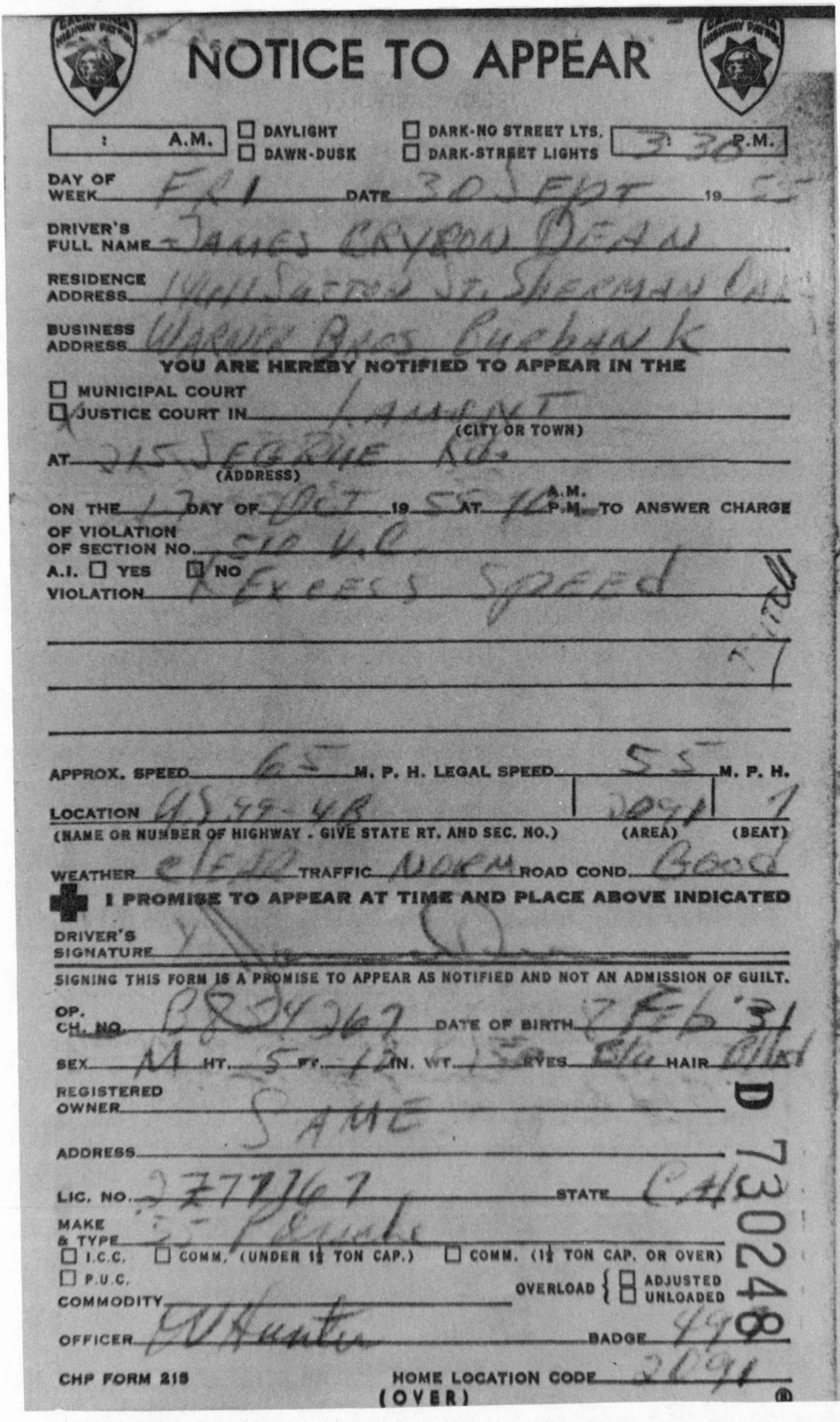

NOTICE TO APPEAR

: A.M. | ☐ DAYLIGHT ☐ DAWN-DUSK | ☐ DARK-NO STREET LTS. ☐ DARK-STREET LIGHTS | 3:30 P.M.

DAY OF WEEK FRI DATE 30 SEPT 19 55

DRIVER'S FULL NAME JAMES BYRON DEAN

RESIDENCE ADDRESS 14611 SUTTON ST. SHERMAN OAKS

BUSINESS ADDRESS WARNER BROS BURBANK

YOU ARE HEREBY NOTIFIED TO APPEAR IN THE

☐ MUNICIPAL COURT

☒ JUSTICE COURT IN LAMONT (CITY OR TOWN)

AT 215 SEGRUE RD. (ADDRESS)

ON THE 17 DAY OF OCT 19 55 AT 10 A.M. P.M. TO ANSWER CHARGE

OF VIOLATION OF SECTION NO. 510 V.C

A.I. ☐ YES ☒ NO

VIOLATION EXCESS SPEED

APPROX. SPEED 65 M. P. H. LEGAL SPEED 55 M. P. H.

LOCATION US 99-4B | 2091 (AREA) | 1 (BEAT)

(NAME OR NUMBER OF HIGHWAY . GIVE STATE RT. AND SEC. NO.)

WEATHER CLEAR TRAFFIC NORM ROAD COND. GOOD

I PROMISE TO APPEAR AT TIME AND PLACE ABOVE INDICATED

DRIVER'S SIGNATURE

SIGNING THIS FORM IS A PROMISE TO APPEAR AS NOTIFIED AND NOT AN ADMISSION OF GUILT.

OP. CH. NO. B834367 DATE OF BIRTH 8 FEB '31

SEX M HT. 5 FT. 8 IN. WT. 150 EYES BLUE HAIR BLOND

REGISTERED OWNER SAME

ADDRESS

LIC. NO. 3777167 STATE CAL

MAKE & TYPE 55 PORSCHE

☐ I.C.C. ☐ COMM. (UNDER 1½ TON CAP.) ☐ COMM. (1½ TON CAP. OR OVER)

☐ P.U.C.

COMMODITY OVERLOAD { ☐ ADJUSTED ☐ UNLOADED

OFFICER OV Hunter BADGE 4491

CHP FORM 215 HOME LOCATION CODE 2091

(OVER)

D 730248

The speeding ticket issued to Dean approximately two hours before he was killed. It was his last autograph. (Author's collection)

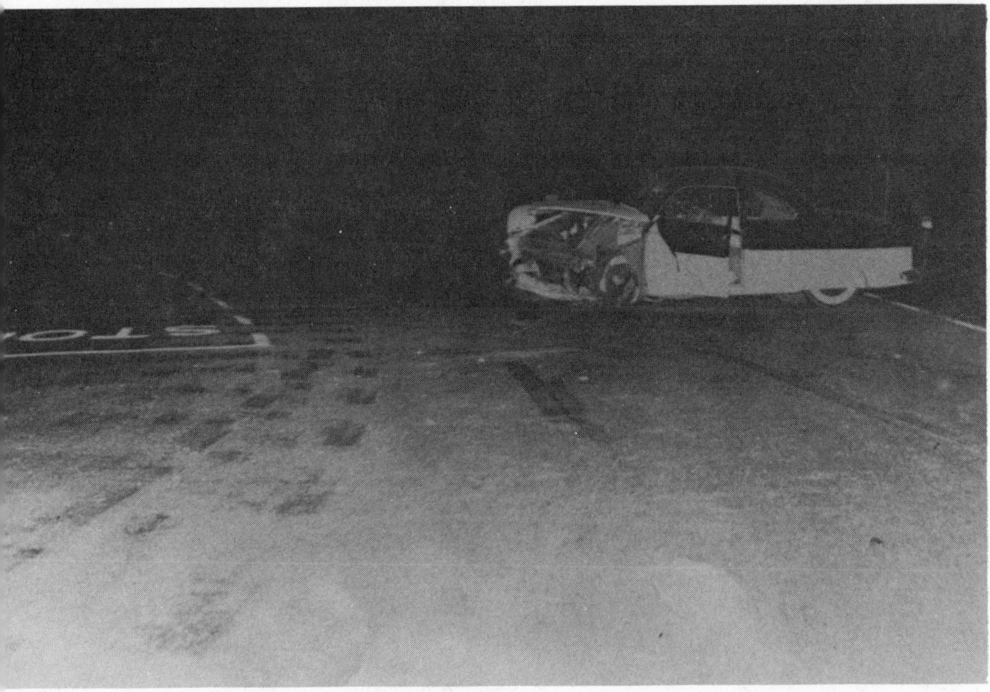

Previously unpublished California Highway Patrol photo showing the 1950 Ford Custom Deluxe Coupe after collision with Dean's Spyder. The skid-marks, terminating at the point of impact, are visible in the foreground. (Author's collection)

Previously unpublished Highway Patrol photo of James Dean's car after the collision. (Author's collection)

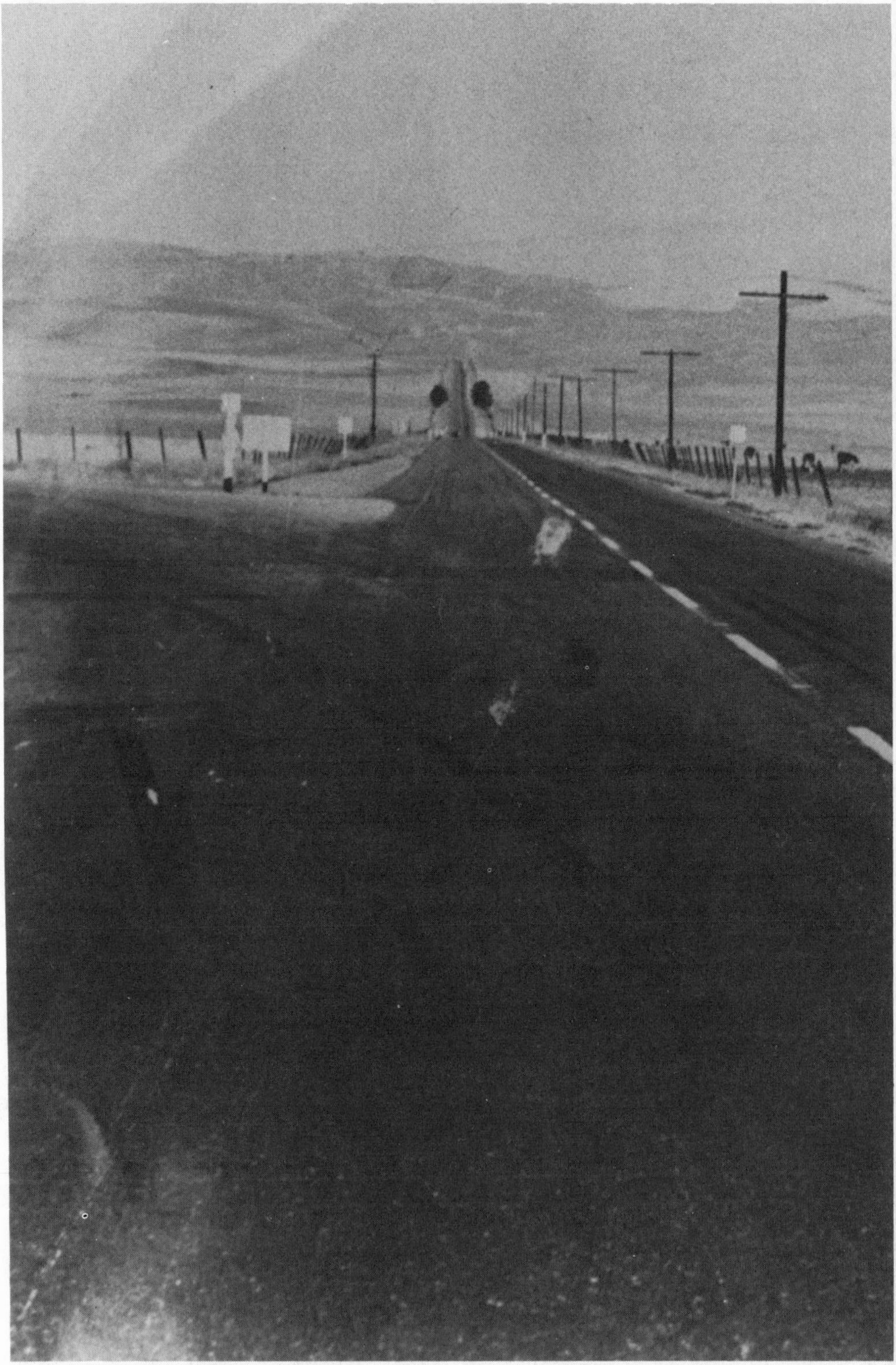

Previously unpublished inquest exhibit showing the intersection, skidmarks and point of impact. (Author's collection)

Previously unpublished photo of Dean's wrecked car in the Cholame garage. The Ford is in the background. (Photo taken by ambulance driver Paul Moreno. Author's collection, courtesy Charles Adams)

The last photo of James Dean: dead or dying, he is carried to the ambulance. (Sanford Roth)

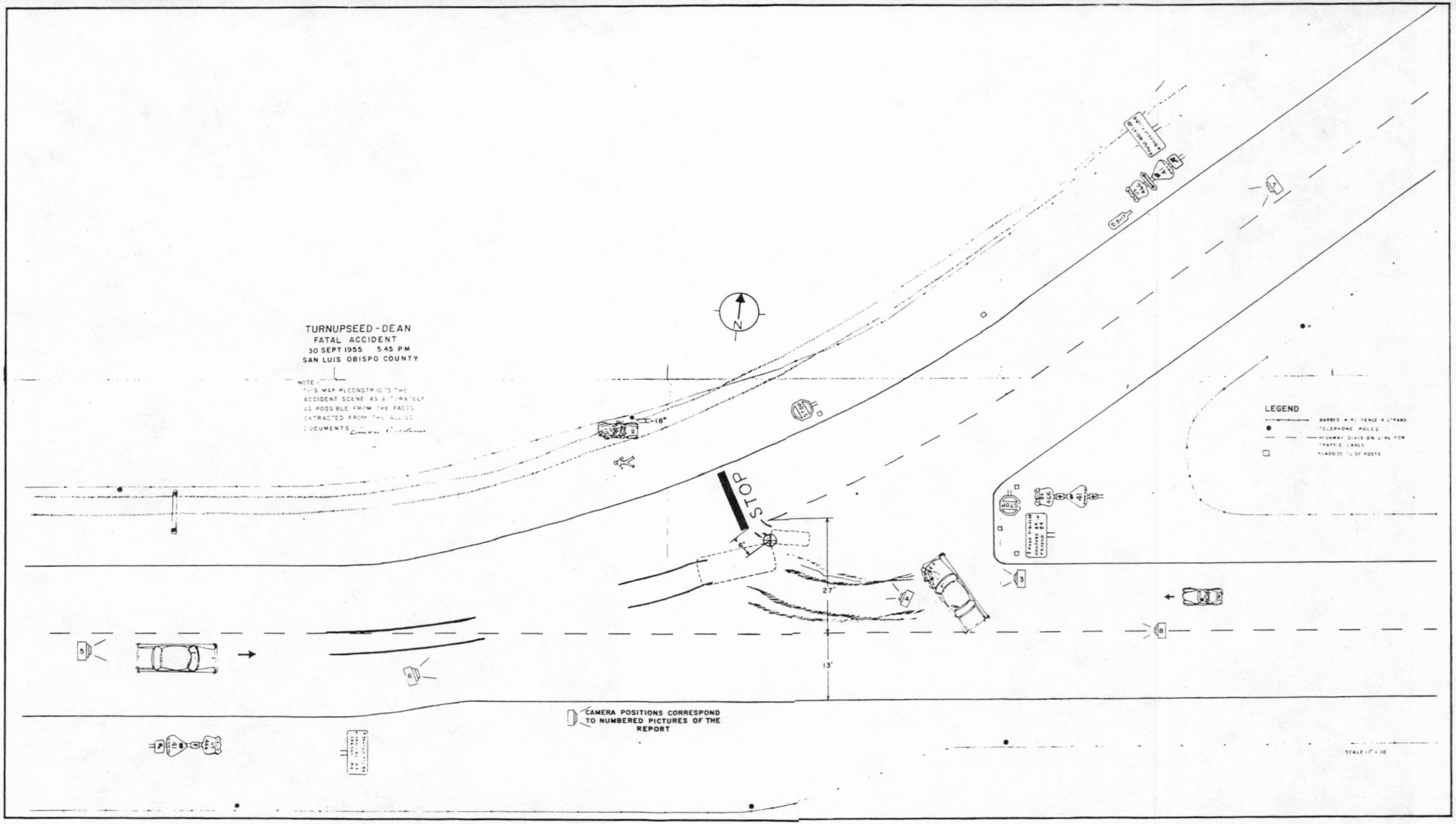

Diagram of the accident, showing Dean's car at upper left, the Ford at lower right and skidmarks. (courtesy Charles Adams)

Dean's Spyder, September 30, 1955 (Sanford Roth)

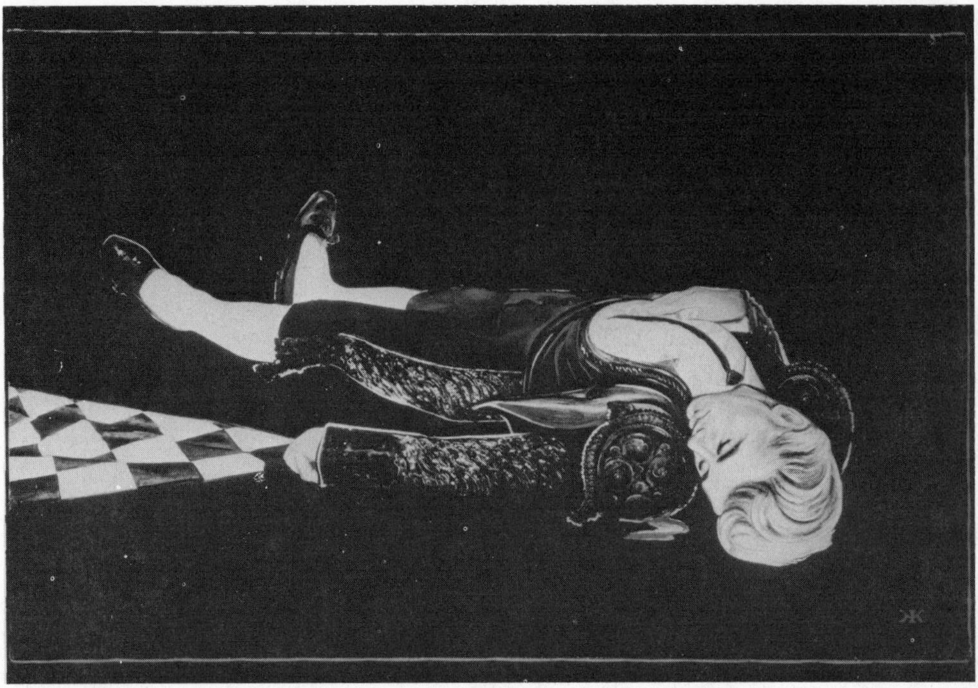

El Torero Muerto by Kenneth Kendall illustrates Dean's fascination with bullfighting. (Kenneth Kendall)

Dean ghoul friend Maila "Vampire" Nurmi in *Plan Nine From Outer Space,* "The Worst Movie Ever Made." (Author's collection)

Kenneth Kendall's sculpture of Dean. (Kenneth Kendall)

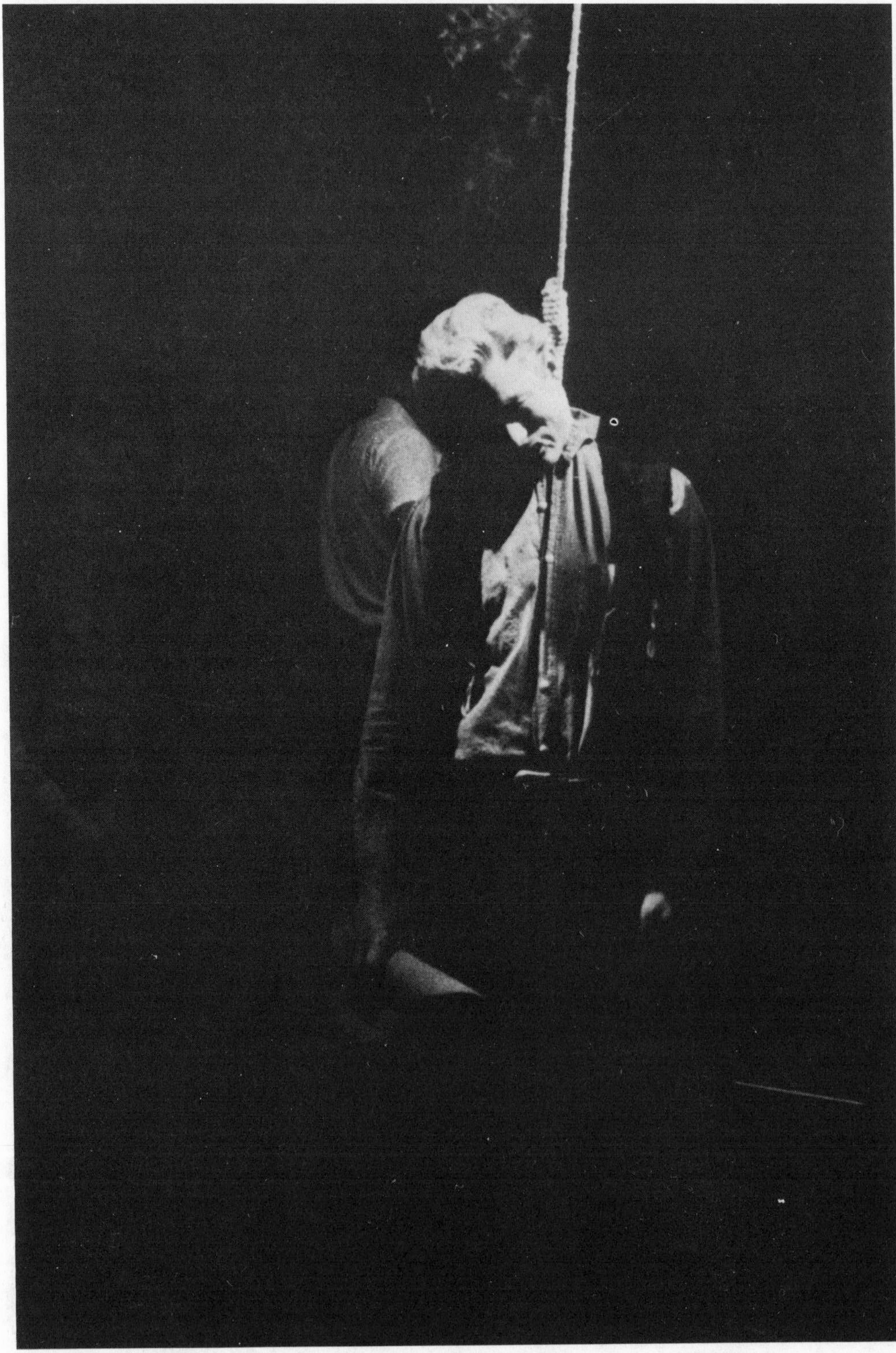

Dean's macabre sense of humor often alluded to his own death. (Sanford Roth)

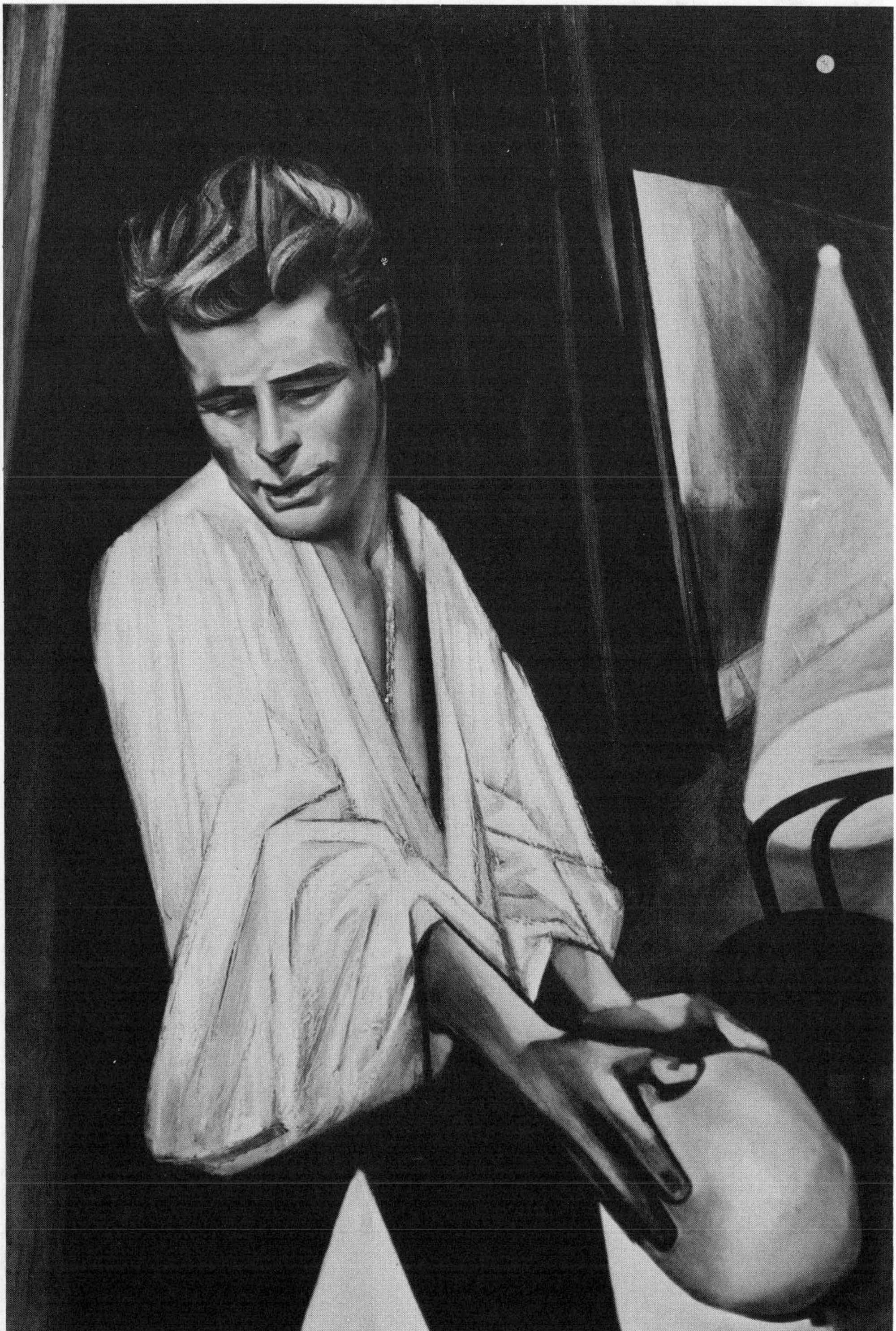

"James Dean Rehearsing *Hamlet*." by Kenneth Kendall. (Kenneth Kendall, photo courtesy Los Angeles County Museum)

Dean's introspection was one of the qualities that attracted fans. (Ray Shatt)

James Dean's grave in Fairmount, Indiana. (Author's collection)

terminated the interview when a female agent tried to photograph a page with a camera concealed in a cigarette lighter. The Dean family did not want the report released. It was not a rejection of his work – it was just not the kind of story about Jimmy they wanted publicized at that time.

Adams was never to interview Rolf Weutherich. The German mechanic had spent nearly a year in hospitals, encased in plaster with his face held immobile by wire structures. Doped and vague on painkillers, he was still never free from pain. When he left the hospital it was on crutches. Three months later he underwent a bone grafting operation. An eight-inch silver nail and several screws were inserted to connect his hip bones. He was, literally, a broken man.

Rolf suddenly found he had a strange celebrity as the man who had ridden to the brink of death with James Dean. He didn't care for it particularly, except when it might help him pick up a girl, but he was a friendly fellow who would talk to the journalists who approached him, like Aljean Meltsir, who was writing an article for the September 1956 issue of *Motion Picture*. His command of English, although improved by the long stateside hospitalization, was still halting, and his recollections dim or nondescript. It had all happened so fast.

In 1957 he finally sold his story to a writer. It appeared in the October issue of *Modern Screen*, prefaced by a comment from editor David Meyers entitled 'The Last Story about Jimmy'. There was a pen and ink sketch of Dean in a T-shirt, Chesterfield between his lips.

> One morning a few weeks ago, I got a phone call from a well known agent, who also happens to be a personal friend of mine. 'Dave,' he said, 'I am holding in my hand right now a story about Jimmy Dean that's gonna . . .'
>
> 'Forget it, Phil,' I said quickly. 'There aren't going to be any more Dean stories in *Modern Screen*.'
>
> 'But this story, Dave, it . . .'
>
> 'Look, Phil,' I said, 'come September 30th Jimmy will be dead two years. Why don't we all just let him rest in peace? Furthermore, all his close friends have already said everything important there is to be said about Jimmy.

They loved him, they'll never forget him. That's it.'

'This isn't written by any close friend of Jimmy's. It's by his mechanic, Rolf Weutherich. He is the only person in the whole world who was actually with Jimmy when it happened. Rolf was right there on the seat beside him. Well, he's out of the hospital at last, and . . .'

'You mean this guy Rolf was in the actual crash?'

'That's what I mean, Dave.'

'Well, how did it really happen? I mean, what's he say? I'd like to know and so would our readers.'

'Meet me for lunch,' Phil said, 'and I'll let you read the story. Then you'll know what really happened on Jimmy's last ride.'

So Phil and I met for lunch. I didn't say much to him – I was too busy reading the story. I left my sandwich untouched on the plate and my coffee got cold. When I was finished, Phil said, 'What do you think?'

For a moment I had trouble focusing on his face. I was still inside the world of the story, still with Jimmy in that last tragic day. Then I said, 'I'll buy it, of course. And Phil, I've never thanked you for bringing me a story before, but . . . thank you.'

The article, illustrated with Sanford Roth's photos of Dean and Weutherich in the Spyder as they set out, was titled 'Death Drive'. The anonymous ghostwriter had fleshed out the skeleton of Rolf's recollections into a picaresque romance – it was what Jimmy's fans *wished* the last drive had been like. It would be quoted for thirty years afterward, and those books on Dean which did not quote it would paraphrase it. Reprinted in a later issue as 'Ghost Drive', it was the most famous and popular story the magazine ever published.

We had been on Highway 466 ever since we went through Bakersfield and now it was deserted. No car except our Spyder and the station wagon as far as we could see. Jimmy went faster now – a very natural thing to do when you are all alone on a good road in a racing car. It was just past five in the afternoon. The sun, a ball of fire, shone directly in our eyes. It was still very hot and the heat flickered and danced on the sandy brown road. To the right and left of us was desert, in front of us, an endless ribbon of road.

'Everything okay?' Jimmy asked.

'Everything okay,' I answered, half dozing. The monotonous hum of the engine was like a soft cradle song. We were not talking now – not of Pier Angeli or of Dean's mother or of anything. The only thought in Jimmy's mind was winning that race. There was no doubt of that: that's all he talked about. I felt a little uneasy again. I glanced at Jimmy but could see no shadow of fear across his face. He had no premonition of his death . . .

A 1950 model Ford was coming at us.

Suddenly, the car swung out toward the centre of the highway to turn onto Highway 41, its left wheels over the centre line.

Then we hit. My head slammed against the dashboard, and my body was thrown out of the car, yards down the highway. I passed out instantly.

Dimly I remembered being lifted by ambulance workers. I came to in the ambulance . . . Then I thought *Jimmy! Where was Jimmy? What had happened to him?* I saw him as though I were looking through a leaden haze. There he was – my friend Jimmy – lying limp, covered with blood, bones fractured, his neck broken. He was beyond help – anyone's help.

Again and again, during the months I lay in the hospital . . . I tormented my memory to recall those few seconds before Jimmy's death . . .

Was there an instant before he died when he knew he was dying . . .

Did he know pain . . .

I do not know. The only thing I can remember is the soft cry that escaped from Jimmy . . . the little whimpering cry of a boy wanting his mother . . . or of a man facing his God . . .

The article did not mention that the anguished Rolf had subdued his grief sufficiently to sue Winton Dean for some of the $100,000 from Jimmy's insurance policy. Weutherich lost. His injuries had been incurred in the course of his employment, which was why Competition Motors' compensation insurance, Pacific Indemnity, had paid for his hospitalization and treatment. Lew Bracker said that it had been Jimmy's intention to draw up a will that would distribute $5,000 of his life insurance policy to Grandma and Grandpa Dean, $10,000 to Markie Jr for his college education, and designate Marcus and Ortense Winslow as the chief beneficiaries of the $85,000 remainder. He had planned to attend to it upon his return from his Salinas racing holiday. But the entire sum went to Winton Dean as next of kin. He kept it all. At the age of forty-eight, he was suddenly a very wealthy man. Marcus and Ortense said nothing, though the people of Fairmount talked. Rolf left the United States, returning to Germany to work for Porsche.

October 1956 had seen the première of Dean's final film. George Stevens's *Giant* was an expensive and impressive production. Its three hours and eighteen minutes chronicled twenty-five years in the lives of a rich Texas ranching family. It presented a strange reflection of reality. The early scenes of Texas were sharp and gritty, with the sets becoming more artificial and studio-bound as the film progressed. The 'ageing' of Rock Hudson and Elizabeth Taylor struck an especially false note – their hair turned blue. But the film had several real and enduring images. Few would forget the first view of the incongruous gothic house in the middle of the flat Texas prairie, or Dean's performance as the surly and ticky ranch hand Jett Rink.

Those detractors who had said that Dean's early death was a 'great career move, kid,' and predicted that one more appearance would reveal him as a flash in the pan, were disappointed. It was a rare critic now who did not grudgingly concede him at least a 'streak of genius'. His characterization of the bitter young hand whose new oil riches cannot halt his loveless deterioration was alternately poignant and acidulous. He stole the movie, and received his second and last Academy Award nomination.

The moment was ripe for another Dean film. His popularity had never been higher. But Warner's biggest star was 2,000 miles away under the frozen ground of a wintry Indiana grave. Perhaps a film biography of Dean? There was much talk and attendant publicity about who might portray him. Elvis Presley was seriously considered. He was a Dean worshipper. Elvis had memorized most of Dean's lines from *Rebel Without a Cause*, and when he had come to Hollywood he had hung around Dean's old haunts, even acquiring some of Dean's old friends, such as Jack Simmons. He had dated Maila. But it was not to be. It was announced that the film would be a documentary.

The finished product was a disappointment to even the most indiscriminate Dean fan. Narrated by a funereal Martin Gabel, it relied heavily on two stultifying devices, the 'distant figure' representing Dean at different times in his life, and motion picture footage of still photographs. Co-directed by Robert Altman, who later went on to better things, the leaden and pontifical script was by Stewart Stern. The Winslows were finagled into it, but most of Jimmy's friends felt that participation would be unseemly. The picture began with a shot of the stretch of Highway 466 where Dean had died. There was a squeal of brakes, the cry of wheeling sea gulls, then the image of one of the birds dead and washing around in the surf.

The title song was sung by Tommy Sands:

> Let me be loved . . .
> Let me be loved . . .
> Let someone care for me.
> Life was so wonderful then . . .
> Let me be loved, again.

The young Nick Adams, his head antlike and rapacious, was present in the lobby at the Indiana première, passing out photos of a car he claimed he and Jimmy had been working on before Jimmy had died. The film flopped.

Normally when people are involved in tragic accidents, time elapses and memory softens and erodes the pain. Horror recedes into the past. But this death and this dead boy were constantly being resuscitated. A year after the wreck, Dean was on the cover of *Look* magazine. His 'new' picture was released.

On the first anniversary of Dean's death, Aljean Meltsir had written in *Motion Picture*, 'White-faced and crying, leaning across the fender of his car, Donald Turnupseed kept repeating, in a toneless, unbelieving voice, never stopping to brush away the tears that trickled down his cheeks, "I didn't see him. I swear . . . I swear . . . I didn't see him." ' In an italicized footnote to Rolf's 'Death Drive', someone had written:

> The driver of the other car was a young student named Donald Turnupseed. When Donald found out that he was responsible for the crash, he broke down in tears. 'I didn't see him, my God, I didn't see him,' he wept. Donald himself suffered almost no injuries.

That he had not been injured was always reported like an ironic accusation of injustice.

On 28 September 1956, Rolf Weutherich amended his lawsuit of $120,000 to include the student as defendant along with James Dean. In early December, Pacific Indemnity, Dean's motor insurance carrier, filed a suit in San Luis Obispo County against the young man for $6,049.37 – the amount of damage sustained by them with the loss of Dean's 550 Spyder (less the $876 recovered by their sale of the wreckage). The sum included Paul Moreno's towing bill of $175.37. The suit charged that the student 'so carelessly, negligently drove and operated his automobile . . . as to cause the same to collide with the Porsche automobile being then and there driven by the said James Byron Dean'.

The young man re-enlisted in the Navy. While the attorneys for his own insurance carrier wrangled with Rolf's lawyers over the $10,000 liability limit of their policy, the trial date in the suit by Dean's insurance company was put off until his discharge in 1958.

Maila's career had taken a disastrous turn after the cancellation of her show. A.B.C. had blacklisted her in revengeful pique. She could find no work.

One evening she was at a party at Bela Lugosi Jr's home when she ran into another Junior – Ed Woods. Woods was a strange man. He was an ex-marine with a deep voice and masculine mannerisms, yet he wore women's trousers suits and panty-hose. He claimed to have been wearing a bra and panties when he made a beach landing in the Second World War. He wanted to be a film director. He came to Hollywood where he became the nucleus of a bizarre coterie which included the psychic Criswell (and his young male 'protégé' of the moment), and 400 lb Tor Johnson. An ex-wrestler and veteran of Gower Gulch horror cheapies, Johnson was a kind man whose immensity and ominous features had won him a 'monster' role in *The Black Sleep* and the title role in *The Beast of Yucca Flats.* Woods confided, out of Johnson's hearing, that Tor broke his toilet seat every time he came over to visit.

Woods demonstrated some ability as a promoter by finding backing for three films. The money was obtained largely on the strength of his ability to supply and extract a performance from the aged and declining Bela Lugosi.

The great screen Dracula had outlived himself. By the mid-fifties he had fallen on pitiful times. Addicted to morphine and alcohol, his memory and English had deteriorated. He was in complete eclipse when Ed Woods Jr gave his career a dubious revival in exchange for the faded star lustre of his name. It was a sad spectacle, Lugosi playing a wizard in the transvestite film *Glen or Glenda* with Woods directing and starring – in an Angora sweater. *Bride of the Atom* followed in 1954. The financing for this production came from an Arizona meat packing magnate whose provisos were that the film star his son, Tony McCoy, and contain an anti-nuclear statement. It was incredibly amateur. When Lugosi blew a bit of menacing dialogue, 'Don't be afraid of Lobo, he's harmless as a kitten', rendering it, 'Don't be afraid of Lobo, he's harmless as kit*chen*,' Woods didn't even reshoot it.

Woods wrote a vampire skit for Lugosi and a couple of showgirls and booked them into the Silver Slipper Saloon in Las Vegas. The seventy-two-year-old trouper soon collapsed under the strain. When Lugosi's wife packed up and left with their son after years of the old actor's addictions and jealousy, Bela fell apart completely. He surrendered himself to a hospital to detoxify, but also to shame and embarrass his spouse. Newspaper photos showed him as withered and skeletal as a skid-row bum. Frank Sinatra sent him a few bucks. But the hospital ward was more horrible than he had imagined. Woods kept the old man's hopes up with talk of new projects. Upon his release, Woods showed him a script called *Tomb of the Vampire*. In it, Lugosi would once more don the Dracula cape.

The hastily assembled company, including Tor Johnson, went off to an old Spanish cemetery in the San Fernando Valley which was soon to be relocated to make way for a housing development. Fortified with drinks, Lugosi helped the crew, including Johnson's strapping policeman son Carl, in moving the tombstones to accommodate Woods's camera angles. The next day's paper carried a story about vandalization of the burial ground. Bereaved relatives calling at the cemetery had been unable to locate the graves of their loved ones.

Woods soon exhausted his money. Worse, he had filmed only about sixty seconds of Lugosi's performance when his star died in his sleep at his Harold Way apartment. Bela was buried in his Dracula cape.

Maila had known Bela from guest appearances they had made together on the 'Red Skelton Show', plus personal appearances for Woods. Bela had once called her, weeping, on Mother's Day. He was heartbroken that his son had not called him.

Now, Woods told her that he had raised some more money and rewritten a new film around the Lugosi footage. It was retitled *Grave Robbers from Outer Space*. Woods offered her $200 for a day's work.

She accepted with distaste. Woods's obsequiousness had always raised her hackles. She thought him a true moron whose one redeeming quality was his tenderness toward animals. But she dressed once more in her Vampira costume and rode on the R.T.D. to Gower Street where she appeared before Woods's camera as the Ghoul Woman.

The script told the story of an evil trio from outer space who plot to take over the United States by reanimating corpses of the recently dead. The film opened with a leonine Criswell grimly intoning, 'My friends, can your hearts stand the shocking facts about GRAVE ROBBERS FROM OUTER SPACE?' Even with looping the film, Woods could produce only two minutes of Lugosi's famous face. For the rest of the picture, he substituted his wife's chiropractor. It has been noted that this man was probably the *only* person in Hollywood who could not imitate Lugosi's accent. He appeared wordless throughout the movie, a cape held over his nose.

Maila's role was that of Lugosi's dead wife, the first cadaver to be reanimated. Her scenes were shot on an incredibly phoney graveyard set. The trees and tombstones were obviously cardboard, toppling whenever an actor tripped on them. The police inspector, played by Tor Johnson in his only speaking role, is killed by the Ghoul Woman and rises from the dead to join her in stalking the cemetery at the bidding of the spaceship trio.

The film was not released until 1959, when it appeared as *Plan 9 from Outer Space*. Laughter and hoots greeted it from the cars parked in premature obeisance before the drive-in screens. The aeroplane cockpit set looked like a shower stall. The flying saucer was obviously a paper plate covered with burning lighter fuel and tossed at the camera. The film's ineptness had to be seen to be believed. Few had the chance, for it sank quickly into obscurity. It was the death blow for more than one career.

Whisper and *Confidential*, two tabloids that reflected the Hollywood underbelly, posthumously linked Maila romantically with Dean. They called her 'Jimmy Dean's Black Madonna' and claimed she had placed a hex on him which brought about his death. She began to receive notes written in blood, death threats from *true* necrophiliacs who thought she'd be more attractive as a real corpse. She found decapitated animals on her doorstep. She virtually disappeared from the public eye.

Sanford Roth said that he would never release the photos he had taken of Dean's body in the Spyder. They were too gruesome. Roth, too, had a newfound fame as a friend of Jimmy's. He had gone ahead and completed the *Collier's* article he had been working on when he left for Salinas with Jimmy that weekend, and it was published the month following the death. Sometimes he claimed that he had begun taking pictures 'instinctively', and at other times he would say he had done it in case there was later any question about who had been driving. The inquiries he received made him aware of a darker, more intense special interest in Jimmy from what was soon being called the 'Dean Death Cult'.

George Barris shared few of Roth's qualms. He was approached by the highway patrol and soon the wreckage was on tour up and down the state as part of a highway safety display. The remains bore little resemblance to the original Spyder, or even to the original 'wreck'. Anything in it worth anything had been stripped and sold. Heralded as 'James Dean's Last Sports Car', the hulk was displayed with a large blow-up of Dean's registration mounted in the seat. 'This Accident Could Have Been Avoided', another placard read. Barris cultivated a mystique about the car, circulating strange stories. Some truly odd things did occur. In March 1959, in Fresno, the third city of its tour a fire had broken out in the Patrol Garage where the car was being stored. The Spyder was scorched and he had spent $1,000 refinishing it. Soon afterwards, he said, the car fell off its display mounts and broke the hip of a teenager.

A few weeks later, the car was reportedly en route to Salinas when the truck transporting it was involved in an accident. Driver George Barhuis was killed when he was thrown from the cab and crushed by the Porsche as it rolled off the bed. The 'curse' next struck in Oakland where the Porsche broke into two pieces which fell onto the freeway causing a minor accident. In Oregon, supposedly, the emergency brake on the display truck slipped and sent truck and Porsche crashing into a store front. In late 1959, the car was in New Orleans when it broke into eleven pieces while resting on its stationary supports.

Barris claimed that No. 130 had been on display in Florida for their highway patrol and was being returned to California when it disappeared. Barris sometimes said it had been shipped by rail; sometimes he said it had gone by truck. He later claimed the Pinkerton Detective Agency had spent years in a futile search. The only certain fact was that the car vanished from public view in 1960.

James Dean had left for New York four days after his January 1955 visit to the Melrose Avenue studio of sculptor Kenneth Kendall. He had promised he would return with photo studies of himself to aid Kendall in 'doing' him like he had 'done' Brando. Kendall, who had never seen Dean in a film, was not particularly impressed. He was slightly put off by the racing emblems on Dean's handsome black leather jacket, and the strident one-legged chick who accompanied him. Dean had time to smoke three Chesterfields in his brief visit. Kendall noticed that Dean removed his glasses to display a gamut of facial expressions for him during the brief visit. Dean was fascinated by Kendall's 'morgue' on Brando – his collection of sketches and photos which had been used in developing the head of Brando which had impressed Jimmy and brought him to his door. He was also impressed by the large zodiacal lithos of muscleman Steve Reeves which covered one wall of the studio. Reeves and Kendall had at one time been close friends.

Kendall came down with a miserable flu and was bedridden for two weeks. When he recovered, he went to the theatre to see *East of Eden*. He was staggered by it and felt awe-struck to think, '*He* knows *me*.' Kendall often worked crowd scenes at Warners. Months passed. He knew there was a call out for extras for the tuxedo set for *Giant* at the Stadler Hilton, but he did not want to risk encountering Dean in any situation other than that of artist–subject and so jeopardize the proposed work. He hoped that Dean was the star he had always dreamt of meeting, who would grant him fame by permitting their mutual immortalization in great works of art. He regretted that he had mentioned a fee during the actor's visit. He began to collect photos of Dean in anticipation of the hoped-for project. But Dean never returned. Kendall never saw James Dean again. He started work on the head of Dean the night he learned of his death.

It would not stay normal size, growing quickly to an eighth larger than life. After four months' work, Jimmy's grandparents visited the studio with Winton and Ethel Dean. They had a good cry when they saw the likeness with its familiar smile and windblown hair. Kendall corresponded with Emma Dean and told her he would like to see a copy of the head erected on the high school grounds in Fairmount. He wondered whether the students could raise the money for a casting in bronze. There seemed to be some local interest, and the kids were to have a drive for old bricks to build a cenotaph on which to display it. Kendall envisaged a crop of corn, or some sunflowers, encircling the platform.

At this point entered Les Johnson, a sort of promoter who had some connection with the James Dean Memorial Foundation, the organization of indeterminate purpose which had been set up to try and channel constructively some of the unleashed enthusiasm for Fairmount's most famous son. Johnson claimed to have located a benefactor with $500 for the casting and lettering. He later told Kendall that he personally had built the cenotaph. But it had been erected in *the cemetery* outside town rather than in the school grounds. Kendall did not know why, though there were whispered hints in Fairmount. Thıe head was mounted atop a steel rod jutting from the 6-foot-tall brick slab.

Kendall had gifted Winton with a replica of the head. Winton reciprocated with a life mask of Jimmy which had been moulded by Warner Brothers' make-up department, an insider's indication of Jimmy's 'arrival'. Winton had found it among Jimmy's things when he and Bill Hickman had cleaned out the Sutton Street house. Winton eventually returned the head. The vibrant and silent laughter beneath the familiar crinkled eyes had been unnerving to live with.

Nine months after the bronze head was erected at the cemetery it was stolen. The hacksawed steel rod stuck up grotesquely like a fractured brain stem. There was a dent in the bricks where it had fallen. It was assumed that it had been taken by an obsessed fan. Some in Fairmount claimed to know it had been removed by an American Legionnaire outraged by a monument to any man who had evaded service in the armed forces by registering for the draft as a homosexual.

The head was never recovered, but the cenotaph was left standing, its bronze letters continually chipped, pried, and cut by outsiders in search of mementos. Kendall often wondered where the head had wound up. He hoped it was not damaged. What had they made of the strange writing on the bottom? Under the base, in Greek letters, he had copied the inscription from an ancient funeral stele. Translated, it read 'Summer was only beginning.'

Chapter 9

In 1969, Howard Hubbell Matson* was seventeen years old and a junior at Dinuba High School in central California. His father had died when he was thirteen, and his mother remarried three years later. With her son and two young daughters she had moved into a new house on two acres of farmland outside the little town of Reedley, two hundred miles north of Los Angeles off Highway 99.

Skinny and angular, with a jutting adam's apple and horn-rimmed glasses (which he hated) on a face always shameful with at least one swollen pimple, the high school years were difficult. He couldn't seem to get popular. The first year of his mother's remarriage he was prey to a fear and sense of displacement he would never have admitted. Once an accelerated student, his grades slipped. He was amazed when he found a girl-friend. Sixteen-year-old Cindy Knight's mother had been killed in a car accident on a rural road. Her father now spent most of his evenings with his new fiancée. Howard and Cindy found much sympathy in one another.

Howard's life had always been very involved with movies. The first horror film he remembered seeing was *Plan 9 from Outer Space*. He had been eight years old. For years afterwards he was afraid of the dark and of the tall, skeletal woman with the cold stare and the long fingernails who had been in the picture, and who now came in through the back door of their house and up the hall to advance one step closer to his bedroom door each night before turning and mysteriously gliding back outside. At seventeen years old, he had let his hair grow and started smoking. He acted tough at school, but he often felt his eyes fill with tears when he sat in a movie theatre.

* not his real name

One Saturday night, Howard stayed up to watch *Rebel Without a Cause* on the late show. He had seen it before. He had been curious because he remembered that his father, who had been a highway patrolman, had told him he had known the officer who had given Dean a ticket on the day he had been killed. But on this night and at this time in his life, it struck him with tremendous force. The image of James Dean cut through the old movie with painful incision and radiance. Much of the appeal was narcissistic: Howard was instantly fascinated by what James Dean had known about *him*. Most devastating was the planetarium scene where Jim Stark moos like a cow at the display of Taurus in the laserium firmament. There was a painful silence, and then a horrible pause as he waited for the approval of the gang. Their disgust and ridicule, *'He's real cute,'* and then the three reflexive emotions flashing across Dean's face – hurt, resignation, and a protective hardness, communicated in a second with the eyes and the muscle of the jaw – hit Howard in the stomach like successive punches. And pervading the movie, like the haunting scent of wisteria, was the sharply edged and poignant awareness that *this boy was dead*. Howard was transfixed until the last strains of the theme music died away.

He stepped outside the screen door onto the lawn and lit a cigarette. He didn't light up in the house because the smoke would be drawn into the air conditioning ducts and wafted into his mother and stepfather's room across the carport. He looked up at the stars and was moved when he thought how James Dean had died somewhere in California under these same skies, on a lonely highway.

Rob Halls, blond, pimply, with a pubescent voice that quavered between two ranges, was Howard's best friend, and he became infected with his enthusiasm. Together, they cut school to watch *East of Eden* when it came on Dialing for Dollars Movie. Howard's fascination grew. He searched the meagre little school library for old film reviews and any scrap of biography about James Dean. He especially wanted to know how and where he had died. No one seemed to know, or everyone said something different. Howard wondered if anyone was still around who remembered what actually happened. With Rob, he drove toward Paso Robles one weekend on Highway 41, stopping at Reef Junction near Kettleman City to ask a weathered waitress if she knew where James Dean had been killed. She said she was pretty sure it had happened at the intersection of Highways 46 and 33. The boys took Highway 33 for thirty miles across the desert to where it hit a barren stretch of Highway 46 – or Highway 466, as it had been in the 1950s.

There was nothing but some charred wreckage. A burnt and blackened metal sign read BLACKWELL'S CORNERS. The trunk and branches of two great cedars were scarred by fire. Howard felt desolate and empty as he walked around and kicked at the rubble. Rob took some pictures before they drove on.

He wondered whether the unquietness inside him would be relieved once he found that spot which he was sure would forever after be secretly and specially *his*. But he needed to know *what* had happened. Howard and Rob drove to Paso Robles and stopped at the cluttered little office of the *Daily Press*. There was a rumpled man at the counter who helped them dig through a yellowed pile of brittle papers nearly fourteen years old. They finally located the 1 October 1955 edition. Howard wondered if there might be only a little paragraph on the back page. 'Here you go,' the man said. There was a large picture of a Ford, the windscreen shot with spider web cracks, the front fender savaged as if a huge shark had taken a bite. Below was a dark photo of the crushed Porsche. *There had been another car involved.* They had been wrong – it had happened at the intersection of Highways 41 and 46. Howard hastily scribbled the news story onto a pad he had brought along. For the first time he read the name of the driver of the other car. He was elated. He would be able to stop and walk around on that spot of highway and know that it had happened *there*.

Though he had passed through many times before, Howard felt strong emotions the first time he and Rob stopped at the intersection of Highways 41 and 46. It was only eighty miles from the farmhouse in Reedley. Each night, he slept only an hour and a half from where James Dean had died. They had driven west to hit Highway 41, which they followed south. The landscape turned arid and sere. There were the rolling hills of Cottonwood Pass until the road fell and levelled onto a vast flat plain. Howard saw the intersection ahead.

It was hard to believe it had happened here. The wind whipped their hair. The light poles and highway signs were crawling with graffiti – 'James Dean Lives!' – or the more cryptic – '9/30/55'. The defacers had come from all over the country.

Howard pried one of the cracked concrete cornices from the centre safety island. He figured it approximated the site of the crash because it was in the middle of the intersection. He lugged it back to the car while Rob took pictures.

They came to the spot again and again. On some trips they would drive eighty miles out of their way, following Highway 99 south to the Famosa turnoff outside Bakersfield, just so that they could retrace the final sixty miles of Dean's last drive. Howard thought of Dean as the highway rolled under them through Wasco, Lost Hills, and past signs with names like BROWN MATERIAL ROAD and KECK'S CORNERS. He wondered what Dean had felt and what he had seen. What traces and resonances were left of that day?

He thought more and more about the driver of the other car. Most of the time, Howard didn't think it likely the man would talk with him. But other times, perspective would be lost in the constant repetition of fascinated thought. He would think, 'It was so long ago', or 'It wasn't his fault, he won't be sensitive'.

One day in November 1969, Howard and Rob were driving back from the coast. They had joked and tossed the idea back and forth until it was a real and possible thing. What was wrong with asking if they could talk with him? Reporters did such things all the time. What could he say, except 'No'? Howard's heart began to race with fear. His stomach grew queasy. They were actually going to do it. Howard laughed with Rob, and he felt a little manic and crazy. They drove through the crash site and onto Highway 41. 'Maybe he won't be there,' Howard thought. But something else told him that he would and that this was supposed to be; something was going to happen. He told himself that by nightfall it would be all over.

They found the shop on a corner in the industrial district not far from the freeway. It had to be near closing time. They walked through the door. The shop seemed deserted. Then Howard saw an older woman behind a desk. She smiled, her face friendly. 'May I help you?'

'We wanted to see Mr Turnupseed, if we might,' Howard said.

She smiled, 'Well, he's right there . . .'

A man near seventy years of age raised his head from a workbench.

'I think it's Donald we want,' Howard said. She walked from behind the counter and leaned into the workshop door.

'Donald, there's some gentlemen here that would like to see you.'

Howard had imagined this moment a thousand times, a thousand different ways. A man in his middle thirties stood in the doorway. He was tall and lean, his light hair cropped short. His complexion was ruddy over bony cheeks. He walked slowly, wary eyes narrow in an impassive face.

Howard found his voice and introduced himself and Rob. Howard extended his hand. The other man lifted his own, slowly. Howard took it. Then Rob shook his hand. The man's eyes seemed a machine metal grey. His expression had not changed.

Howard said, 'We're doing a project for our college and we ran across your name several times in our research – and we were wondering if you could tell us anything,' his voice faltered, then hurried on as numbness spread over his face, '– about the accident in fifty-five?'

Howard had been barely able to finish the sentence. He was struck by the sudden change in the light in the man's eyes behind the frozen facial muscles as the words called back to memory that twilight in 1955.

The man's voice was firm and clear.

'Not a chance.'

The silence was sudden and awkward. Howard was full of shame. The man's father was working a few feet away. Howard's peripheral vision had shrunk until he could hardly see. He scratched in his throat for his voice and thanked the man.

The man saw his embarrassment. He said softly, 'Sorry.' The kindness and grace of that wistful smile were shattering. Howard had known something unimaginable would happen. He felt desperate and craven gratitude. He was oblivious of Rob as he walked the thousand miles to the door, aware of Turnupseed's eyes on his back until he stepped outside.

Howard was filled with awe. He had held in his own hand the same fingers that had turned the wheel of the Ford across Highway 466 fourteen years before. He hadn't really expected Don to tell him anything. All he had really wanted was to stand with him for a second on that lonely highway, just the two of them, isolated by the memory of a horror the man had lived. It was important to Howard that he had looked into the man's eyes at the same moment they both felt real pain.

Rob gave Howard a present he had made. It was one of Rob's photos of the fatal intersection, but superimposed on the rough road and the highway signs was the ghostly image of James Dean. Howard framed it in his bedroom. The floor was crowded with his piano, his weights, his desk, and his stereo.

Underneath the picture he taped a card with an inscription from Antoine de Saint Exupery's *The Little Prince*, one of Dean's favourite books: 'This is, to me, the saddest landscape in the world. It was here that the little prince appeared, and disappeared.'

Something exciting happened in January. Howard received a letter from Ernie Tripke. Rob's mother had known him when she had worked in Paso Robles years before. Howard had written to the officer and mentioned Rob's mother. Tripke had xeroxed a magazine article about the accident. He said it was authentic. He had also sent a diagram in pencil which showed how the accident had happened and where the cars had come to rest. Howard bought a binder with plastic sleeves in which to keep them.

Howard saw the address of a bookfinder company in an ad in the back of a science fiction magazine. He sent them $20, and several weeks later he received in the post a 1962 issue of *Popular Photography* which contained an article about Jimmy Dean by Sanford Roth. A footnote said that Roth had died in March of that same year in Rome at the age of forty-five. He had suffered a heart attack. One photo showed James Dean and Rolf Weutherich heading down the freeway out of Los Angeles in No. 130. The wind blew Dean's hair, while Rolf's, more wiry and curly, stayed firmly in place. Howard had never seen the death car before. It was beautiful.

Another photo was incredible. It showed Howard something he had never thought he would see: the wrecked car, the two ambulance attendants, and the injured Rolf in the dirt. The man in the foreground, thumbs in his pockets, even bore a strong resemblance to Don Turnupseed.

Howard and Cindy drove out to the intersection one Saturday. He brought his magazine. He wanted to try and identify where *exactly* the Spyder had come to rest. He compared the terrain in the photo with the actual terrain. The clue was the little arroyo from the culvert under the road. In the photo, the fence stakes fell into this same depression behind the Spyder. Though the phone pole was now gone and the original intersection had been widened and obliterated, he could still estimate where the car had landed. When he found the spot, he asked Cindy to take a picture of him. When it was developed it showed him as small and skinny, his glasses in his pocket, a young boy smiling awkwardly on a gravelly roadside before the broad sweep of Highway 41.

Howard wanted to go to Fairmount. He and Rob would graduate from high school in June. They began to plan a drive across the country. Neither of them had been anywhere or done anything like that before.

It was hot July when they set out. They drove through Texas, Louisiana, and Mississippi. When they slept it was in the back seat of the car. A few days later they drove into Fairmount, Indiana.

They followed a lonely country road north out of town. They came upon an old graveyard under tall trees. Howard pulled the car slowly into the gravel drive. They set off searching in different directions.

On a flat green swath by a creek, Howard came upon a slab of brick on a circular base. The bronze letters were burnt and sawn: JAMES DEAN.

A steel rod poked up strangely from the mortar at the top. Howard was surprised at the crude plainness of it. This had to be the grave. He felt empty. Rob took some pictures.

They left the car and walked further up the road, past fields of corn along country fences. Howard had read that the Winslow farmhouse, where Dean had grown up, was not far from the cemetery. He wondered whether the house was still standing.

They came to a mailbox with the name MARCUS WINSLOW. Howard was amazed. He was *there*. The boys stood and stared at the house. Two pink flamingos on metal rods were perched on the lawn.

A man appeared behind the screen in the door. Howard had no idea what he was going to say. He hadn't expected this, but he began to walk across the broad lawn toward the porch, gangly and bewildered. Howard was awkward and filled with emotion that made him shake the man's hand and tell him how far he had come. The man studied his face seriously.

The man did not ask what he wanted. He didn't even nod his head. Howard struggled to tell him why he was there, when he wasn't even sure himself. The man stepped out of the door and sat on the porch chair, motioning for Howard to do the same. Through the dusky screen, Howard saw Ortense working in the house. Howard was oblivious of the fact that he was probably delaying the man's dinner. Marcus Winslow said nothing about it. He wore a white T-shirt and blue jeans; his skin was ruddy and his eyes as clear as a baby's. Howard couldn't guess his age.

Marcus lit a Marlboro and talked to him man to man, like an adult. Howard was proud. For a moment Howard thought he was supposed to interview him. But Marcus sort of dismissed the subject of Jimmy Dean. 'He was just like any other boy,' he said. Marcus knew that the boys were not there to find out something new. Howard talked about himself and about living on a farm in California. Marcus asked him about crops and irrigation. Howard tried to answer. His stepfather was a farmer and he lived on a farm, but he hated to work on it and never paid it any attention. Now he wished he had. One of Marcus's Marlboros burned down. He stamped it out on the porch with a heavy shoe, then shredded the filter. The wind eddied and whirled it away.

Howard asked if many people still came to the house. 'Yes,' Marcus said. 'From all over. There's a gal from Japan who comes and stays with us sometimes. There's a young man, a merchant marine. He travels all over the world, and he's adopted us as his parents. He'll come to visit Jim's grave and stay a while. I'll get up of a morning and there will be his car in the drive, two feet sticking out the window. And I know we'll be having company for a few days.' He said they come just to be there, to spend some time with the people who had been so close to Jim.

Mr Winslow understood. Dusk was falling like ash on the road and the cornfields. Howard shook his hand again, and he did not feel empty as he walked with Rob back down the road to their car at the cemetery. He knew the trip was over for him. Something had been breathed inside him.

Howard had never really worked, and he did not work the rest of the summer. He started Junior College in September. For his philosophy class, he wrote an essay called 'Notes on Dying'. His teacher was compiling an anthology to be published widely as a college textbook. He was impressed with Howard's talent and included it in his book. The essay was about the fear and fascination of death. Howard mentioned in the pages that he never drove by the spot on Highway 41 where James Dean had died without stopping.

He found an old *Life* magazine with a picture of Dean's grave. He realized for the first time that he had not been there at all. He hurt.

Howard was restless a lot and spent much time staring out of the window when he was in class. He had bouts of depression and he would get in the car, light a cigarette, and head out toward Highway 41 and the intersection, only to turn back before he had driven for twenty minutes. He began to have dreams which he remembered in the morning. Many were about Dean's grave. He would sometimes be in a cemetery, looking for the headstone in the grass and weeds. Sometimes he would come upon it unexpectedly in a strange place, like the bank of a canal, or strangling in the overgrown roots of a great tree.

Howard broke up with Cindy when he found a new girl-friend. In September 1972, he moved to Fresno to attend the university. His subject was English. He lived in a house his mother had bought for him. Away from home, he began to drink more. His drinking was different from that of his roommates: once he started, he could not stop. He did not know when he would get drunk, or what he would do when he drank. He had blackouts. He was twenty-one years old and he wondered what was going to happen to him. He had always assumed he would be a writer, but he had no story. Only one thing excited his imagination, and that was not a story or a theme, but an image: a lonely stretch of highway across which blew dry tumbleweeds, and a beautiful long-dead boy who had been killed there.

He began to write. The boy he named Jimmy Dalton. The time was the 1950s. There was no story, except what resulted from the tremendous strain of sleepless contrivance. He drew huge graphs and charts and lines to interweave several characters, each of which was born only when the last one he had been writing about became lifeless under his pencil. All were pale reflections of Jimmy Dalton, who was himself an echo, a shadow of a sharper real image in Howard's mind. He believed none of it himself, but tried to follow his imagination and energy where it might lead him; and it led him to the one landscape which alone was real and alive and where he lost himself in yearning descriptions. It was a flat land, endless and desolate, with brittle rolling tumbleweeds and stark barbed wire fences along a hot dusty highway where heat shimmered up like the corrugated air over a summer radiator. There was a petrol station, blistered and isolated, past which white highway lines shot straight to distant horizons and burning brown mountains. It all existed long ago and was lost and irretrievable. He felt very emotional as he wrote about it.

He had to finish his project, but when he wrote about the people his frail plots blew over in the wind of his own disinterest. He wanted desperately to *have written*. He had always deferred to his potential, and to the promise made long ago to himself that at this time in life he would get serious and do something. But he knew nothing and had nothing to say and there was nothing, really, he cared much about, besides himself.

Disappointment and frustration became more acute. The day came when he could not figure it out and could not go on. He dropped his 80,000-word manuscript into the rubbish bin. It was impossible. Everything was impossible.

He experienced more and more symptoms of a worsening alcoholism which he could not recognize or admit. He was too young. The best nights he could hope for were those when he merely got drunk at home and crawled into bed oblivious and sick under the brooding gaze of the large poster of James Dean which stared down from the wall. Sometimes, in the hungover mornings, his eyes half closed, the eyes on the poster seemed to move. He dropped out of college. His mother supported him. He tried again the next term after a drunken summer, but the very next month he was arrested and jailed for drunken driving. In December 1974 he turned twenty-three years old. This year would be different, he promised himself. Three nights later he smashed into a parked car in the early morning hours. He got out, staggering in the roadway. The dogs of the neighbourhood began barking and howling. He ran away into the night.

Chapter 10

Stan Pierce* was three years old when James Dean died on the highway to Salinas. He would say years later that ever since he grabbed a movie camera at the age of thirteen and convinced the neighbourhood kids to perform in front of it, he had known how he wanted to make his way – in films. He graduated magna cum laude from the University of Portland in 1974 with a degree in communications. After a 'dues paying stint' as a copywriter, he headed for Eugene and Oregon University of Medicine, where he filmed interviews, examinations, and surgery for in-house viewing. Corpses were queasy subjects, and he often wished he were somewhere else, doing something else. A succession of jobs followed. His late twenties found him again in Portland, where he thought of himself as a freelance television writer, producer, and director. A course in psychology qualified him for part-time work as a drug counsellor at an addiction centre, which he found 'fulfilling and rewarding'. Fortunately, his blonde and attractive young wife, Gloria, had a good job as a legal secretary. Her income helped to make ends meet and maintain their apartment and Stan's enthusiasms. For Stan, children were out of the question for the present; he had too many things going. The Pierces were an active young couple. He and Gloria were always 'hitting the road', taking advantage of her professional association travel discounts.

Trim, with an engaging smile and modish hair, Stan's appearance gave no hint that as a child he had been bespectacled and fat. He had weighed 200 pounds. As he grew older and elected to follow communications where svelte youth and vivacity were at a premium, he began, like Gatsby, to refashion himself in his own platonic image. He

*not his real name

dieted on a regimen of water, soup, and salad. The inner vestiges of a sensitive and self-conscious adolescence remained. His father had been an insurance executive, and it had been hard to make and keep friends when you moved around all the time. Fantasy was his refuge. Horror and science fiction films had become his passion. He later became fascinated with the images of Judy Garland, Marilyn Monroe, and especially, James Dean.

In the mid-seventies a book by David Dalton, *James Dean, the Mutant King*, was published. Stan bought the biography and lingered on the photos and descriptions of sleepy Fairmount, Indiana. It stirred in him that feeling which he described unabashedly as a love of nostalgia, a yearning for another place and time. Stan and Gloria began to save, and by 1979 they were able to fly to Grant County and Dean's home town for the anniversary of his death.

Little Fairmount had no motel; they checked into the Hart in Marion. Renting a car, they joined the other fans at the tiny Fairmount Museum above the Western Auto store on Main Street. There were buttons, pins, postcards, and amateur paintings of Dean. Stan gazed at the black polished boots the actor had worn in *Giant*. They drove north of town and Stan stood silently at the rust-coloured stone in Park Cemetery. He was moved. But his most exciting experience was meeting Adeline Nall and Ortense Winslow.

Marcus had died in 1976, but Ortense still resided in the white farmhouse outside town which had seen so many generations of her family. Stan was thrilled to talk with the woman whom James Dean had called 'Mom'. Her kindness filled him with emotion. In her late seventies, the importunities and hysteria of unremitting fans had once brought her nearly to a nervous breakdown, and her daughter Joan was protective of her. But Ortense felt she owed it to Jimmy to be nice to his fans, so she answered the same questions for the millionth time. She was a wonderful old woman. Stan was hurt that Joan did not respond to him and seemed to have no interest in letting him know her. Neither was Markie Junior impressed by Stan's description of himself as a television producer, or the accompanying paraphernalia of film camera and microphone. Markie sold tractors in town and lived in a more practical world. Stan was hurt, but deflected the pain by saying they seemed 'burned out' by the whole 'Dean business'.

Adeline was more receptive. She still performed in community theatre. Once jealous of the fame her pupil had achieved, she now settled for a celebrity of reflected light. Stan collected Adeline and Ortense, drawing their images and voices onto his film and tape. He listened, absorbed, as Ortense shared some recollections. Stan treasured them. Candid detail and unpublished anecdote sharpened the internal feeling for how it really had been, and it made him feel closer to the man he now started to call 'Jimmy'. He was grateful, and also jealous. There was a proprietary cast to his attitude when he described his feelings toward these 'Dean People' as 'protective'. Once a Dean fan, he was now an insider and a special friend. He spoke of 'well-meaning' fans, less sensitive and tactful than himself, who had hurt these people and so been denied admittance to the circle of those who had been loved by Jimmy Dean in his life. Full of memory, story, and atmospheric colour, Stan was elated on the flight back to Oregon.

A warm sadness came down on him as he returned to the frustrations of work and of no work. The thing that really vitalized him and excited his imagination was James Dean. What he often envisaged was Dean's death. He read again and again the descriptions of the final drive until he could nearly recite them. He wouldn't admit to his fascination. It didn't seem healthy, and he didn't want anyone to think he was morbid. It became a recurring fantasy of strange joy to relive in his mind the stops, hours, and stations until the orgasmic release of the crash. His heart knew what his mind could not admit: the death itself was the essential thing. He was transfixed by the unthinkable, the grotesque and unnatural shattering of the beautiful and gifted. Garland, Monroe, and Dean, all awakened in him a painful and delicious rush of feeling. He felt a *hunger* to draw closer to Jimmy, to step into the charmed circle and be privy to the most naked and horrible moment of his life.

He thought more and more about the other driver. Who was he? What was he like? What had happened to his life? That would be something, to know him and to talk with him. His was the unknown story, and his secrets were the deepest. To touch him would be to enter another inner circle and cross another burning line in the dust. Perhaps it would be like standing finally before the enigma itself. But even just to be able to say, 'I talked to him,' or, 'He told me this . . .' would be marvellous. Stan had started to correspond with other fans in a Dean club, and he had discovered among them a friendly hierarchy based on rarity of collectibles, extremity of acts of devotion, and intimacy with the family. Stan longed to have sensitive information to treasure, hint at, and mete out like scraps to ravenous crabs.

On 24 October, less than a month after his return from Fairmount, Stan connected his tape recorder to the telephone and dialled the home number of the driver of the Ford. A woman answered. Stan's arteries tightened and his blood rushed faster. Modulating the nervousness in his voice, he said that he was organizing a reunion of Cal Poly graduates, and, to this end, he was checking up on people who had attended the university in the 1950s. But the man was not home.

Stan could hardly believe he was going about it in this way. He told himself that reporters did it all the time. But it was so unlike the kind, respectful young man who had approached the aged Mrs Winslow the month before.

He dialled the man at work. He repeated his story to the receptionist. The man came to the phone. Stan was excited, elated, and filled with disbelief. And he was *cautious,* he told himself. He didn't want to hurt the man. That was why he was lying.

The other man's wariness was palpable over the line. Stan made his own voice sound cheerful as he again told his story. Cal Poly. A survey. May I ask some questions? Stan hoped it sounded plausibly innocent.

The man's responses seemed slow and suspicious. The voice was clipped, abrupt, and to the point. He offered nothing. Stan wondered whether it was his own guilt that was making him hear such defensiveness and distrust. He could not tell. But what was unmistakable was the *sadness.* Something within Stan wanted to cut through it all and to say, 'But I'm different, you can *trust me.*' But he knew he would not, and that the other could not.

With each question, Stan felt a reticence and an arctic coldness through the phone. Had he been attending Cal Poly in 1955? 'Yes, I was there,' the man said as the tape spool turned. No, he had not graduated. He had joined the service. The call soon came to an end. He wondered whether he should have done it.

He began to assimilate the experience even as he rewound the tape he had recorded. He told himself he had been sensitive. 'Well-meaning, misguided fans can be a terrible strain on some people,' he thought. He had 'trod softly'. Stan made the man his own and absorbed him into his 'Dean People'. He would be protective of him, shielding him from further invasions of his privacy by fans who wouldn't be nearly as careful as he had been.

But what a scoop! He could hardly wait to tell, with appropriate cautions and appeals for secrecy, of the 'contact' he had made, like a magneto wire sparking to some charged plug of initiation and special knowledge.

Stan had cultivated correspondence with Adeline Nall and followed the shaping of events at Fairmount for the twenty-fifth anniversary of Dean's death in September 1980. The quarter century mark, the resurgence of interest in Dean, and the added lustre of the involvement of a *live* Hollywood movie star, promised to make it the biggest Museum Days ever. Martin Sheen, a successful film and television star of the Dean school, called Jimmy 'the greatest actor who ever lived'. He had donated a $1,000 plaque commemorating Dean to the Fairmount High School, and he had helped form a Memorial Committee whose members included Adeline and Charles Nolan Dean, Jimmy's uncle to whom he had given a ride in the Spyder on that fatal day. Fairmount had always called the annual festivities near the date of Dean's death 'Museum Days' and attempted to celebrate local history and other Fairmount luminaries, which included a Wright brother and the inventor of the hot dog. But this year the ruse of 'respectability' was so transparent as to be laughable. A record crowd was expected, and all events centred around Jimmy Dean and the theme 'To Commemorate His Talent and Time Among Us'. Stan knew he could not miss it. He made early reservations.

The Hart Motel in Marion was the assigned rendezvous for the We Remember Dean club members who had been able to make the trip. Stan was able to meet for the first time some of the people with whom he had corresponded. There was Tom Nickel, the club president. In his early thirties and unmarried, he still lived with his parents. Stan was especially glad to meet Phyllis Hirsh, an accounts clerk. Originally from Chicago, she had been a Dean fan since 1954 when Jimmy was *actually alive*. When she moved to Hemet, California, she had carried all her scrapbooks with her on the plane, not willing to entrust priceless and irreplaceable remembrances to an airline. Like most Dean fans, she said she would starve before she would sell any of her collection. As club secretary, Phyllis typed and edited the newsletter. She had never married. Correspondence with fans and involvement with the club filled up most of her time. There was some trouble brewing between Phyllis and Tom; after all, she did all the typing and all the work, while he was the president and did all the *interviews*. But the rift was subdued out of respect for the memory of Jimmy as they donned Dean T-shirts, swapped stories, and thumbed through scrapbooks in the motel bedrooms.

In Fairmount the next day, Stan was saddened to see some of the changes. Ortense had finally moved into town, closer to her doctor. Markie had put his foot down. The last straw had been the night when a hysterical woman, drunk and crazy, had terrified her by beating on the door of the darkened old house and screaming for Jimmy. Ortense had moved into the house vacated by Winton, who had moved again, this time to Florida. Markie had moved his wife Marylou and the children into the farmhouse. Little Chuckie slept in the room which had been Jimmy's. Stan was dismayed to hear that a Farrah Fawcett poster now hung on the wall alongside Jimmy's watercolours.

Festivities began on Saturday. Fairmount's Main Street was thronged with outsiders from all over the United States, Canada, and the whole world over. There were pavement stalls with vendors hawking pennants, buttons, and hot dogs. Activities included the James Dean Rock-Lasso Contest. That evening featured a concert by the Old Timers' Band in the high school gym, followed by a screening of

Rebel Without a Cause in the cafeteria of the Madison-Grant High School in Marion.

Sunday was more sedate in the Quaker community. There was church, and then a service and tribute to Jim at the Marion High School, followed by another matinee showing of *Rebel*. But the evening whooped and shouted with Walt Riddle's 'Grand Ole Opry' show, featuring Elvis's former drummer and the former husband of the late Patsy Cline.

Monday morning found Stan and Gloria on an organized 'Tour of Dean Country', visiting old haunts, high points, and the various houses where Jimmy, Winton, and Mildred had lived when Jimmy was a toddler. That afternoon they followed Adeline on another tour, this time of the old high school Jimmy had attended. Stan stood on the stage where Jimmy had first performed, and where he had played a papier-mâchéd Frankenstein's monster in his class's production of the spoof 'Goon With the Wind'.

At twilight, a star was unveiled in the pavement at 4th and McClure in Marion, the site of the house where Dean had been born, and the street was renamed 'James Dean Avenue for a Day'. Everyone went to the Armory at Marion for a programme of slides of Jim's youth. Ortense was in the audience, and so was Markie. Stan was excited. He had been invited to take the podium and speak on behalf of the We Remember Dean fan club. He had been the best candidate because of his media experience. He stood before the assembled crowd and had hardly begun when he heard a shrill cry. A nearly hysterical woman was yelling at him, demanding to speak and be heard. She shambled up, wild-eyed, to the stage. She was Flora Bonniani and she said she was the current president of the *original* Dean club which had been founded in New York in the 1950s by Theresa Brandes, since deceased. She told Stan that her club *was still active,* and that it was the *oldest* club. It was a nightmare for Stan, standing there on the stage while she raved, the worst kind of fan, incoherent and obsessed. She was everything Stan hoped that he was not. It was harrowing.

The vastly swollen crowds and the influx of out-of-town and even foreign reporters and journalists signalled that Tuesday the thirtieth, was the Big Event. It was the anniversary of Dean's death. The tribute convened at 1.30 p.m. in the once-tranquil Wesleyan campground tabernacle. It was the same hall in which Dean's high school commencement had been held in 1949. Phyllis found herself being interviewed outside while Stan set up his microphone and recorder near the podium. The crowd milled and buzzed. Television cameras whirred, and ball point pens clicked like summer locusts. Reporters and photographers leaned through the windows with microphones and Insta-cams as the pews filled under the high vaulted ceiling. There was a rainbow of licence plates on the cars choking the little country lane. They had come from New Jersey and North Carolina and Vermont and Spain and next door. A group of fourteen men and women from Japan filled a centre pew, led by seventy-one-year-old Razubo Komori, a Tokyo talk show host who had brought an entourage of a camera crew and several students. 'All people from Japan remember Jimmy Dean,' she said. There was a group from England, one of whom incited waves of applause when he corrected a commentator who had called a youth a 'fan'. 'No,' the Briton said seriously, '. . . *a disciple*.'

To Jerry Miller, the reporter from the *Marion Chronicle*, they seemed an army of worshippers drawn by a spiritual magnet. Hard-pressed when asked to explain why they had come, they seemed a little awestruck and blinded by an intense charisma which they could only follow where it led them. For some, just to be there was the fulfilment of a lifelong dream. One man had driven 3,200 miles in a van from Canada, listening to the recorded soundtracks of Dean's films until he had memorized all the dialogue.

There was a short address by Linda Milligan, a wan and vague young girl from Fairmount who had felt such a spiritual kinship with Dean that she had followed his path to Hollywood, where she was an aspiring actress. Then Martin Sheen took the podium, and the crowd rippled with excitement. Strangely, over the years, few Hollywood stars had come to Fairmount. Nick Adams was one. 'Nick was so funny,' Ortense remembered, 'he could make a dog laugh.' Sheen spoke to the congregation of 600. 'He created one of this century's most unique inventions,' he said, '. . . *himself*.'

When the service was over, the fans formed a new

pilgrimage which moved slowly up the highway to Park Cemetery with Sheen at its centre, the coat of his grey suit draped over his arm. Suddenly there was a roar, and a tall and forbidding black-jacketed figure appeared on a huge motorcycle. Inscrutable behind black moustache and sunglasses, he took the head of the parade in fulfilment of another tradition as inviolable as Biblical prophecy. He came every year. He said his name was Nicky Bazooka, and he never answered any questions. 'I'm from around,' was all he said. Some claimed he was from Bloomington, leading to the suspicion that the truth, in his case, would only be disappointing. He dismounted grandly at the grave and took a spray of flowers from the handlebars of his bike. He laid them against the pitted marker. He roared off.

The rest of the crowd waited at the grave for Sheen, who was escorting Adeline Nall. Wreaths now covered the tombstone. James Dean had been dead longer than he had been alive. Sheen, a young man with a heart condition, wondered for a moment about his own mortality. Ortense found the merciful shade of a tree and looked on spryly at the crowd assembled on the hills where so many Deans, Winslows, and Woollens had been laid to rest. *Amazing Grace* and *Rock of Ages* filled the air like the throat of a pipe organ.

At the bottom of the hill, a helicopter roared and buzzed to life, ascending hotly like a dragonfly. Stan photographed Gloria with Martin Sheen, who obligingly hammed it up a little with her. Then Gloria photographed Stan with Sheen. 'It was a very moving experience,' Stan told the Marion reporter, after identifying himself as a television producer. 'It was quite fulfilling.' He put a finger to his chest. 'It stays in here. If we can save the money, we'll be back.'

Marcus Winslow Junior had not gone to the cemetery or the service. He could have got off work, but it was the busy time at the farm centre west of town where he sold Massey-Ferguson tractor parts. He had enjoyed the slide show at the Armory the night before. One picture had showed him as a small boy being pulled in a wagon by a teenaged and bespectacled Dean, the cousin who had been more like a brother to him. Markie had been eleven years old when

Jimmy had died, but he remembered the funeral like it had been yesterday.

He felt he shouldn't get involved in the hoopla. It didn't seem right, since he was family. He didn't feel like he was letting Jimmy down, or his fans. The family had accommodated them a lot over the last twenty-five years. His parents had always been kind to the pilgrims. They had felt they owed it to Jimmy's memory. Markie had done his part without having to go and be with a lot of people. He had never advertised he was Jimmy Dean's cousin, but he had never denied it, either. He had always been patient with the fans and never refused to answer a question. He had always let them take pictures of the house from the outside. But it was a home, not a museum. The fans were nice people, but crazy as hell. He was relieved when they all left town and things calmed down back to normal.

When Stan returned home he wrote and recorded the narration and soundtrack of a video cassette which he titled 'The Legacy'. It was a pedestrian hash of bland Dean biography and Stan's psychologizing, but it displayed his recordings of the voices and recollections of Ortense and Adeline. It was his proof that he had been there. And there was a surprise. For the part about Jimmy's death, Stan adopted staccato Walter Winchell cadence – 'September 30, 1955 – *dateline*', and he described the approach to the intersection and the squeal of brakes on the dusky highway. But then came the punch. 'When asked about it recently, the driver of the other car had this to say –', and there was a voice, distant, scratchy, and tape-looped as he mindlessly intoned, 'Yes, I was there, yes, I was there, yes, I was there . . .' Stan added, 'and so were the thoughts, hopes, and dreams of our nation's youth.'

In early February 1981, Hugh Caughell, who had been Jimmy's biology teacher, local booster Glen Allen, and Adeline, had a celebration of Jimmy's birthday at the Armory in Marion. Several fans were there. Jimmy would have been fifty years old. Stan's video cassette was shown. He was very touched.

Inspired, Stan began work on the script for another cassette. It was about the aftermath – the cult figure and myth. When he was objectively commentating on it all, he felt relief from discomfort with his absorption. It set him apart from the morbid, maudlin, and hysterical. He drew on his psychology course for an analysis of Dean. 'In the end,' he summed up, 'recklessness, self-hate, and self-destruction were the names of the demons that drove his Porsche down that road to oblivion.' His real question, though, was: 'The Dean fans – who are they?' And who am I? 'This new group that persists to this day is a stratified assortment from various walks of life. Some are nostalgia buffs who mourn the loss of a former lifestyle and fantasize about a happier time; others are drama fans or artistic types who recognize Dean's sensitivity; some are wistful romantics who wish they had known and loved him; others are morbid, troubled souls that identify with and desire a type of power and charm Dean exhibited . . .' Stan's own hope was that he was mainly one of the artistic types who recognized Dean's sensitivity.

There was a purgative relish in describing the 'darker side of the Dean cult phenomenon'. He reported, 'People would camp in and around his home, tear up the ground in front of his house for remembrance. A fan even stole some of Jimmy's belongings from his aunt and uncle. The headstone of his grave has been mutilated by morbid souvenir hunters, and his name on the marker is now a memory. A monument to Dean was desecrated when an avid fan ripped his bust from atop the pedestal.' Stan wrote with foursquare loathing of the ghouls and violators. He never made the cassette, but he sent his narration to Phyllis for her newsletter.

Stan learned that a club member from California, Roger Cannon, had organized a memorial rally for the last Friday in September. Participants would retrace the death route, starting at Farmers' Market in Los Angeles, and meet at the monument at Cholame. 'It is a life experience,' Roger had written in his flyer, 'a poem, a song, an exercise, a discipline, a dance along California highways . . . This is a day for celebration of personal freedom. Leave your troubles behind and venture the open road.' It sounded good to Stan. He decided to make the rally instead of Fairmount in 1981. He would re-create Jimmy's final day. He sent Roger the $5 entrance fee for the map and rally guide.

It was with great excitement that Stan and Gloria jetted to Los Angeles International Airport where they rented a 1980 Firebird. Stan had brought along three paperback Dean biographies to help him navigate; Roger's map had been lost in the mail. They drove to 14611 Sutton Street, the site of Jimmy's 'log cabin' home which had burned down years before. After doughnuts at Farmers' Market, they took Cahuenga to the Ventura Freeway, then headed west to Sepulveda Boulevard. As they cruised north on Highway 99, Stan felt they were really on their way. It was like 'unravelling a mystery, or following a "treasure map" as "familiar" location after location flashed before our eyes'. Tips, the diner where Jimmy and Rolf had stopped on the Ridge, was now called Castaic Junction. It was closed and boarded up. Stan and Gloria settled for a hamburger and milkshake at a Sno-Queen in Bakersfield.

They turned west onto Highway 46. 'Contrary to what we had been led to believe, the route was not "monotonous" at all, but was quite breathtaking. We were not in a desert, but instead, we passed a landscape laden with lush greenery, shrubs, and palms, followed by large tree-encrusted mountains that supported beautiful rolling hills and valleys. Fields of cotton were followed by rows of carnations, cotton crops, and grape and orange groves.'

They stopped at Blackwell's Corners. Stan learned from the girl behind the counter that the original building had burned to the ground in 1967 in an electrical fire. But the lightning-scarred cedars still stood at the front. Stan took out his camera and Super 8 for photos and film footage.

As they drove over Polonio Pass and down Antelope Grade, Stan saw for the first time that intersection he had pictured so often. They parked and alighted. Stan stood and watched the cars coming down the slope and the opposite traffic that turned north-east across Highway 46 onto 41, envisaging the crash that had occurred at dusk so many years ago. Gloria was silent. She knew he was having a *moment*.

They continued on around the bend to Cholame, where they met Roger and Marge Smith, from San Jose. Roger was an intense man with a red beard and ascetic features. Stan was dismayed to see that fans were already chipping away at the lucite covering of the medallions of Dean which were set in the wooden benches around the monument; they were also stealing the polished stones around the base for souvenirs.

They drove on to Paso Robles to register at their motel. They followed Roger and Marge up 15th Street to the top of the hill. The old War Memorial Hospital was now a Nazarene School, but it had hardly changed. Neither had Kuehl's Funeral Home. Stan and Gloria posed in front of the brick mortuary for pictures.

That evening they all shared dinner. The driver of the Ford came up as a topic of conversation. Stan could not resist telling them that he had talked with the man who had driven the other car at the collision where James Dean had died. Marge and Roger questioned him, and he finally admitted the ruse he had used to question the man. Roger said he felt that the man ought to be contacted. He was the one man whose story had never been told.

Stan's reaction was violent. The man should never be asked about the accident, he said. It would be cruel. Stan and Roger argued and nearly came to blows. The evening was wrecked.

Stan and Gloria did not stay for the festivities at the Dean monument the next day. They headed back down the coast, stopping at Cal Poly to take pictures of one another before the entrance. The student had enrolled there in 1955 at the time of his accident with Jimmy Dean. On the drive south, Stan raged about Roger Cannon, his obstinacy and insensitivity. The couple had dinner that evening with Phyllis in Los Angeles.

Stan wrote an account of their trip which appeared in the newsletter the next month. 'Needless to say, we all had a great time talking about James Dean with each other and sharing our thoughts, feelings, and opinions. That's the greatest part of the James Dean phenomenon to me: how through Jimmy many different kinds of people from various walks of life have been brought together for good friendship and camaraderie. Thank you, James Dean, for what you lived for and for what you left behind . . . because that continues to reach out and move people.'

Chapter 11

In October 1981, Howard Matson was twenty-nine years old. He had not had a drink in over six years, not since his first meeting with Alcoholics Anonymous. Recovery had been slow. It had been almost two years after that first meeting that he had gone to work. He was now the assistant manager of a wholesale tyre store. In 1980, he had been transferred to Bakersfield. He had started dating Leslie, another member of the A.A. programme. Within six months they were married, and now they had a six-month-old boy, Junior. The wedding had been at his mother's two-storey house at Cayucos on the coast. They enjoyed the ocean and drove there on many weekends. If they had had to pay for a motel room, they would not have been able to go nearly as often.

Howard always stopped at Stella's at Cholame. He was startled to see some handmade colour postcards of the intersection – labelled 'James Dean Crash Site' – on display in the glass case by the register. They were from Roger Cannon Productions in Carmel Valley. Howard bought them, fascinated that someone else had been drawn to Cholame as a special place. He studied the postcards over the weekend.

The drive across Highway 46 was more important to Howard than the weekend at the beach. He was silent as they crossed the hard, flat plains with hundreds of oil pumps strewn across the ground like black beetles. They would stop at Blackwell's for coffee and Howard would study the bulletin board for messages. Twenty-seven miles up the road, he would park near the intersection and dart across the path of whizzing cars and rushing trucks to stand in the middle of the highway and snap pictures. He carried rocks and chunks of concrete back to the trunk. On the way home on Sunday, when Blackwell's was closed, he would stop and pry up some of the foundation of the original garage. He kept the boulders in the bedroom of their apartment.

One afternoon, they returned from Cholame and Howard sat down at the kitchen table and wrote two letters. The first was an inquiry to Roger Cannon concerning his postcards. The second was to O V Hunter, the Bakersfield patrolman who had ticketed Dean on his last drive. Howard asked him what had really happened. He watched the mail expectantly.

He was just leaving work a couple of days later when Leslie called to say that Mr Hunter had just phoned. He had left his number, saying Howard was welcome to call him. Howard dialled him from the back office.

Mr Hunter remembered Howard's father well. They had been on the same Central Valley championship pistol team. Otie Hunter and his wife had thought a lot of his father. Howard asked about the ticket he had given James Dean, and he listened enraptured as Hunter told how he had crossed the median and given chase to the silver Spyder. It was a good talk. Mr Hunter told him that if he had any more questions, he was welcome to call or even to stop by. 'I'm around here most of the time,' he said. Howard was thrilled as he hung up the phone.

In early November he went to Mr Hunter's home to visit him and his wife, Judy. They told him how it had been in Bakersfield in the fifties. They told him stories about his father, things he had never known. Howard discovered that Mr Hunter had taught at the college. Retired, he now worked part-time as a traffic court judge. He retained the sharpness and chiselled authority of a patrolman. Howard was drawn to him.

He exchanged letters with Roger Cannon. Cannon believed that the Spyder had come to rest past the Parkfield Road west of the intersection. He had even posted a plaque on a phone pole which he estimated marked the spot. Howard disagreed, and was upset when Roger did not immediately accede to his arguments. Howard set his alarm early one morning. By the time he left for work, he had composed a long letter which Leslie typed and initialled. The tone was sharply officious. He restated his arguments, telling Roger that if he did not believe *him*, he could contact Ernie Tripke.

Howard bought scrapbooks and began to save things. There were the letters he had written and received from Roger, the notes of his conversations with Mr Hunter, and the stray items and articles he had run across. He requested from the library the microfilm of the Paso Robles newspaper for September–October 1955. He sat in the darkened research room and grew dizzy reeling the ghostly screen before his eyes. Leslie tried desperately to entertain the roisterous Junior among the sedate stacks under the glare of pinch-faced librarians.

He dug out his old college essays on Dean, and the scraps from the journal he had kept. He was fascinated by the *continuum* of his interest, and fascinated that there were others with a similar vision. There was one, at least. He wished he hadn't been so sarcastic with Roger. He thought of Dean and the Spyder all the time. He wrote to Ernie Tripke again. Great disappointment filled him each day that there was nothing in the mailbox.

Had a transcript been made of the inquest? Did it exist still? It seemed an impossible dream that he might hold in his hands that rarest of documents. Sometimes he sat in the back room at work and called San Luis Obispo County. He talked with the offices of the sheriff, the coroner, and the Hall of Records. He even inquired at the Superior Court. He was always put on hold, or told that the records did not exist or could not be found, or that the files had been purged. Once he was told that they existed, but were sealed. Oddly, the most helpful fellow was the cheery man at the coroner's. But his files were meagre.

One Saturday, on an impulse, Howard dialled the Shandon number of Clifford Hord, whose name he had found in the old newspaper accounts. He was nervous as he dialled the number, sensitive about what sort of reaction he might get from the man who had testified at the inquest.

Mr Hord was now elderly and hard of hearing. He yelled into the phone. But, yes, he said he would meet Howard and talk with him. Leslie quickly packed, and after work they headed west on Highway 46. The Hord farmhouse was on a bluff over a country road not far from Creston.

Mrs Hord was very kind and charming. She, too, had a hearing problem. Wary at first of Howard's interest, they were soon enchanted with the baby boy. Mrs Hord made coffee while her husband brought out a box of toys. He wound a toy frog which hopped across the carpet.

The couple told Howard about their 30 September 1955 encounter with James Dean as they had been on their way to the football game. A chill went through him when Mrs Hord, without rancour, remembered the smiles on the faces of the boys in the sports car. Howard was engrossed by a deep and dizzying terrible truth.

The memory of the inquest still rankled with Mr Hord. He had only tried to do his duty, to tell the truth. They had asked him to come and testify. He hadn't volunteered. He had been nobody important, like Dean, but that was no reason to boo a man and treat him that way. He had no hard feelings against Dean. 'Kids, you know, they've always acted that way. I'm sure they still do.'

Mrs Hord thought someone ought to plant flowers around the monument. It would be much prettier and more colourful than the stones. Cliff showed Howard the points of the antelope he had shot on his last hunting trip, even giving him some antelope steaks.

Howard felt a new excitement as they drove down the winding road. The day, the highway, and the accident had not been like he had read in books and magazines. Could Dean have been distracted as he recovered his car from the near collision so near to the intersection? Did it contribute to the crash? It wasn't far-fetched. If Dean were travelling at 120 m.p.h., as Hord had said, then the incident with the Pontiac occurred only thirty seconds before the impact at the intersection a mile to the west. Lance Reventlow had told officers that Dean had claimed at Blackwell's that he had driven as fast as 130 m.p.h. that day. At that velocity, the time elapsed between the near collision and the fatal wreck would be even slimmer. What if Dean, in those last crucial seconds, had turned his head to look back at the Pontiac, or to yell a smart-ass comment to Weutherich? There would be a lapse in attention. This could have had a bearing on the crash. Howard wanted to tell someone.

He broke down and wrote to Cannon, sending him a conciliatory cheque for more postcards. He also enclosed several copies of an appeal which he had written and xeroxed. It stated that he, Howard Matson, had an objective: the first complete and accurate account of the events of the day Dean died. His point of departure was that extant accounts were inaccurate and had been produced for the fan magazine mentality. He felt he was dropping a bomb when he included a line, which he thought tantalizing and irresistible, about how Dean's Porsche had nearly hit a Pontiac containing a San Luis Obispo County family. Howard hoped to correspond with individuals who had collections of material about the fatal accident. He hoped, too, that others would write asking *him* what had really happened. He had more nervous energy and enthusiasm about that day than he could discharge through replies to merely occasional letters.

A letter arrived from Captain Tripke, who was most considerate and polite. He invited Howard to contact him with any further questions. Howard framed the letter and hung it on the wall in the front room of the apartment. There was a warm note from Roger. 'I will pass on your appeal to a few people,' he said, 'but you must realize you are more knowledgeable on this subject than anyone else.' Howard studied the words.

He received copies of the highway patrol accident report from the coroner's files and pored over them. They described in detail the skid marks west of the impact. No account in any book or magazine had mentioned that. The Ford had apparently crossed over into Dean's lane and begun to brake some distance prior to impact. The Highway Patrol report read:

> FACTS: There were two sets of skids west of impact, one 22 feet and one 39 feet with a 33 feet gap in between, but the skids are in the same arc.

There was a pathologist's report describing Dean's wounds. The accident was much more immediate and vivid.

He fantasized about the inquest transcript. He wanted to read it more than anything else. It would answer all his questions. He could not believe that he was not meant to have it. Hunter had thought a record must have been made, and that it had to be available to the public. News reporters were quoting inquests all the time, weren't they? Howard went into the back room at work when his boss was out, and he followed the telephone wires down the false trails and blind halls of the judicial, administrative, and enforcement bureaucracies of San Luis Obispo County. Meanwhile, he duplicated and replicated again the police documents to share with anyone who might respond to his appeal. But there were no letters.

During the Christmas holidays in the waning days of 1981, Howard and Leslie drove to Los Angeles where Leslie's folks lived. They visited Hollywood and located the 1955 site of Competition Motors on Vine Street. It was now a Goodyear tyre centre. Howard peered through the hurricane fence at the back yard where Dean had posed in his new car on the morning of the day he died. On their way home they stopped at Griffith Planetarium. The day was overcast and foggy. The grounds were abandoned and the planetarium had not yet opened. Howard climbed the gate to clamber alone to the roof. He paused at the spot where Dean and Sal Mineo had stood and he gazed down at the parking lot and telescope alcove where the knife fight had taken place. The air was cold and fog curled around the Hollywood Hills.

On the first day of January, the Matsons again visited the Hords, this time to talk with their son Phil, who had stopped at the crash before the dust had even cleared. A handsome man in his early forties, he was suspicious. 'You're the James Dean guy,' he said. Howard felt that Phil was only suffering him at all as a favour to his mother. 'What is this,' Phil asked, 'just curiosity, or an obsession?' Howard was embarrassed and told him the story that he had come to tell people, about how his interest had begun with his father who had known the highway patrol officer who had given Dean a ticket. Phil relaxed after a while and memories stirred. He even went into the other room to get his high school annual to find out who had won the football game in Bakersfield that evening. Howard stood up to leave after a short time, as the Hords were expecting guests. Howard wished he had called before he had come. Cliff walked them to their car. He drew lines in the dust with the toe of his boot to show again how the silver Porsche had driven him off the road at the bottom of Antelope Grade so many years before.

Howard enlarged the colour photos he had taken of the crash site. He framed them on the wall of the apartment. Leslie would sometimes catch him staring at them, lost in the highway beneath the rolling grey clouds.

The trips to Cholame became more frequent, and the rituals more rigid and involved. Howard found a spot where he could park the car on Antelope Grade. He would leave his wife and child on the side of the highway as he became lost in walking the old abandoned stretch of Highway 466 around its desolate curves and collapsed twistings. He would think of Leslie and the baby alone in the car then run on a little further, imagining the shiftings and accelerations Dean must have executed, knowing Leslie must be worrying. They'd probably have a fight. Where were you? You said you'd only be gone a minute. You don't think of anybody but yourself.

He dragged back two battered and rotting highway reflector signs. He cleaned them and put them in the bedroom. The signs held the mud-built nest of the larvae of Cholame bees, which hatched and buzzed around the apartment. An irritated Leslie had to take the corpse of one to the Health Department to find out what it was and from where they had suddenly come.

It became more and more difficult to work on the novel he had been writing during his lunch hours and to which he had pinned so many hopes. His imagination was totally absorbed in his scrapbooks and correspondence about the car wreck in which James Dean had died. Weekends and even holidays were subsumed.

At Book City Collectibles, a Hollywood memorabilia shop, the girl behind the counter showed him three photos which she said were *original* stills from *East of Eden*. Beautiful and glossy, their livid WarnerColor gave a blush to Dean's face as hot as a film projector on the third reel of a second matinee. She said they were much sought after by collectors because they were so rare. Howard inquired how much she was asking. All three cost nearly $150. He concealed his shock; they were definitely out of his league. He settled for some photos and a couple of posters. Yet he couldn't get the stills out of his mind. 'Go ahead,' Leslie said. 'You never spend anything on yourself.' He ordered them, then watched the mail every day. Whenever he heard brakes in the parking lot below, he wondered if it was United Parcel. When they finally arrived he hung them on the wall over the piano.

He had been three years old when they were made. They were objects of special mystery. Had they been displayed in lobbies twenty-five years ago when Dean's pictures had played in movie houses? Had Dean, himself, seen or held one of these? The only time he was really comfortable looking at them was when Leslie was in the other room. The deep coral colours were hypnotic.

Chapter 12

One Sunday, the Matsons returned from Cholame to find a letter for Howard in the mailbox. It was from a Stan Pierce in Portland, Oregon. Howard read it with mounting excitement. Stan described himself as a writer/producer and director of T.V. whose interest had been piqued by Howard's appeal in the Dean club newsletter. By way of credentials, Stan said he was well acquainted with Adeline Nall and Ortense Winslow. Incredibly, Stan said, 'I also feel lucky that I was able to talk with the driver of the Ford briefly in 1979. But that's another story.' His letter was obviously intended to pique, too. The writer was intelligent, and like Howard, was fascinated by Dean.

Howard typed a long reply after working on several drafts. 'You are the only person besides myself,' he wrote, 'who has approached the student. I would appreciate any details of your contact with him. What was said?' He begged for the whole story. 'No detail is beneath my interest.'

Stan answered immediately, quizzing Howard anxiously about *his* meeting with the driver of the Ford. 'Please fill me in, in more detail. What exactly was said by both parties? What was the tone, attitude, nuances, etc.?' He went on, 'I must digress for a minute to ask you to what end you are pursuing this research? I'm wondering what will it prove?'

Howard responded excitedly in a letter of six typed pages. He tried to be thoughtful and reflective, but in his anxiety to impress Stan and his defensiveness at the other's implications his language came out pompous and stilted.

Stan eagerly opened the envelope. He was absorbed by the xeroxes Howard had sent, but his amusement at the affected writing bordered on annoyance. He told Howard he was himself a professional 'word-smith – (writer/producer/director)', and he had found some of the statements 'abstractly philosophical or perhaps a little heavy on the metaphysical.' He quickly added, 'But I truly enjoy the correspondence. What I'm trying to get at is, feel free to be more relaxed in your writing. Informality is no problem for me.'

Howard was hurt and embarrassed. He was irritated by Stan's comment, 'On the serious side, you've convinced me of the legitimacy and sincerity of your quest. You are a Rebel *With* a Cause!' He told himself he hadn't been trying to prove anything to Stan; but after a couple of days' reflection, he admitted that he had, and that he had been pretentious. He confessed to Leslie that he had been trying to impress people. 'And to keep them at arms' length,' she added – from himself, and from the heart of his interest. Stan had taken care to be tactful. He obviously wanted to know Howard better – he had sent a photo of himself, plus a biographical article that had appeared in some educational community publication when he'd been hired to run projectors. Stan, too, was eager to impress, besides being self-consciously vague about current employment.

Howard wrote a reply which he hoped was more casual. He only rewrote it once, and it was just four typed pages. He adopted Stan's style of sentence fragments, dashes, and slashes. To become more vulnerable, he told Stan about himself and his hobbies. He also asked a personal favour that was important to him.

Months earlier, Howard had written to Roger that he wished he could locate Maila Nurmi, Dean's intimate friend who now found new fame as one of the stars of the cult classic *Plan 9 from Outer Space*. In the intervening years the film had acquired a new fascination for a younger audience, who were curious to see the *worst* movie ever made. Howard would stay up until 3 a.m. on any Friday night when the film was shown on television. He remembered how Maila had frightened him when he was little. Now he found her unsettlingly sensual. How he would treasure a letter, or just an autograph from her. He often wondered where she was and what she was doing.

Now, amazingly, Stan had written that he had just finished a letter to her. Howard asked how he had found her. He was interested in contacting her, too.

He also wrote to Stan about his efforts to find the Dean

inquest transcript. Stan replied that he had checked with a legal friend who said that if Howard went *in person* to Paso Robles and filled out the right forms, he could petition to open the file under the Freedom of Information Act, and they would have to show it to him. 'It's possible, I was told,' Stan said, 'that when records are lost, bought off, or destroyed, local officials might just tell you it's "closed", because they can't say anything else. Please look into it, as you're so close out there, and it would be absorbing for all interested parties.'

But Howard's heart sank when Stan did not offer him the address to reach Maila Nurmi. His contact, Stan said, was a friend of a friend of a friend, who saw Maila Nurmi three to five times a week. He said that his own letters had been hand delivered to her.

Stan enclosed several xeroxes, as Howard always did. The last was engrossing. It was a copy of a receipt from a registered letter. The signature, in a graceful, flowing hand, was that of the Ford's driver.

'Now you know,' Stan wrote excitedly, 'who I also corresponded with very recently. Also talked with him on the phone – yesterday, as a matter of fact. Very discreet. I was tactful, diplomatic, sensitive. Spoke more or less like I was taking a general survey – that was my approach. He was more good natured this time. A *bit* lighter, I'm glad to say. I asked him (ready) about the whereabouts of his two-tone 1950 Ford. He said, "yes", he owned it, but "no, I have no idea . . . now . . . where it's at." He said the car was taken to the junk yard. It was never bought by anyone, "not to my knowledge . . . no", and never restored. Thought you would enjoy this info.'

Howard suspected that Stan had taped the call. He had also enclosed a xerox of a photo of himself and actress Mercedes McCambridge, whom he had located at a book signing session at a Houston store. She looked stiff and uncomfortable at Stan's importunate arm around her. His smile was ingratiating for Gloria's camera.

Chapter 13

That week, Howard again closeted himself in the back room at work and started calling the gamut of San Luis Obispo County offices. This time he wound up at the county clerk's office. The woman who talked to him seemed to be trying to be helpful. She did not tell him flatly that the inquest transcript was lost, or did not exist. She said she would talk with Mr Cooney, the county clerk. He was out. She promised to call back.

When she rang again, she said, yes, they had the inquest transcript. *She was holding it in her hand.* Howard's heart started to beat quickly, and he was startled at the plaintive quality of his own voice as he asked her to describe it to him. She said that he could have a copy, but the charge to reproduce it was 90¢ a page.

He felt sick as he hurriedly calculated the total cost – over $70. At half the price it would have been too much. Each time he had spent a lot of money on his obsession he had promised Leslie it would be the last. Those three Japanese books on Dean had cost over $60 – and he hadn't even been able to read them.

He went home for his lunch hour, and he let her see how downcast he was. When she asked what was the matter, he told her he had finally found the inquest transcript, but it was too much money – $70. She did not argue, and he felt worse.

He racked his brains until he got an idea. He tried to call Stan Pierce from work, but he got a message recorder. He tried Portland a couple more times. Finally, he left a message on the tape: his phone number, and that he had something important to discuss 'of mutual interest'. If Stan would go in with him halfway it would still be a lot of money, but it might be possible.

Stan did not call. He was still out. At five o'clock, Howard locked up and sent everyone home. He tried Portland once more. The nervousness was eating at his stomach. These damned long-distance calls, charged to his home phone, were so expensive. He hoped he would have the inquest transcript by the time the phone bill came. If Stan would pledge him the money now, then he could tell Leslie that he was only going halves. He could order the transcript tomorrow. How long would it take to arrive? He was sure Stan would go for it.

Stan answered the phone. He had evidently just stepped in. Howard was surprised at the man's voice, which was high-pitched and twangy. He quickly told Stan that he had found the inquest transcript and how much it cost to duplicate it, and suggested they go half and half. He was shocked when Stan balked. 'Forty dollars is a lot of money,' he said slowly. He said he would go halfway on the photos – he would really like to see those. He suggested Howard try and enlist several more people, like Phyllis, and they could all share the expense.

Howard felt sick. Stan seemed chatty, and why not? He wasn't paying for the call. Howard got off the phone quickly. He stood there in the dark warehouse and felt desperate.

He hadn't corresponded with Roger in a long time, but he didn't know who else to call. But Roger wasn't home. Howard left a message with his wife.

Howard was completely crestfallen when he arrived at the apartment. He couldn't believe he had come this far and now would not be able to obtain the transcript. Leslie felt a little satisfaction as Howard told her about his conversation with Stan. She had always said he was a prissy jerk. Howard hoped that Leslie was feeling sorry for him.

It was uncomfortable at the dinner table. Leslie knew what he wanted her to say. But it was so much money. They argued. But afterwards, she told him that she would not stand in his way. She knew how much it meant to him. He loved her for that. He felt terrible, and so guilty when he looked at Junior. And there were things which Leslie wanted and could use, but which she had denied herself. It had been years since he himself had bought any new clothes. The hours passed, and Roger did not call.

It was after nine when the phone rang. Roger, too, thought

it was a lot of money. But he said he would invest forty. He supported the work Howard was doing. Howard was moved. More than that, Roger was interested in getting together at Cholame, perhaps with Marge from San Jose. They made plans for 27 March, a couple of weeks away. Howard was elated. The next morning, Leslie got a certified cheque at the bank which she mailed to the county clerk's office.

He didn't mention the inquest transcript in his next letter to Stan. Stan said, 'So hope you get ahold of the photos, at least. At 90¢ each, I'll go half on that with you. Let's do that as soon as possible! So wish we could spring for the whole 56 pages. This Dean thing is getting out of hand! We're both feeding and stoking each other's fires!'

Page three of Stan's letter was in red ink and titled *Vampira News*. Green envy curled in Howard's stomach as he read it. 'I was *thrilled* to hear from Maila Nurmi last week! I will share a bunch of info with you I think you'll be interested in. I would give you her address or phone, but she wants her privacy guarded. I'm not "playing secrets", or keeping her to myself. This is the way she wants it, and I don't want to jeopardize our correspondence.' The jealousy sharpened as he read he next sentence; he knew Stan must have felt delicious satisfaction as he wrote it. 'Maila mentioned no one had approached her the way I did. She said in all her years, no one was so nice. "It's the first really literate and intelligent one *ever!*" She was kind and thought I was "highly evolved". We know better!?!'

Later the next week, Howard received a call from Leslie at work. The inquest transcript had been delivered. He was emotional when he walked through the door of the apartment after work. For the first time, he saw copies of photos of the intersection as it had existed at the time of the wreck. He studied the stark deathscape. The scene was more primitive than he had thought. Howard felt he was drawing nearer. There were skid marks, and the gouge and the scrape in the road where the cars had actually hit. He assembled the large diagram. It showed the paths of the cars, the width of the road, and the points of rest of the smashed vehicles. There was a copy of the traffic ticket Hunter had issued to Dean. The actor's signature was arched. Howard pictured him writing awkwardly, arm bent, in the little cockpit of the Spyder.

The next morning, Leslie called again. She had gone for a pregnancy test, and it was positive. To Howard, it seemed God's will that he had just obtained the transcript; one more week, and the money would have seemed a lot more crucial.

Howard was disappointed to discover that the driver of the Ford had not testified. But the inquest was still remarkable. He read the transcript again and again, reliving that time and that day until some of the testimony was committed to memory. He carefully placed the pages in the plastic sleeves of some albums he had bought. He got out of bed early at the weekend to sit alone in the front room, poring over the xeroxes of the photos.

Howard savoured his next letter to Stan. He knew it would gall him to know that Roger was to have a copy of the document and he would not. He did send Stan a xerox of the large diagram. He couldn't decide whether to send copies of the inquest photos, the exhibits of most interest to the Oregonian. He had a compulsion to share and show, but he was resentful that Stan hadn't helped him obtain them. He knew it was silly, but he felt betrayed.

He received a gift from Stan in the mail. Opening the little package, he found a tape cassette. Stan had recorded snippets of dialogue and music from Dean films, plus a dub of *The Legacy*. Howard softened. He was still hurt. Perhaps Stan just hadn't had the money. The last words of Stan's next letter were, 'Any and all inquest xeroxes are treasured.'

Howard made another copy of the inquest transcript and sent it to Stan. He had known all along that he would, eventually. He was grateful for the correspondence. Writing to Stan, putting it into words that would impress, shock, and intrigue, gave him the most satisfaction. A lot of the thrill of his discoveries was the anticipation of sharing.

Howard counted the days until Saturday, the 27th. He worked until noon, as usual, when Leslie picked him up. He felt it was a historic occasion: he was retracing the death route, with the sweeping, yearning Dean soundtrack music on the tape deck, on his way to deliver the Dean inquest transcript at the site of the fatal accident over twenty-five years later.

The Matsons were the first to arrive. Leslie was in a lot of discomfort from the pregnancy, and Junior was restless and irrepressible. Marge and her husband pulled up, and then Roger in his Volkswagen. They all sat at a circular table under a suspended wagon-wheel ceiling light.

Lilly Grant, Cholame's postmaster, had come in on her day off to join them at Roger's invitation. She had brought the great scrapbook in which she had pasted newspaper articles about Dean and the monument, and mementos from the many people who had stopped to ask questions. She had known both Paul Moreno and Collier Davison. She found Moreno's obituary in her scrapbook. Strangely, he was buried only a couple of miles from the apartment where the Matsons lived in Bakersfield.

Howard presented three transcripts to Roger. Later in the afternoon, as the wind became sharper and the light was fading, they all drove up Highway 46 and around the curve to the intersection. The roadside was muddy as they walked to the death site. A truck blared its horn as it roared past. Roger had brought a reel of tape; he wanted to try and estimate where the Porsche had come to rest. Howard walked west along the road to pace off the skid marks which the inquest diagram had shown in the same thirty yard arc tracing the Ford's path across the white line and the westbound lane to the point of impact. They took a few photos as the sun dropped behind the Cholame Hills. They said their goodbyes and headed home on the dark road.

Chapter 14

Howard had kept a secret from Stan: he had learned from Marge at Cholame that Phyllis was in touch with Maila Nurmi. Of course, Phyllis must be Stan's contact. Stan had been careful to disguise that it was someone Howard knew. He was sure Stan had told himself he was fudging on the truth to protect Miss Nurmi's privacy – from Howard. But he also knew that Stan couldn't help but be relishing his delicious exclusivity and specialness as he gave Howard 'full details' of the compliments Dean's old friend had paid him. It would sure take the wind out of Stan's sails if he could tell him that he, too, had received a letter from her. But what if he wrote to her and she didn't respond? He would feel terrible, and embarrassed. That was the other reason he didn't tell Stan he was writing to her.

He rewrote the letter a couple of times before he typed it. There were two pages of compliments and questions – about herself, Bela Lugosi, *Plan 9*, and James Dean. He mentioned the book he now hoped to write as explanation for his intense and rampant inquisitiveness. He sent the letter to Phyllis and asked if she would forward it. He tried to assuage the excitement of waiting by ordering two lobby cards from San Francisco. One was from the original release of *Rebel*, the other from the 1957 reissue. Together, they had cost over $60. Leslie rolled her eyes.

Stan thanked him profusely for the inquest transcript. He had just returned from New York, where he and Gloria had seen *Come Back to the Five and Dime, Jimmy Dean, Jimmy Dean*. He had loved the city and the play. The curtain had opened with the theme from *Giant*, and his eyes had filled with tears. Backstage afterwards, Stan and Gloria had introduced themselves to the cast for the inevitable celebrity photos with one or the other of them smiling with their famous catch. Stan reported that they had visited Jimmy's old room at the Hotel Iroquois, sneaked into the Actors' Studio, visited Sardi's, the Cort Theatre, the site of Croyden's, and other touchstones, haunts, and legendary places of Dean's life and career. He was writing an article on the trip for the club newsletter.

Stan mentioned something which irritated Howard, who had commented in a previous letter that he had spent 'a romantic day retracing the death route'. 'Interesting, for sure,' Stan commented, 'but those terms connote some morbidity, or maudlin quality.'

Of course it was morbid. Why all this *drooling* and chortling over inquests and crash photos? But he knew Stan was nowhere near comfortable enough with his own interest in the death to admit it, much less discuss it. Howard could expect him to make occasional defensive comments. Stan was probably a little touchy because Howard had asked him pointblank in the previous letter if he had recorded Don without his knowledge. For the first time Stan owned up to it, perhaps because he figured Howard had already put the story together from others. Stan closed the letter with, 'No news from Maila yet. I hope she writes soon.'

Howard checked his own mailbox every day at his lunch hour. If it was late, he called Leslie to ask her to run down the stairs and across the parking lot to check whether it had arrived. Sometimes he woke her from her nap.

A day did not pass when Howard did not study the xeroxes Marge had sent him from a French biography on Dean. They showed Rolf, Bill Hickman, and Jimmy in the Vine Street garage checking the Spyder before setting out. He mounted the pictures in their own special volume in his scrapbooks. The homely Indiana newsletter came and it contained a poem from a fan: 'I had to go to Fairmount . . . where he's laid under the ground. To kneel at his grave is unlike anything else you can know. It's sort of like finding the End of the Rainbow. For the Treasure laid there we will never forget – ' A week did not pass when he did not dream of the cemetery. He wanted to drive into Fairmount, park his car, and then walk along the country road to the gravel drive of the graveyard. He shook his head of reveries. There was no way they would have enough money for a trip like that. He felt bad enough spending as much as he already had on

Dean. It had been *hundreds* of dollars in the last few months.

'No news from Maila,' Stan wrote again. 'I'm waiting patiently with the growing realization that as more time elapses it will become increasingly unlikely she will respond.' Howard was relieved. He hadn't received a letter, either. 'Sorry you can't make Fairmount this year,' Stan went on. 'Wish you could. Many fans were there this time. And, Ortense and Adeline were *not* getting younger. Know you'd love to meet them. We could "open some doors" that otherwise might be hard to get access to, if you were to go alone in years to come. Comment?' Stan evidently figured he had Fairmount sewn up.

Howard wrote to many of the fans whose names he found in the newsletter, saying he was interested in trading for items or accounts about Dean. He offered in exchange articles that seemed irresistible to him: the inquest transcript, the map by Tripke, and the crash photos. He was surprised when hardly anyone responded. He reread his letters. Maybe he came across as odd or morbid. He began to think he had misunderstood the way most fans felt about 'Jimmy'. Maybe some were offended by his rough handling of the details of the death. He had recognized an extension of understanding and tolerance from Phyllis and Stan. They admitted to a *pained interest*.

He wondered if the thing he had been saying for months was not really true – that he would write something about the death of James Dean. He wasn't sure what, or how. But the crash itself had become a real thing to him. The events were now arranged and the impressions of witnesses absorbed as perceptions in his own imagination. He could see the Porsche. He felt the highway, the cool air, and the dusky texture of the light. It was not a vague thing. He could see the gravel of the dirt shoulder and the strands of dead weeds around the shattered car as sharp and distinct as a pointillist painting. He saw the dust drifting across the road and stood in the terrible empty silence after the impact. He felt the fear of the first people to step from their cars to walk numbly across the highway. Language was born, adjectives and sentences arranged themselves until he could not stop them. He finally set the whole sequence of events down on paper.

As if it were a sign, the post brought something from a Colorado fan. It was a xerox of the 1957 *Modern Screen* article 'Death Drive', which contained Weutherich's ghostwritten recollections. Howard was fascinated. He had always wanted to have it. You never knew when you were going to come into possession of something tremendous. The phrase 'death drive' haunted him. It worked on his imagination with strange resonances. It was pulpish, to be sure, but it was also descriptive of a potential of acceleration, an ultra-gear or overspeed torqued to intolerable tensions which could only be released *once* because the explosion of energy vaporized its own mechanism. Howard could not express or explain it, but it was *incredibly significant*.

Stan wanted to do something wonderful for Maila Nurmi. He wanted to effect a miracle in her life. He wrote to the promoter of a nostalgia convention and recommended her as a speaker. It was all secret, though he sent a copy of the letter to Howard. No doubt he would have loved her to travel to Portland. Howard pictured Stan meeting her plane. He knew Stan wanted desperately to be her friend. Howard felt a little sickened. What had been wrong with his own letter that he had received no reply? It had been weeks.

One day at lunch, he walked to the mailbox and found an envelope self-addressed in his own hand. A thrill rippled through him. The packet was stuffed. He opened it and studied the strange hand. It was a terrifically long letter, a flowing epistle scattered across the back of large xeroxes of articles about – Vampira! Leslie saw how excited he was. He did not even go up to the apartment. He was late for work, but he sat numbly on the steps to read his treasure.

He had never been regaled before, but she charmed him with stories about Ed Woods Jr, Bela Lugosi, and James Dean. He was devastated by her candour and self-deprecating humour. He could not believe she had written to him at such length.

He waited a couple of days before writing to Stan, savouring the anticipation. He saved the news about Maila Nurmi for the bottom of the second page. 'It was incredible,' he told Stan. 'My transcription of her letter came to three and a half typed pages.' The image was of a woman spending hours and tremendous attention on his letter. Stan would get the point. He recounted enough of the anecdotes and high points to impress and intrigue. 'I love her!' Howard said.

He looked forward to Stan's reply with almost vengeful satisfaction, though he knew that such gloating usually preceded hurt or disappointment. True enough, Stan answered that he had received a letter from her too. Howard felt a let-down.

Chapter 15

Howard's mother felt sorry for him and his family, living in a cramped apartment which would be even more crowded when the new baby arrived in October. She helped him to buy a house in Oildale, at the north end of Bakersfield. The area, known as 'North of the River' to estate agents who tried to avoid the cruder local connotations of 'Oildale', was to Bakersfield what Bakersfield was to Los Angeles. Howard and Leslie did not mind. They were to have a real home. They moved late in May. On their first morning in the house, Howard rose very early and carefully unpacked his photos and lobby cards and hung them on the wall of the front room. It became 'the Dean Room'. Leslie fixed a little gate in the entrance way so that the baby could not come in and wreak havoc on the little cosmos arranged there.

Howard wrote to Stan, 'Now that we're settled, I hope to get some serious Dean writing done.' He was more and more convinced that he was supposed to write the story of the accident. The letter from Maila was a strong sign. He had come so far and into possession of so much information he had never thought he would get. Howard decided to set down on paper the events as they developed in his mind to the point where they were real and he could *see* them. He wrote a description of the ticketing incident, which had come to life for him as a result of his conversations with O V Hunter. He arranged it in a form that he could submit to the newsletter. Phyllis had said she was sure it would be interesting. She had just circulated Stan's account of his New York trip. It was titled 'Traces of Dean', and ended ' – Jimmy passed through this City changing his life, and touching ours. For this, we remember Dean.' Howard knew he could write at least that well. He promised to show it all to Stan for his reaction when it was finished.

Stan had told him that things were tough in the job

department in Portland. 'I need some luck,' he said. 'This is a *rough* business.' Stan's candour melted the little resentments Howard had accumulated. There had been some abrasive spots in their correspondence, but they had worked through them. Howard told Stan he should try his luck in Bakersfield. It would be great if his friend lived in town.

Not long after the Matsons had moved, their phone rang on a Wednesday night. Howard was excited to hear the voice of O V Hunter. Howard had sent him a copy of the article he had written and asked for any comments or corrections. Before they hung up, Mr Hunter gave Howard the name of a local radio personality who had had his own programme in the 1950s and 1960s. Hal Laffoon, Hunter said, had done special shows on Dean on the fifth, tenth, and fifteenth anniversaries of his death. He could have much information that would be of interest to Howard. Perhaps he had interviewed people since deceased, like Paul Moreno.

Howard tried immediately to call Laffoon, but his number was unlisted. Hunter had said that he still heard Laffoon's voice on radio spots for a local car lot. The next day at work, Howard waited until the manager stepped out, and he called the car dealer. They referred him to an advertising agency; the agency told him Laffoon worked at McMahons as a salesman. Howard dialled McMahons, and had Laffoon on the line within a few moments.

Yes, Laffoon said, he had done radio specials on Dean, but Howard really ought to talk to a local man who had been a guest on the shows and who was a great, great Dean fan. This man had coroner's reports, inquest documents, anything Howard might want. Laffoon even looked the number up. He told Howard to ask for Charles Adams.

Howard quickly dialled the number, which put him in touch with the office of the County Employees' Association. The receptionist corrected him. Adams was not an employee, but the *president*. She said he was in and out. Howard told her briefly that he was interested in Adams's involvement with James Dean. She took his number. The call was returned within five minutes.

Howard told Adams that he had been interested in James Dean for many years; his experience of 'fans' was that they warmed immediately to other fans. He told Adams how he had discovered his name, and the pains he had taken to locate him. It was incredible that there was someone else in Bakersfield who shared his intense interest.

Adams's voice was gruff as he quickly made it clear he was not a Dean 'fan'. He had been appointed in 1956 to conduct an independent investigation of the accident for Winton. The mention of the name of Dean's father, a man only a little less secretive and mysterious than the driver of the Ford, was for Howard the imprimatur on the authenticity of Adams's involvement. Just this week, Adams said, he had intended to write to Dean's grandmother for a copy of the report he had written. His own copy of the main exhibit, the large map, had been taken from his desk at work. Howard's heart was beating fast as he asked Adams whether he still had a copy of the text. Was the report available? Adams calmly said that they could sit down and go over it some time.

The pregnant Leslie had stopped by the store, Junior in tow. And now the manager had returned. He stood by at a polite distance, chatting with Leslie, waiting for Howard to get off the phone. Howard started to sweat. He couldn't relinquish the receiver. He was gripped by the voice on the other end of the line. This was the man he had been looking for all these months. He began to whisper into the phone, the admiration obvious in his voice.

Howard felt the man warm to him a little. Adams wanted to put a personal question to him. Was Howard married? Adams asked what Howard's wife thought of the time he spent on this thing. Howard said it was difficult for her to understand – especially when he spent a lot of money. Adams laughed. His wife had never been able to understand it, either.

Howard was trying desperately to fathom the man. He sensed that Adams had in the past been obsessed with the accident, as he himself was. His vehemence implied that he had been, or had become, more than an impartial investigator. Perhaps, because Adams had operated outside the perimeters of 'fandom', he did not have the trust or the language to admit to his absorption by Dean.

Howard was uncomfortably aware of his wife and his

boss behind him, but everything Adams was saying was fascinating and as heady as a sugar rush to a hypoglycaemiac. The other man had warmed to the subject and seemed to be enjoying himself.

Howard began to ask a flurry of questions. He was amazed that Adams began to discuss skid marks, velocities, relative weights of the cars, and the points of rest of the vehicles. It was the most irrefutable credential.

Howard told him that everything he was saying was of great fascination to him. He wanted to get together as soon as possible. When? His heart sank when Adams told him to call in a couple of weeks, because he was leaving town on Thursday to pick up his daughter and grandchildren, who would be visiting for a while. He was afraid to set a definite date after that, as his association was involved in contract negotiations and meetings were called on short notice. Howard could not stop himself from pressing the man. 'Call me in a couple of weeks,' Adams said. 'I'm sure we'll get together.'

Howard could hardly contain his excitement as his imagination flared to incandescence. He wrote Stan a detailed letter, saying, 'When things fall together this way, I feel I was born to discover something about this thing, or be involved in it somehow.'

Howard did not disclose to Stan the name of his new 'contact'. He didn't want anyone to jeopardize his chances of obtaining the report. More than merely obtain it, Howard wanted to be *the only one* to have it. He had suddenly become very serious about his account of the accident and inquest. The writing had become the climactic experience where he put all the diverse strands of his knowledge together; when he wrote, he *relived* the accident. And now this report from Adams promised to be everything he had hoped the inquest transcript would be, but was not. He was sure it would be the crystal he would hold to his eye and *see it all*. It was so hard to wait. Two weeks seemed forever. He felt suspended, as though his life had been put on hold. He couldn't write another word until he had seen the findings of Adams's investigation.

By Sunday, his anxiety peaked and he could no longer restrain himself. He wrote Adams a two-page typed letter of frank admiration, pleading with him to contact him immediately if a sooner convenient time arose. He could think of nothing but the report. He could hardly concentrate on work. Thursday crept up. It was two weeks, exactly, since his phone call to Adams. He was depressed by the paralyzing possibility that Adams might *not* talk to him – that he might have come this far and got this close and not know *everything*.

That night he paced the floor until after the dinner hour, when he placed his call to Adams. The man said that his family was still visiting, and for Howard to call the next week. 'Monday?' Howard asked. Adams laughed, irritatingly, at his eagerness. 'No, Tuesday would be better.' Howard felt horrible. He tried not to let Leslie see how miserable he was.

Stan was intensely interested in Howard's discovery. 'You have possibly struck oil!' he wrote. He asked dozens of questions, trying to assess the credibility of the man whose name Howard would not tell him. He was hurt, but he had always made confidentiality such a big deal himself that there was nothing he could say. 'Is he president of a big association, or a little one?' he found himself reduced to asking, with a little resentment.

Things were not going too well for Stan in Oregon. He had finally got a job with IBM. '*Not* my style environment, or work for that matter –'. Well, Howard thought, Stan's wife worked, so he could afford to be fussy. 'Wish me luck,' Stan said, 'I need it. Pontiac broke for $250. Buick needs a water pump *now*. My eyeglasses were crushed.'

Howard was moved that Stan was confiding his troubles. Howard had no friends in Bakersfield. He did not believe in socializing with the people he worked with, and the Dean accident occupied what leisure time he had. He revealed to Stan for the first time that he was a recovered alcoholic. Stan had mentioned that he was running low on xeroxes to exchange. Howard told him not to worry about it.

Stan's letters were becoming more meagre. Howard felt that he himself was moving onto another plane of involvement, leaving Stan behind.

He had sent Phyllis a copy of his O V Hunter article in which he had inserted a note to the effect that an independent investigation had been conducted in 1956 which disputed much of the testimony at the inquest. But she decided not to include it in a newsletter. 'Once you have your facts in order, that would be something else.' He felt crushed.

The long Fourth of July weekend arrived. Howard hoped to use the holiday to write up his findings on Adams's report. But there had been no word from the man. Howard told Leslie how miserable he felt. He didn't have the energy to try and hide it. All the long weekend, he didn't know what to do with himself.

On Monday, the fifth, the phone rang in the early afternoon. Charles Adams told Howard he would meet him in about forty-five minutes at the headquarters of the employees' association. Howard listened to a cassette of soundtrack music from Dean films as he turned onto 17th Street in Bakersfield.

Adams was waiting. He shook Howard's hand and asked him to sit while he finished balancing his chequebook on a desk calculator. He was a small man, with alert and bird-like features. He was probably in his early sixties. In a moment, he sat across from Howard at a desk and opened a folder. It was the report. On one side was the text, and on the other were the letters of inquiry he had written and the responses he had received. Howard saw the letters from Winton Dean.

He went over his report with Howard, his intensity increasing as he reviewed the work he had done so many years before. His contempt for the inquest returned and flared, then subsided in a weary cynicism. It seemed to him that a strange aureola had formed immediately over the accident because of who was involved.

They talked for several hours. Howard asked Adams if he could have a copy of the report. Adams said again that the most important exhibit had been the diagram, and his own copy had been stolen. He said he was going to write to the family in Indiana to try and locate the original. When he recovered it, he would make Howard a copy and present him with a xerox of the text. Howard got the impression that Adams sincerely wanted him to have a copy but that he did not want to break the report up. On the other hand, perhaps he had no intention of letting him read it. At no time during their meeting had he put the report in Howard's hands or let him inspect any of it himself. Howard was confused.

When he got home he sat at the kitchen table and immediately wrote down all that he remembered of the conversation. He knew it might be the only record of Adams's investigation he would ever have.

Chapter 16

Stan told Howard that he had left his new job. 'Didn't like the environment, duties, or people. Oh, well, that leaves me looking.' He added, 'Don't work too hard; not worth it!' That irritated Howard. Easy for him to say, with his wife working. He was jealous of the time Stan evidently had on his hands.

Stan told him more of Maila, and Howard saw that he, too, was completely smitten. Of her most recent letter, Stan wrote: 'She went on to pay me some very kind comments about my writing and personality. She's so very *nice*. I thoroughly respect her. She's so warm and generous. So real and modest. "Jimmy is lucky to attract such worthwhile fans," she wrote. "Perhaps it's a natural affinity rather than luck." I think she is totally marvellous.' Howard wanted to write to her again, but he wanted it to be something special. He would send her his completed manuscript. Then she would really *know* him. There was little more to Stan's letter. Their correspondence had subtly changed. Howard felt more and more that Stan was looking over his shoulder as he worked, wrote, and investigated. All Stan really had to contribute now was his opinions, which Howard was beginning to feel were unqualified.

Howard was charged with inspiration. The accident story was constantly on his mind. It had begun to write itself in his head, and he felt an obsessive need to set it down on paper before he lost it. He punched the alarm clock for three o'clock in the morning so that he could work on it before the family got up and he had to report to his job. Once Junior was awake there was no chance of accomplishing anything. The little man would crumple his pages, steal his pens, or climb in his lap.

Yet Howard felt an underlying discomfort as he wrote. It sharpened into an almost paralyzing anxiety. There was one thing which kept his manuscript from being truly revelatory. What exactly had happened? It was all that was keeping him from being a real part, even the last chapter, in the story of James Dean. He felt a desperate need to cross the last line and find out. To re-live the death.

What would Dean have said, had he been able to testify at his own inquest? Howard pictured his face, contorted with emotion, as they tried to lead him through testimony; he shook his head to clear the vision.

The inquest was so strange. Testimony had been elicited from Paul Moreno about the colour and height of the Spyder and the quality of sunlight at that time in the afternoon. But what of the tyre burns? The Highway Patrol accident report, the inquest exhibits, and the official diagram confirmed that the investigating officers believed both sets of skids west of impact had been made by the Ford. At the time of the crash, the Ford had been proceeding in the westbound lane, Dean's lane. Had the other driver begun to brake for the Spyder thirty yards before impact?

It could be argued that a light coloured car would stand out in relief against a black highway, especially when that road descended on a grade as 466 did east of the crash. What about the colourful shirts of Dean and Weutherich? The racing number was painted large on the hood and side doors in red. Clifford Hord had seen the car instantly, and from a distance.

The issue which had been made of whether or not Jimmy had been wearing his glasses would have been comic were it not so sad. Of course he had been wearing his glasses. Without them, he couldn't have seen to drive. It was ridiculous to expect them to still be on his face after the car had rolled several times. Why hadn't anyone asked about the other driver's eyesight?

Two witness's testimony had mainly prejudicial value. The speeding citation issued by Hunter had been introduced and entered as an exhibit in evidence. But evidence of what? Whether or not Jimmy had been pulled over for speeding two hours and 107 miles prior to the crash in which he died had no bearing on the issue of the inquest. No-one had backtracked the other driver, though Fredericks had testified that the Ford passed him just west of the accident at a speed over the legal limit. Supposedly, the ticket had been introduced to confirm the time it took Dean to cover the 107 miles. But the only time stated on the summons was 3.30 p.m. – the time Dean had been stopped, *not* the time he had left the scene. Had it taken thirty minutes to write two tickets?

Clifford Hord had been subpoenaed by the Sheriff's department for his story about the Porsche forcing his family off the road. Whatever Jimmy had done up the road, he was in his own lane at the time of the collison. And not even the other driver, in his statement to the patrolmen at the scene, had claimed Jimmy had been speeding at the time of the crash. Would a speeding racer travel only 45 feet after a 'sideswipe-head-on collision' as the Highway Patrol report classified the impact?

Why all the business about the aluminum skin of the Spyder? Was Dean's death his own fault for driving a car made of 'not ordinary' material? Jimmy seemed to have violated some unwritten statute of this little backwater and been found guilty of being 'not ordinary'.

Tripke's testimony and his diagram had established the point of impact – it was deep in the westbound lane, Jimmy's lane where the Porsche had the right of way. The Deputy D.A. had entered the Highway Patrol daylight photos in evidence to support testimony about the blending propensity of the highway and hills at Cholame. What Tripke had also intended them to show was the sets of skid marks showing the Ford could have travelled nearly ninety feet in the westbound lane. Was that the proper way to make that turn? No one pursued the possible importance of these tyre burns. No one even asked whether the other driver had signalled his intention to turn – and he had not. Instead, the next question of the witness had been. 'Was there anything else in the area – was there glass from the cars or dirt?' It was idiotic.

The final oddity was D.A. Grundell's charge to the jury prior to the deliberations in which he estimated for them, as part of his instructions, that Jimmy's average driving speed had been 'between 85 and 90' miles an hour for the time elapsed and the distance covered.

But the elapsed time was an hour and a quarter only if the

wreck had occurred at 5.30 rather than near 6 o'clock. White's call from Moreno's store – a mile away – had probably been placed in less than five minutes. It was more than likely that the Highway Patrol had been notified within ten minutes, and perhaps within five. Tripke had received his call at one minute to six – that was the only time that was beyond dispute, because he had made a note of it. It was unlikely that the crash had happened before 5.45 p.m. That would make the average speed closer to Weutherich's estimate. Adams had talked to Payne, the owner of Blackwell's Corners, who swore that Dean hadn't been there for quarter of an hour, just seven to ten minutes at the most. That dropped the average speed even lower.

All conjecture was improper. The facts were that Jimmy had been in his proper lane, there was no evidence that his speed was a factor in the crash, and the other driver had crossed over into Jimmy's right of way possibly thirty yards before the intersection with no signal or warning.

Howard heard that the D.A. of a nearby county had taken a hand in influencing the inquest. He began making long distance phone calls from work, charging them to his home number. When someone walked in to ask him a question, he cupped the phone and answered them cursorily, almost angrily. He called the County's library. They promised to do research for him, then became annoyed at his successive and insistent calls. He called the County's Clerk's office, and the Hall of Records. Who had been the District Attorney of the county in question in 1955? It had been so long ago. They referred him finally to the office of the current District Attorney. He had to call several times. It seemed, to him, a simple question, but he was pressed by the secretary to explain *why* he wanted the name of an ex-District Attorney. He was vague. Eventually, he got a call back – from the present District Attorney. They talked. The D.A. was amiable, but disturbing. 'You don't think there was any impropriety, do you?' he asked.

It was a shock when the man finally revealed to him the identity of the District Attorney in 1955. Howard felt numb, as if something he had been doing had suddenly turned back upon him. Bill Hapton. He recognized the name. He knew Bill Hapton. He remembered back when he was twelve years old and his father, an ex-Highway Patrolman, had been alive. For years, Hapton had been one of his father's best friends. Howard had known that Hapton was an attorney, and now he seemed vaguely to recall that he had held some official position at one time.

Howard called one of the county's newspapers where he located a reporter whose memory went back to the local politics of the fifties. He recalled that Hapton had resigned as D.A. due to some sort of scandal. Perhaps that was why Howard could not remember it being discussed, though the family had seen Hapton often, until his father's death. Short, balding, and roly poly, Hapton now seemed a figure of mystery, perhaps of jovial evil.

He felt so close to an answer. Impulsively, he tried to call Hapton's law office where Howard's mother had told him Hapton now had a practice. Hapton was out of town, but when Howard arrived home that evening, he typed a letter. He felt a little sick in his stomach as he reminded Hapton of his friendship with his father. Then he mentioned his 'hobby'. He wrote, with studied casualness, 'One person I have talked to was even under the impression that there was some connection with you as District Attorney of your county in 1955 . . .'

With that letter, he came to admit to himself that he would do *anything* to find out the whole story. He could not wait, and he had to be prepared for the likelihood that Hapton would never reply. From the back room at work, Howard phoned water districts, bar associations, libraries, and newspapers pleading for any thread which might lead from someone of influence to the events in San Luis Obispo in 1955.

Howard's guilt became a deep sore with the arrival of the phone bill. His long-distance calls had run up a bill of $120. Worse, he had found out *nothing*. Things got rough at home. Leslie sat him down for a serious talk. She hoped this was the end of it. Howard assented, but inside himself he felt more desperate than ever. He resigned himself to the thought that the draft he was working on would be a tool. He would submit it to some of the people involved, and hope he could perceive in their reactions whether he had struck a nerve of truth.

Stan was the only one who could come near to understanding Howard's agitation and sense of excitement as the manuscript neared completion. He wanted finally to meet Howard in person. He hoped Howard would come to Fairmount for the Museum Days on the anniversary of Jimmy's death. Stan and Gloria had decided definitely to make it. Stan wrote, 'I think you belong there this year. So much has happened. You're at fever pitch now, and so many will be there, and the fine older people so far are doing okay. Next year could be another story entirely.'

Howard began seriously to consider it. The dreams had increased. In them, he would find himself in a cemetery which looked one way this time then different the next, but always he was searching for the grave of James Dean.

He finished typing the rough manuscript around 20 July. It was nearly 20,000 words. There was a description of the accident, then an account of Adams's investigation. His questions about the inquest were near the end, followed by a brief follow-up on what had become of the people involved in the intervening years. The last sentence read, 'They still come to Cholame to walk silently around and feel the wind that courses through the hills to rush and flap their pant cuffs like the invisible wake of something passing by at great speed.'

That same day, Leslie made three copies for him. The very first he mailed to Maila Nurmi, care of Phyllis. He was glib in his covering letter, pretending that he did not think it was a fine piece of work with much of his heart in it or that he would be crushed if she thought it worthless.

The other two copies he mailed to Ernie Tripke and Ron Nelson. He wrote to the ex-officers, 'I do not think the inquest verdict was wrong or unfair, but it seems to me a very biased proceeding. I would really like to have the whole story, and anything you say would carry a lot of weight with me. Please tell me if I am off base in the direction I am headed.'

He made another copy which he sent to Charles Adams. He had not heard anything further about his report and was afraid that with each day his chances of obtaining it faded. If the manuscript impressed or flattered him, perhaps he would renew his efforts.

Stan's next letter left him acutely jealous. 'Latest here,' he had said, 'is that I've been asked to "work-up" the "Vampira" interview for the We Remember Dean Club newsletter. It will be "pulled" from audiotapes of a "rap-session" Phyllis and a couple of friends had with Maila. I'm thrilled.' Howard was hurt. He had written to Phyllis that if ever there should be an interview with Maila in the newsletter he would love to be involved, even if it meant driving to Los Angeles. He guessed that she had decided Stan was the professional.

Around the first of August he received a note from Phyllis acknowledging that the manuscript was in Maila Nurmi's hands. 'I'll be seeing Maila hopefully on the seventh,' she closed. 'A few of us are getting together and I sent her an invite. I think if her schedule allows, she'll come. Keep you posted!'

Howard replied almost immediately, saying, 'I'm presumptuous as hell, but I would like to meet her, and if your get-together is composed of Dean people, I figure I won't be too obtrusive. If ever there is an opportunity for me to meet her, please let me know.'

That week he received one of his manuscripts back with a note – from one of the retired California highway patrolmen. It was exciting. He had never written to the man before. The ex-patrolman, one of several who had responded to the Dean accident scene in 1955, wrote, 'Suggest the next time you're over this way you let me know in advance and we can go over some of the things that bother you.'

Howard wrote to Stan, 'I'm intrigued because he *didn't* say I was on the wrong track, and because he gave the impression he didn't want to comment on the issues in writing.'

Howard was a little reluctant as he sent this copy of his manuscript on to Stan. 'I'm pretty aware of its shortcomings,' he said. 'It is merely a starting place.' But he still invited him to make notes or comments.

His heart sank when he checked Friday's post. Nothing from Phyllis – and the meeting was tomorrow. Perhaps she would call during the day. But the hours passed and the phone did not ring. A tremendous depression clouded him. It was a strange, dull shock. He had been sure he was meant to meet her.

It was nine o'clock, and they were getting into bed when the phone rang. Finally, it was Phyllis. Howard was surprised by her Chicago accent. She had talked to Maila, who had consented to Howard's presence. The meeting would be at the house of Cindy Arnvel, another club member. Sculptor Kenneth Kendall would also be there. Howard could hardly sleep for his excitement. With Leslie he hurriedly made plans for the next morning's trip to Hollywood.

The meeting was at a little house in an old neighbourhood near Santa Monica Boulevard. Several people waited on the pavement. Howard recognized Phyllis from her pictures. Leslie dropped him off. He was introduced to Lois, another club member, and her husband. Leaning against their car was a gangly fifteen-year-old boy, his son from a previous marriage.

Cindy was late. She had run to the market. A small car pulled up. Cindy was wraith-like and friendly, with large eyes behind pink and delicate lids. Howard helped Phyllis carry her large scrapbooks into the house.

It was warm in the small front room. A makeshift bookshelf was filled with paperback editions of popular plays. Cindy was a drama student. The sullen profile of Dean stared across the wall from a framed lobby card of *Giant*. Cindy turned her radio to a station playing a marathon of Beatle songs. Howard sat on the couch and chatted nervously with Phyllis. Kenneth was bringing Maila, and they were late. Someone said, 'Here they are.'

Kendall was a striking man in his early sixties. He wore a western shirt and jeans. Tall, his hair was combed back and tied, giving his refined and moustached features an aquiline cast. The strong hands sharpened the impression of a journeyman artist.

Maila was wonderful. Howard could not guess her age. She wore a black caftan which set off a large crucifix on a chain around her long and sensuous neck. Her hair was pulled away from her face and fastened in a bun at the crown of her skull where large, swept-back sunglasses were arranged in an effect that was Egyptian. Her skin was clear. Under the feline lashes her eyes were deep, penetrating and luminous. When they fell on Howard as they were introduced, he felt a thrill. She smiled graciously, tilted her head to laugh, and he saw that the teeth on the left side of her face were missing. There was a flash of softness in her eyes, and there was vulnerability in the giggle she tried to suppress as she covered her missing teeth a little self-consciously. It was feminine, poignant, and electric. Howard realized that for the first time in his life he was in the presence of one of the great beauties, the *ageless*, kept forever young and sexually vibrant by either extreme purity or meticulous evil.

His mind began to play the strange games it had in high school. When she arranged her chair to sit between him and Kendall to hear their conversation better, he thought, 'She likes me.' But then she would seem to lavish attention on Lois' stepson – who began to irritate Howard. All angles and adenoids, he was a reflection of Howard when he was that age.

The little cassette tape recorder was on the coffee table. Maila asked whether Stan Pierce's wife Gloria looked like Marilyn Monroe. She had seen a resemblance in the snapshot Stan had sent. Kendall said that he had a genuine relic of Marilyn: a flaxen strand that had been removed from her studio hairbrush and pressed in a little glass square. Maila, who had known Marilyn, said that she also had a 'remembrance'. She arched her eyebrows. 'A booger.' There was a moment of silence. She threw her head back in a laugh as a ripple of shock ran like a current through the room. Howard felt a rush of affection. He was aware of her even when he was talking to someone else. He found himself sending silent and yearning waves of emotion to her below the chatter and bustle.

'You must write your memoirs,' Phyllis said to her. Maila said she had written them, once – then thrown them away. She savoured the aghast expressions. She said an agent would not even read them because they had not been typed. Phyllis said that she would type them. Lois, too, offered help. Howard wondered if Maila remembered that he, first, had offered to type any memoirs in the letter he had sent with his manuscript. If anyone, it should be him. He offered again.

Cindy had fixed manicotti for dinner. Her pantry was filled with health foods. In line at the table, Howard listened for Maila's voice somewhere behind him. Even as he talked absently with Cindy, invisible antennae were trying to pick up what Maila was saying. She was telling Lois's stepson that he was a gorgeous young man, and that he would have to be careful of her were he older. She asked him what his astrological sign was.

Howard was jealous, wishing she were interested in him. He had not been able to strike up a conversation. All he had asked were goofy questions about *Plan 9 from Outer Space*. Maila was so vital, she was interested in *today*. All Howard's questions were about dead people and yesterdays. He had been so absorbed in that past of which she had been a part that he could no longer make conversation about real life. When Maila stepped back to the screen door to look out at Cindy's garden, he followed, suddenly desperate to be alone with her. He saw again the image of Vampira, pale hands outstretched, walking from behind the crypt and advancing towards the camera, eyes wide, lips tremulous, dead but flushed with passion. It was an image which had haunted him for most of his life. He wanted to communicate in some way. He told her that you had to water plants a great deal in Bakersfield because of the heat. There was a silence. Amazingly, he felt a little self-consciousness in her, too. After a moment of awkwardness they went back to the kitchen.

He was flattered when, after dinner, she asked *him* to fetch for her a piece of Cindy's carob cake. Phyllis had a camera. Lois's stepson took a place by Maila on the couch, easy and unself-conscious, and she moved close to him, peering intently into his eyes for the photo. Howard felt pain. Maila did not sit as close to him when they posed for their picture together.

It was near nine o'clock when the party broke up. Howard was sad. He told Maila and Kenneth how very excited he had been to meet them. He watched as they walked out of the door, still talking to Phyllis and Lois. Howard did not follow. He felt hollow. When he had said goodbye she had seemed so formal. He felt he had not made an impression. She had not liked him. He felt a failure. He did not like himself. He had been sure that something was supposed to happen, and it had not. He had not been equal to the experience, and now he would not see her again. He would probably not hear from her if he wrote.

He felt empty when he returned home, and it was a while before he felt up to writing any more letters. There was a thank you note to Cindy, in which he included a copy of the Tripke map of the accident and a xerox of the Roth crash photo. He did not hear from her again. He realized she probably thought he was terrifically morbid.

His heart was hardly in it, but he wrote to Maila. He had to try once more. The short note was desperate and direct, just the opposite of the obsequious 'fan' letters he had sent previously. A half page, candid, personal, and, he hoped, disarming. He felt compelled to tell her about himself. He renewed his offer to type her memoirs, and closed with some remarks of calculated self-deprecation in case she thought he was pretentious. He sent it off.

He heard from Stan that he had finished his own Maila interview article and had sent it to her for comment. Stan was *collaborating* with her. The piece would probably appear in the next month's newsletter. Stan was really the logical choice to type her memoirs, if she liked the way he handled this project. He tried not to think about it. 'How marvellous,' Stan wrote about Howard's meeting with Maila. 'Please details. Know you must have been thrilled. Lucky!' Howard's smile was rueful. Most of the letter was irritating evaluations of Howard's speculations about the accident, with requests for *more* information.

He received his manuscript back from the Portland man. A letter followed a couple of days later. The first page of the typescript was slashed and peppered with comments and question marks, pencil corrections of grammar and syntax, and underscoring of dangling participles. 'I read all 41 pages,' Stan wrote, 'but only commented on page one. The raw data is there, but needs reworking. Some sections are muddled, inconclusive. Sources should be documented. The opening pages are the most difficult. (Please remember all comments are offered as *constructive* criticism. *Your possible sensitivity worries me.*)' He thought that much of it was disjointed, distracting, and disconnected. Howard's treatment of Dean's death he found clinical and lacking compassion. A little self-consciously, Stan tried to leaven his negative remarks with humour, inserting a joshing footnote, 'Hey – do I get to exact a fee?!!'

Howard was stunned, then angry. But he *had* asked Stan for his opinion. He realized now that he had been dishonest. He hadn't really wanted it. But the letter rankled. He thought of a hundred replies before settling on one that was thick-skinned, oblivious, and sarcastic. 'Thank you for your kind remarks,' he began. 'I was surprised you had trouble with the chronology and organization. So far, you are alone.' There were a couple of examples to demonstrate that Stan's reading of the account had been inattentive. The implication was that, perhaps, it was a bit beyond his range. They evidently had different tastes, Howard said, because he had not been much impressed by Stan's writing, either. He suggested they just stick to 'substantive' matters, and things of mutual interest.

It was painful for him to write about his meeting with Maila and Kendall. Perhaps it had already got back to Stan that she had found Howard a bore. He mentioned the meeting only briefly, adopting a glib and cynical tone. Howard was staggered when he shortly received two letters from Maila. He read them in wonder. She wrote glowingly of his manuscript. 'It's thrilling, of course – I'm so happy that a divine destiny has somehow chosen you to execute it!! I had to tell you how strongly and favourably your account affects me. I read and reread.' There were seven closely written and detailed pages of further memories of Jimmy Dean. Howard was thunderstruck. *She liked it* – and she liked *him*. It was so unexpected, and such a violent reversal of what he had been thinking, that he felt close to tears. And when she wrote that she would accept his help in typing a chapter from her memoirs he felt truly *appointed*. He was charmed and helpless against her sweetness, humour, and intellect. He studied her pages and savoured their memory. He spent vacant moments at work or in the car perfecting the wording of his reply as though selecting flowers for a bouquet.

Two weeks passed and he did not hear from Stan. It was the longest time they had gone without corresponding since they had first written to one another many months before. Maybe Stan would never write again. He told Leslie to call him at work immediately if a letter arrived, and when the call came he asked her to open it and read it to him. Stan said he had found Howard's letter disturbing. 'Some people do not wish to hurt your feelings,' he said. 'Perhaps I have been too polite in the past. Howard, you haven't been getting opinions on your effort from literary professionals. You have repeatedly insulted my intelligence. I am usually paid for my comments. I'm not being granted the respect I'm owed for the help you needed, and asked for. I'm sorry your ego was slightly bruised.' He objected to the irreverent remarks Howard had made about Maila. 'Where is some decency and respect?' A section had been cut out with scissors, and the letter taped back together. It was not signed, as usual, 'Your friend,' but only, 'Stay in touch.'

Howard tried not to let Leslie see his shock when he arrived home, or his anxiety to study the letter. She knew he was hurt. A terror was setting in, too, that Stan might contact Maila and say that Howard could not be trusted. Leslie said she wouldn't put anything past Stan. Howard suddenly wanted Maila to cut Stan dead. When he calmed down he recognized that perhaps Stan's remarks had cut so deep because they were *true*. The manuscript had been written frenziedly, and at three in the morning, which, as Stan had offered, perhaps wasn't his best time of the day. But he couldn't accept that Stan was the better writer. He reread all Stan's articles which had appeared in the newsletter. Was it only because of his resentment that they now seemed so flat and unimaginative?

They had both gone too far. Howard knew the relationship was beyond repair. The mature thing would be not to reply at all. But he found himself chewing over some of the expressions from Stan's letter, '. . . problems . . . pompous . . . I usually get paid . . .' and he would become furious and start talking to himself. He wanted to slam his fist into Stan's simpering face.

One day at work, he was beside himself. He wrote a note, 'I agree with the prevailing attitude of *professionals* that the standard of writing in Portland is best served by your continued unemployment.' He also said that Stan's best point was on his head. It was pompous and awkward, he knew, with pain transparent in his spluttering anger. But he couldn't stop himself from stuffing it in an envelope and running down to the post office to throw it violently in the slot. He felt a twinge of regret almost immediately. There was a knot of rage in his stomach.

Chapter 17

Howard did not go to Fairmount at the end of that month for the twenty-seventh anniversary of Dean's death. He had to work on the last Friday in September, the day of Roger's rally. But on Saturday the whole family took Highway 46 to Cholame. Leslie was eight months pregnant and very uncomfortable. On their doctor's advice, this was the last trip she would make out of town before delivery.

It was raining. The sky was dark and the pavement wet. There were many vintage 1950s cars on the highway, participants in Will O'Neil's nostalgic parade in honour of Dean. Howard passed an old Ford pick-up hauling one of their props, a replica of a tombstone with the inscription:

JAMES DEAN
1931 1955

They met Roger at Stella's. He was alone. A family of three had made his rally the day before, but they were the only ones. Outside in the mud, the 1949 Mercs lined up past the gleaming chromium of the monument. Howard saw that there were several 1950 Fords clustered around the sculpture. Rain spattered the windows.

Leslie went into labour on 30 October, and Maggie arrived on Halloween. Howard was in the delivery room. He had seen both his children born.

It was near the end of November when Howard finally arranged a meeting with Ron Nelson, the patrolman who had testified at the inquest about his investigation of the Dean accident. The first time he had called him, in late August, Nelson had told him he was just leaving town and would be gone for two months. In the meantime the baby had arrived. Howard would be making the trip to Atascadero alone. On Saturday the twentieth, he left straight from work at noon. In a half hour, he was heading west on Highway 46. The sun shone on the highway as 'The Secret Door', Rosenmann's theme from *Rebel Without a Cause,* played from the tape deck.

Howard was excited. Now he was really going to get some answers. Three months earlier he had received his manuscript back from Ernie Tripke. The accompanying note had been terse and cold compared to the familiar tone of previous letters he had received from the retired captain of the highway patrol: 'My comments are noted on your manuscript. I have no comments to make on your opinion of the inquest, the D.A., and Sheriff Merrick. I never heard that Turnupseed had any "clout" in that county and/or city politics . . .'

Tripke had ignored entirely his suggestion that they get together some time in person. Howard felt badly. He had been insensitive to send his manuscript, with its scattergun imputations of wrongdoing, to a man who had been very generous and considerate to him. He had cast no credit on anyone involved in the investigation, implying that everyone was, at best, a tacit accomplice. Howard winced when he thought how he had even asked Tripke why Turnupseed had not been cited at the scene. He was sick with himself.

He drove through the intersection where Dean had died, glancing as he always did at the phone pole to make sure Roger's plaque was still in place. It was about two o'clock in the afternoon when he pulled up in front of the spacious house on a steep hillside on the outskirts of the little town of Atascadero. A man in a sports shirt was stepping out of a blue pick-up piled high with switches and branch cuttings. In his early fifties, he was tall and trim. He had not noticed Howard. He walked to the house and went inside. Howard followed quickly, knocking on the door to introduce himself. The handshake was firm and strong. Howard saw that Nelson's arms were scratched from the branches he had cut and carried. 'So your father was on the highway patrol?' Nelson asked.

He seated Howard at the dining room table. It was a nice house. Did Howard want any tea? Nelson brought himself a cup to the table, and a glass in which to place the soggy teabag.

Howard had brought a volume of his scrapbooks and a copy of his manuscript. Nelson thumbed through it. Howard was embarrassed at the title page, A Death at Cholame, with its photo of the crumpled Spyder. Nelson said, 'You've got a lot of time in on this thing, huh?' He tapped the picture of Paul Moreno. 'I knew him – he had a bad appendix operation. That's him there, without a coat. Not that he needed one to stay warm, with all that fat. I heard that they had a hell of a time getting to his appendix. They had to cut through all those layers.'

Howard was curious. 'Did every patrolman have a camera in his car?'

Nelson smiled. 'When I was working with Ernie, I usually wound up taking the pictures. These other daytime photos, I don't remember.'

Looking at the inquest exhibits, Howard remembered a question. 'Did the Spyder hit this bracing cable anchoring this pole? It seems to be in a different position in these two pictures, as if it were knocked loose from the ground.'

If the Spyder had struck the cable, perhaps that was why it had gone only forty-five feet after impact.

Nelson studied it. 'No, no, it's just the angle. Right here I was looking right on, and then over here, it's seen from the other side.'

'So the Spyder didn't strike the pole, or fence, or anything?'

'No. I was never, and I don't think Ernie was either, I think he'll bear me out . . . there was never in our minds any evidence that the Porsche was travelling at any speed. There's a lot of damage to the Porsche, but if he'd been going that fast, I think it would have looked different. Worse. I think Dean had slowed down, either by changing gears, or by braking. If Dean had lived, I would have cited Turnupseed for illegal left-hand turn.'

'But because he was killed, you did not?'

'When there was a fatality, we conducted an investigation and turned it over to the D.A. for review. It was his determination whether or not to prosecute for manslaughter.'

'Turnupseed must have seen the Porsche.'

'He said he didn't.'

'Clifford Hord told me that, after the inquest, Turnupseed had come up to him and told him that he had seen the Porsche, but that by the time he saw it, he couldn't go ahead, or turn away, to miss him.'

Nelson stirred. 'He never told us that. He never came forward with that.'

'Why was the visibility of the Porsche such an issue? The skid marks were physical proof that Turnupseed saw the car.'

'Probably the skids weren't that long.'

Howard showed him the inquest diagram of the accident. The skid marks *were* longer than Nelson remembered. 'I drew this,' he said, mulling. 'What Turnupseed probably meant was, "I didn't see him *in time*." I don't remember, but it seems to me the skids showed he tried to turn away at the last minute. But these skids don't necessarily mean he was braking for the Porsche.'

'He might have been braking for the intersection?'

'It's possible.'

It made sense. There were always skid marks at the intersection, and certainly they did not *all* represent collisions or near collisions.

Howard asked Nelson, 'Do you think there was a cover-up?'

The other man reflected for a minute. 'An inquest was not that common,' he said. 'There probably wouldn't have been one, at all, if it had been someone other than *James Dean* who had been killed. *None of these people knew what they were doing*. The sheriff-coroner was just a citizen who was elected. He didn't have any training. He was a *politician*. That's the way it was in these little towns. *Anything* could happen, and did.'

'You don't think the D.A's office manipulated the interrogation in a certain direction?'

'I think he just asked the next question that popped in his mind. It wasn't relevant at all whether Dean was cited for speeding outside Bakersfield, or whether he drove someone off the road five minutes earlier. That had nothing to do with the accident. Once, I cited a guy for passing a car on the right. He told me, "The guy in front of me was turning, but with no signal." I told him it was not relevant. Like this thing. Someone should have said, "Let's don't talk about Dean's speed or what he did up the road. Let's talk about *the other guy's speed.*'

Howard was not satisfied. He read Nelson some excerpts from the inquest where it seemed patent to him that a case was being built against Dean. Nelson had not recalled all the testimony. He thought he might even have been required to leave the room when he was not actually on the stand. He pursed his lips. It did seem fishy.

'I guess the D.A. had decided not to prosecute.' He paused. 'This frustrated us patrolmen so much. We would build cases and then nothing would ever come of it. One boy ran a stop sign and killed someone. It never came to trial. Turned out he was the crony of the judge. They had coffee every day.'

'So, you feel that, while someone could read this inquest, and find all kinds of inflammatory things, it was not by design?'

Nelson said, 'An inquest isn't like a trial where a judge is there to impose some order. At an inquest, they can do any damn thing they want. No one around there knew what to do, or how to conduct one.'

As Nelson thought, he often covered his mouth with his hand. He asked Howard, 'What do you hope to accomplish?'

Howard was startled. 'I figured talking to you would be the end of it for me. I'm sure that if there were anything to a lot of these allegations, it would have come back to you.'

Nelson showed Howard his garage on his way out. He had made it into a workroom. The air was warm and sweet. He was heating the vines and branches he had cut so that he could twist them into handmade baskets. Howard bought one for $5.

On the way home, Howard stopped at Stella's for a cup of coffee. It was near dusk as he neared the intersection. He pulled onto Parkfield Road and stepped out to look east up the highway. In the distance, he saw old Highway 466 where it climbed over the two knolls. The wind was sharp and rippled the grass in waves across the plain.

A conspiracy was not always an 'arrangement'. It might be two guys, perhaps a sheriff and a district attorney, who had coffee together a couple of times a week and who shared the unquestioned biases of the rural community which had elected them – and which they hoped would elect them again. The 'design' might be as tacit and subtle as the inbred values and prejudices of a way of life acknowledged and affirmed at local meetings of the V.F.W., the Cal Poly Boosters, the Republican Central Committee, the Chamber of Commerce, the Elks, the American Legion, the Daughters of the American Revolution, the Rainbow Girls, and the miscellaneous roasts and football dinners and church socials.

The other driver had been a *local boy*, even though he was from Tulare. Like many of the local kids, he was a student at Cal Poly.

Dean was an *outsider* from *Hollywood* – a place which in the McCarthyist 1950s connoted to the ruralities a sort of Communist Sodom.

The other driver was a navy veteran.

On the other hand, Dean was a *movie-actor* – and not a *beloved* one like Gary Cooper. Those who knew anything of his career knew only that he played bad boys and represented a disturbing new wave which exalted rebellion against old values.

Anti-German sentiment still existed in the county ten years after the Second World War. Many of the locals had lost friends or loved ones in a conflict the memory of which was still painful. Howard still detected enmity toward Ohnishi – and this was nearly thirty years later. The local press had pointedly described Dean's sports car as 'German-made'. He had been accompanied by a *real German* who spoke no English. What if they had known that Weutherich had been in the Luftwaffe and was, in fact, an ex-Nazi?

The other driver had a pregnant wife. The thought of prosecuting a clean-cut veteran who was a head of household was unsavoury – especially because the inevitable attendant publicity would make it a spectacle which would enhance no one's public image with the local electorate.

Perhaps prejudice, compassion, and self-interest had confused themselves until they were indistinguishable within the district attorney, the sheriff, and the jurors.

The local view, expressed rather than reported by the local

paper three days after the crash, was that Dean had been 'speed-loving' with a 'reputation for fast driving'. His car had been 'careening' at the time of the crash, and, worst of all, he had driven several *local people*, en route to a football game, off the road. He had been on his way to a sports car race, a rich kid's sport, in a car which had cost more money than many of the local farmers would scratch from the soil that whole year. The roads were undoubtedly a safer place without him. Howard had himself detected the still existing community sentiment which, while never quite saying that Dean deserved what he got, implied that he had certainly been asking for it.

Whatever had happened, this was the climate that had made it possible. Howard knew, because he had grown up in the same kind of town with the same kind of people, only eighty miles away.

Howard looked up the road, squinting. He had never been here alone, before. The Spyder appeared on the old highway at the top of two knolls, suddenly zooming around the car ahead of it to drive a Pontiac off the road right at the two trees, before sliding quickly back into its own lane. It flew down the slope, its engine a high whine, Dean's hair whipping in the wind, his hands racing-gloved and his face inscrutable behind the clip-on sunglasses he had worn as Jett Rink in *Giant*. Then he slowed. He had seen the Ford coming around the curve.

The black and white paint job gave the immediate impression of a police car – and Jimmy had already been pulled over once that day. He warily took his foot off the gas and wind resistance slowed the car to 65 m.p.h. He saw that it was not a police car – but it *was* moving erratically. It had crossed into his lane, and then back.

In the highway safety spot, Jimmy had said, 'Half the time you don't know what this guy's going to do, or that one.' It seemed like the guy was going to cut in front of him, but now he was hitting the brakes. Jimmy's reflexes kicked in as he realized the man in the other car was confused and could go either way. He pulled the wheel to the right, veering away and around to give the Ford more room. Something in the sports car's hesitancy tipped the Ford's calculations to one last and committed power lurch to the shortest line across the intersection, before the brakes were slammed on again in desperate awareness of misjudgement.

The Spyder exploded into the grill and flew up like a silver trout breaking water, hanging there for a noiseless instant before it crashed and skittered across the intersection in a shower of dust and hurtling fragments before sliding to a stop eighteen inches from the barbed wire fence.

Howard felt so sad for the boy who had sat in the Ford and tried to comprehend the impossibly grotesque and horrible thing that had happened. And he heard a giggle and quirky laugh as Dean threw back his head and raised his eyebrows in strange and quizzical delight. 'Turnupseed?'

Darkness fell quickly. Howard got back in the car. On the other side of Polonio Pass, he hit the straight stretch where the traffic was sparse. The road was his. He pressed the accelerator and the needle of the speedometer trembled between 75 and 80 m.p.h. until he had a floating sensation as if the car was going to lift off the road and into the stars. He wanted to be home.

Chapter 18

Rolf Weutherich never lost his love for speeding cars. Even before the Cholame crash, he had survived two bad racing accidents in Germany. Yet in the 1960s he was still active as a rally driver for Porsche. The high point of his track career came in 1965 when, with Stuttgart driver Eugen Bohringer, he placed second at the Monte Carlo Rally. But he never recovered physically or spiritually from the crash in which he had nearly died with James Dean. He returned to the Federal Republic a haunted man. He had four unsuccessful marriages. He attacked one wife with a knife and was confined to the Weissenhaur Psychiatric Hospital for a period. After eighteen years with Porsche, he left the firm in 1968.

In March 1979 he moved from the Cologne area to Hohenloren, where he was hired by Honda dealer Roland Eckert. 'He was car crazy,' his employer remembered. Eckert recalled giving Rolf a ride in a racy new B.M.W. 'He was in seventh heaven.' But Weutherich could not stay put, or stay away from Porsches. He turned up in Neuenstein, mounting turbo engines in the cars that had been so strangely involved in his life.

Restless and worn out, he still maintained a reputation among his friends as a man gregarious and fun-loving. Which was to say, he liked women and he liked to drink. But his health was broken, and he never long escaped his fame as the man who had lived when the idol had died. He even received fan mail. He ridiculed the senders to a friend. *'James Dean was rotted away before they were even born.'* But in 1981 he signed a contract with an American publisher to tell his story about his time in the United States with James Dean.

On the night of 20 July 1981, Rolf visited a bar in his home town of Kupferzell in the county of Hohenloren. He was scheduled to leave for the United States in a couple of weeks. He was under the influence when, later in the evening, he got behind the wheel of his Honda car and gunned the engine. He headed for home. As in 1955, he ignored his seat belt.

A witness on the street at 10.50 p.m. saw a tiny car speeding down Market Street toward the centre of town at about 65 m.p.h. The pavement was wet. As Rolf tried to make the long curve near the People's Bank he lost control. The car skidded across the road to the right and smashed through a chain link fence and into the front of a house, inflicting $4,000 worth of damage. Fortunately, no one in the house was hurt. But Rolf suffered massive injuries. The Kupferzell fire department rushed to the scene. This time it was Weutherich who was pinned in the car. The emergency doctor tried to revive him, but it was futile. He was that county's seventh traffic victim that year. He was only fifty-three years old.

The driver of the Ford returned from the navy in 1958 to face two lawsuits against him arising from the accident. In the summer of 1958, his own insurance carrier settled with Dean's and that action was dismissed 'with prejudice' – the waiving of all future claims.

Rolf Weutherich's suit was a different story. That complaint had been amended to name only the Ford's driver as defendant in late March of 1958. The attorneys for the student's insurance began the standard flurry of motions – to quash, to change venue, to dismiss. They requested a trial by jury and claimed that Dean's own recklessness was the proximate cause of the accident, and, anyway, Rolf had consented to Dean's negligence and bore responsibility himself.

Ultimately, it was Rolf's absence from the Country which ended the filings and motions. Unavailable for questioning, the trial date was reset three times in 1959. Both sides agreed to a re-continuance. On 16 October 1961, six years after the crash at Cholame, a judge dismissed the action for failure to bring to trial within five years. Only the defendant's attorney was present.

Though he had never granted an interview, the other

driver was required to give a deposition in Fresno, California on 8 March 1958. A.H. Brazil, attorney for Dean's insurance company, questioned him about the accident.

Don said that he had left Cal Poly for Tulare between twelve and one o'clock in the afternoon of 30 September 1955. He had been in no hurry. He was travelling at about 45 or 50 miles per hour when he started the turn less than 100 feet west of the point of impact.

Q And had you been looking in the direction of 466 which runs straight east?
A Yes.
Q And was there any traffic on the road at that time as you observed before you started to make your turn?
A No, not that would even call my attention to it.
Q But you were looking directly up that highway?
A Yes.
Q Did you see any vehicle coming in the opposite direction?
A No, I sure did not.

He said that he had been looking directly up 466 but had seen nothing at all. He had just started his turn.

Of the collision itself he said, 'I was driving along and then I heard this screaming of an engine, or saw it first, I am not sure which, in other words. It both happened and I had – it was right under me then, or there was a collision.'

Q How soon before the impact would you say that you heard the sound of the engine?
A Maybe three seconds, or, it was very very fast, right there.
Q Three seconds would be one, two, three.
A No, it was closer than that. It all happened right about the best as I could tell, at the same time.
Q A snap of the fingers, you might say, is that right?
A Yes.

What had happened when he realized the car was upon him? 'I made a distinct movement of the steering wheel; that part I am sure of.'

'But not enough reaction so as to get your car out of the path of this oncoming automobile?' Brazil asked.

'No sir, I sure did not.'

He said he had not seen Dean's car until after impact. 'Well, I heard the car and I looked right down into the seat after the impact, but at the time of impact I seen an arm come up over my hood.'

> Q Now you mentioned previously of having seen this arm rise up and – being raised up and covering the face. Could you at this time know as to whether it was the person on the left or on the right side?
> A No sir, until after the accident I had no idea whether there was one or five of them in the car.

He thought he had applied his brakes with great force as soon as he heard the other car. After the crash, he said he saw that he had left four or five feet of skid marks with each tire. He said Dean had not applied the brakes at all.

Since he hadn't seen Dean's car, Brazil said, the young man could not say whether it was going fast or slow.

'Just from the sound of the engine would be the only way,' the Ford's driver said.

The attorney asked where Dean's body had been situated. 'He was on the right hand side of the car hanging over the door face down.'

The attorney asked, 'He was dead at the time as I understand it?'

'That is the way I understand it,' Turnupseed said.

Under more questioning, he said he might have been going as slow as 20 miles an hour when they crashed. He was sure he wasn't doing 60. He revised his earlier estimate and said that 45 was the top speed he could have been travelling.

He said there were no restrictions on his license, that he did not wear glasses, and that his sight and hearing were good. He said that the Highway Patrol had not arrived until two hours after the crash.

Today the death of James Dean is a part of his life he does not discuss. Situated on the corner between his two companies is a large carpet cleaning outlet with the prominent name in bold and cheerful script five feet high: DEAN ENTERPRISES.

In September 1982, Stan and Gloria returned to Fairmount for Museum Days. Jimmy's films were shown again in his honour. Ortense was up to attending the screening of *Rebel.* Hugh Caughell, Dean's old biology teacher, was the projectionist. When the lights came up, Stan was moved to hear Adeline and Ortense comment how good Jim looked.

Again, there were the familiar rituals. Adeline led a tour of the high school, and there was a visit to the Winslow farm. They stopped at the site of Marvin Carter's bicycle shop, and inspected Vernon Hunt's funeral parlour where Jimmy had played in a casket for photographer Dennis Stock on his last trip home. There was a quieter time at Back Creek Friends Church, where Jimmy's funeral had been held and where Ortense had been organist. At Park Cemetery, Stan stood for a silent moment at the chipped and scarred stone over the grave.

Members of the We Remember Dean club who had made the trek had luncheon at Jewel's De La Shure Cafe. Twenty-five members from all over the country had showed up. Adeline was guest of honour. She remembered the last time she had seen Jim. 'Don't forget to be kind,' she had told him. They were the last words she ever said to him.

Upon their return to Oregon, Stan wrote an article for the newsletter at Phyllis' request. 'All of us took a piece of Fairmount home with us in our hearts, and left a piece of ourselves there. One day in the not too distant future, we'll have to return, and exchange the pieces once again.'

Howard read the account. Now that he did not correspond with Stan, his visions and psychic energy were turned inwards. One night he dreamed again that he was in Fairmount, but this dream did not end as the others had. It was as if he had come to a gate which had always had a chain around it, but this time it was ajar. The cemetery became a churchyard, and there was suddenly a white house that was also a church. He went inside.

There was a small dark room, cosy, comfortable, and crowded with antiques and bric-a-brac that were part of a real and lived-in room from which someone had only just stepped out. Howard passed into another room which was similar to the first. But in the middle of the floor was a bier. A blade of sun sliced through the parted curtains to fall on the polished wood of the casket. Howard was startled. He realized that it held the body of James Dean. A man dressed like a priest approached him out of some shadows. The man looked like himself, only slimmer, with finer features. Howard felt awkward, as if he had been discovered in some place he should not be. The priest had not come to turn him out but to set him at ease. He pointed to the foot of the catafalque, and for the first time Howard saw that there were *kneeling rails*.

The dream was strong and stayed with him with clarity. Over the months, he came to realize that while other fans that he had sought out and met had seemed unable in many ways to admit the death of James Dean, he had been unable to admit his love for him.

In December 1982, he bought an autograph of James Dean from a Santa Monica dealer for $500. The economy was rough and his company had shown a loss all year. There had been no rise and only a small bonus for many months – and there was the expense of living in his new house for the first year. He had had to borrow the money from his mother, and he would have to make payments to her every month. Leslie was furious, then hurt. She couldn't understand. They had just spent $240 for twelve original movie stills from Dean films, and Howard had promised that that would be the last thing. It was right before Christmas, and it seemed like the worst time.

That night in bed she relented. He told her it was something he had wanted for most of his life. But, God, it had cost as much as their refrigerator, or their bed, and almost as much as the washer and dryer. Sometimes Leslie wondered whether he was *really* crazy.

He was emotional the day it arrived. It was in a large frame, mounted museum style. There was a portrait of Dean in a leather jacket. On a small square of thin paper, the pulpy kind with big lines which he had used in elementary school, was the light signature in ink – 'James Dean' – underscored with a flourishing squiggle. He recognized the familiar low-slung penmanship and could hardly breathe. It had been obtained by an assistant soundman on *Giant* in the final months of Dean's life. Howard hung it in the corner of the room and no other thing hung beneath or near it. Howard had a strange impulse to write to Stan and tell him. But that was impossible.

The February 1983 We Remember Dean club newsletter arrived. It included a page from the December issue of *Hollywood Studio Magazine*. The title of the article, written by Stan, was 'A World of Dean Memorabilia'. It began, 'Never before, and not since . . .' Stan threw bouquets to the 'top-notch' fan club. 'My prized Dean memorabilia possessions include a chunk of plaster from the set of "Reata" used in *Giant*.' He wrote, 'Luckily, my wife shares my hobby, which helps "stoke my fire"! My wife and I have followed the "James Dean trail" to his home town and resting place, Fairmount, Indiana, more than once. There we've met warm, kind, sensitive, respectful people that any town would be lucky and proud to have as its citizens. We've had personal contact with several of Dean's relatives, friends, and even costars, and our lives are all the richer for it. The W.R.D. club, the collection we have (valued in the four-figure range), the friendships we've maintained, the trips we've taken, all add up to a beautiful experience that has touched and changed our lives in a moving, positive way.'

The photo above showed Stan, tanned and smiling, sporting a moustache, his shirt opened halfway down his chest. He held a large chunk of Reata plaster in one hand, and the small Kendall head of James Dean in the other. Around him he had gathered and arrayed his talismans and icons, myriad images of Dean. Then he had got Gloria to stand on a chair and photograph it all. That was his marriage to Dean: to be seen by many, to create an image in the consciousness of others in which he was identified with Jimmy. It was like all the 'star' photos he had asked Gloria to take, the flash image of Stan intruding himself momentarily into the bright aura of some celebrity, smiling, seizing the instant to half frighten the famous with the ferocity of his sudden semblance of intimacy.

Howard visited Kenneth Kendall's studio in April 1983. The walls were hung with hundreds of portraits of Dean of all sizes. In one large room was displayed his masterpiece.

Kendall flicked on an electric light and there on the easel was *El Torero Muerto*, a fantasy on the death of James Dean. It portrayed the outstretched body of Dean, in a torero's costume, trickling blood. The limp cape in his still hand was a checkered racing flag.

Kenneth took a zippered plastic bag from the cupboard and removed from it the coat which Dean had worn in costume tests for *Eden*. He clucked disgustedly at the discovery of a moth hole. They sat on an old bed where Kendall produced from a carved wooden box the two ties Dean had worn in the same picture. Howard held in his hands the 'distressed' jeans that Jimmy had worn in *Rebel*, and the cummerbund from the final tuxedo scene in *Giant*.

Kenneth stood, opened a bathroom door, and snapped on another light. Howard was suddenly face to face with James Dean. Winton had given Kendall the plaster life mask that Warner's make-up department had made. Kenneth had bought two artificial glass eyes and installed them under horn rimmed glasses, then dressed the head in a *monk's cowl*. Howard stared for a long time. Dean stared back. 'Once he entered your life,' Kendall said, 'it was never the same. He had the strangest effect on people.'

In the next room, the artist reached into a glass case and handed to Howard an awesome relic: pressed between two postage stamp sized pieces of glass was a fleck of silver paint. It was a piece of the Porsche which Kendall had peeled from the aluminium skin when the wreck had been displayed in Hollywood.

Howard's 'Dean Room' in Oildale continued to accumulate items. It began to resemble a museum with a multiplication of accretions that was almost cancerous. The effect was overwhelming. There were large posters of Dean, and nearly a hundred framed photos. There were hundreds of dollars' worth of lobby cards and movie stills, including one autographed by George Stevens and another signed by Julie Harris. There were rare records of dialogue and soundtrack music, plus tapes of 1950s tribute songs to the dead star. There were letters from Ernie Tripke, and colour studies of the intersection. There were Dean buttons, and even a Dean pencil sharpener from Italy. A pilot's flight map charted the death route while two large framed topographical maps detailed microscopically the intersection and the old highway. A stand-up cardboard cutout of Dean lounged insolently in a corner, opposite two highway markers and several large rocks from the road near the deathsite.

But the pulsating heart of the room and of Howard's imagination was the Dean signature. Sometimes in the early mornings before he went to the gym as he did each day before work, he would dress in the room so that he could see the autograph.

In April he suddenly began to work seriously again on the accident manuscript. He stopped going to the gym. He dragged himself out of bed at three o'clock every morning to drink coffee and work himself into a febrile incandescence of imagination, reporting to his job at 7 a.m. enervated and exhausted. He remembered how his father had died at the age of forty-two of a heart attack and he worried at how run down the lack of sleep left him.

He had never had many friends and now he had none. He drew emotional sustenance from Maila's long and increasingly affectionate letters. She had become smitten with him and he had become infatuated with her. She lived in a cottage behind the Los Angeles restaurant where she worked as a waitress. He commiserated with her when she lost her beloved cat. He sympathized with her bitter rage at the studios which had abandoned her and then stolen the image of her beloved child Vampira to resurrect her as the slatternly 'Elvira', the bosomy hostess of an L.A. television horror film showcase, without so much as a nod of recognition, much less any money. From her close and candlelit room Maila ridiculed Stan Pierce and wrote torrential assurances to the unpublished Howard of his star of destiny, which moved him nearly to tears. His A.A. meetings had fallen off drastically as he receded into an inner world whose colours were more vivid than real life.

In the deep early morning hours when the rest of Oildale was asleep, he would sit at a card table among his photos and items of emotional significance, writing letters to Harry Murphy, the assistant D.A. at the inquest, or one of the witnesses, or a juror, or George Barris or William Eschrich, who had figured in the history of No. 130 after the crash. He shuffled papers and made notes, typing desperately about the inches and seconds and skid marks and velocities and speculations, arranging and mounting the meticulously collected facts into a reality so near and sharp that he could almost step into it. He knew more about the accident than anyone in the world. Once it occurred to him (the only time he really frightened himself) – what would he do if he were walking along *that* highway, and the silver Porsche pulled to a stop beside him and Jimmy Dean motioned him to get in? He felt a queasy recognition of an irresistible gravity. He knew that the symmetrical ending for his insoluble manuscript would be a footnote saying that he himself had died in a car accident while working on it.

He eventually framed the inquest photos of the highway and hung them on the wall where they formed a stark triptych. After a longer while, he wound up doing something he had only joked about in macabre moments: he framed the other inquest photos showing the wrecked cars, the ugly hulks freshly split open. Finally he did the unthinkable – he framed and displayed the picture of the crushed Rolf beside the mangled Porsche, and the photo of Jimmy being carried on a stretcher across the highway to the ambulance.

Looking up from his writing in the mornings, he would stare at the Tripke photo of the intersection taken on 1 October at the approximate time of day when Jimmy had died. It was the last scene to fill Jimmy's eyes and mind. The sun was setting and the granulated road surface in the foreground was speckled with dying light. But at the intersection itself the sun's rays flared and reflected up, turning the highway into a molten river that swept west and around the bend. The classical identifications of the west and the setting sun were not lost on Howard. What a magical picture, he thought. He followed the highway in his mind and was rushed up into it.

He knew there were others who shared the obsession and responded to the same implanted vision. A chauffeur at a Howard Johnson's in Colona, Illinois, wrote to him: 'Having gone over that fateful day on a map and in my mind, your study is of immeasurable interest to me . . . I would like to obtain photos of the crash site and shrine at whatever cost.'

The graphics, posters, and cards that were coming out – he

had them framed on the walls – rendered in visual terms the crystallization of the myth. Jimmy was shown with smashed stop signs, skid marks, and white lines that receded in the distance. Car keys were tossed on discarded photos, or held in racing-gloved fingers. A pale, vampirish Jimmy smiled enigmatically through a swirl of smoke while the Spyder, a spectral silver, beckoned behind him. Another portrayed him insolent and hellbent, his shirt open, while visible in the background No. 130 waited, parked in the telescope alcove of Griffith Observatory, the HOLLYWOOD sign discernible in the far hills. Then there was a card titled 'The Legend' – a licence plate crumpled on a highway, while above the illimitable horizon the yearning image of Dean spanned the sky and clouds.

On a Monday in May of that year Howard drove across town one evening and up the bluffs to the home of Charles Adams. It was not far from the darkening cemetery where Paul Moreno was buried. Adams had called the night before and invited him over, and now he was waiting at the front when Howard arrived. Howard wondered if he had met him outside because his wife was still irritated at his involvement in this thing.

Adams led him around the side of the house to the den. After nearly eight months he had finally received the original of his report and diagrams from Indiana. Howard pored over the map, studying its tragic story with oddly affectionate familiarity.

It all represented so much work. Adams admitted he had been obsessed. He drew on a Winston cigarette.

'You've followed this thing and its developments all through the years,' Adams said. 'By the time I was finished with the report, I just washed my hands of it. You can't go on at things forever.'

Adams was curious about the monument at Cholame. 'We had always thought we'd stop and see it when we went to visit our son,' he said. 'He was a student at Cal Poly. But he died before we could make the trip.' He had been killed in a car crash. Adams had established a scholarship in his memory. Gary had been a fine artist. Adams showed Howard some of his son's pen and ink work which was framed on the wall.

It was nearly 10.30 p.m. when Adams walked Howard outside to his car. The night was cool. Adams said, 'There are just so many loose ends to this thing. Someone could spend the rest of his life, and he would never know what really happened out there.'

Howard continued to write. The story of the death of Dean became not just the measurements and skid marks, but the way he himself had felt when he was sixteen and had first *really* seen *Rebel Without a Cause*. It was Mr Turnupseed's wistful smile, and the moment with Marcus Winslow on the Indiana porch while the corn rustled across the road, and the way the wind felt when he walked the old Highway 466 near the intersection. He wrote about his friendship with Stan Pierce, for it had been so long since he had had even such a friendship as that, and he described all the naked and vulnerable feelings he had had for Maila.

When he had put it all down and typed it, he sent it to her like a live and quivering piece of his heart.

He received it back in a few weeks with a covering page that consisted of the single word 'No!' written large. He was shocked and hurt. Maila had recoiled in horror from the story he had told. Had he too roughly spelt out a fantasy romance whose comic elements she could not admit? After all, Howard wrote from the warm and secure household of a wife and two children while Maila lived alone. There were also strange symbols on the paper, and as he studied them he thought of the hex she was rumoured to have placed on Jimmy Dean.

That same month he did not receive a newsletter from Phyllis. Maila must have told her and Stan about the manuscript. Howard now admitted that there was much that was small and mean in it. His description of Stan had been unfair and his anger at any fan or person who had not responded to him, perhaps repelled by his absorption with the accident and death, had resulted in cruel caricatures. He had burnt some bridges and there had been people on them. He had been excommunicated from We Remember Dean. It was with relief that he realized something was over.

One night the phone rang. It was Bill Hickman. Howard was thrilled. He had written to Hickman a couple of weeks earlier. It had been with some trepidation. He was such a grim and villainous presence in the films Howard had seen. If he wasn't shooting someone he was trying to force Steve McQueen or Roy Scheider off the road in a car chase. And there had been Maila's description of him as dour and unimaginative. Howard was pleasantly shocked.

After Dean's death Hickman had gone on to become the top stunt driver in Hollywood, co-ordinating the car chase sequences for such films as *Bullitt* and *The French Connection* before retiring in the late 1970s due to a bad back and a dismay at the direction the movies were taking. There was so much vulgarity that he hardly cared to be a part of them anymore.

Now he was ailing, his tongue thick and burnt from radiation treatments, and in and out of hospitals, but his voice was warm on the phone. Howard recognized how jealous Maila must have been of this lanky car friend of Jimmy's whose company he had preferred to anyone else's in his last months.

Howard was able to talk to him and hear him, to sense the man and his faith without the oblivious pressure of trying to pry from Bill's memory whatever jigsaw impressions he possessed of the day Jimmy Dean had died. Bill's was the deep sadness of a helpless friend who had knelt on a dusty roadside with his broken pal in his arms. Through Bill, Howard was able to feel again that which all the diagrams and police reports had served to obscure even as they brought the factual event closer: his own young sense of personal loss.

Bill and Howard talked for a long time. Bill liked Howard, too. 'Anytime, ol' buddy,' Hickman said as they got off the phone. Howard knew that the long conversation must have been a tiring effort for the man. He thought often of Bill, so ill and yet so grateful to be alive, and hoped he would hold on.

One Sunday morning, Howard and little Junior drove twelve miles up Highway 99 to park at the U.S. Army Air Corps barracks at the edge of a field. They walked out across the cracked and desolate tarmac of the old airport where, on a May day nearly thirty years before, Jimmy Dean had raced his white Speedster to third place, and where he had seen the silver Spyders win decisively. Junior, who could not yet speak, ran enchanted and laughing, blond head upraised at the tiny charm of a distant aeroplane floating noiselessly skyward at the far end of the waste.

Dennis Hopper descended on Portland, Oregon, on 12 June 1983 like the title of his new film, *Out of the Blue,* which he was in town to promote. Stan and Gloria Pierce were in the audience at Portland College. Stan was in awe. Hopper was the only surviving actor to have appeared with Jimmy in two films. At the age of sixteen he had played Goon, one of the gang members who had tormented Jimmy in *Rebel.* Then he had played Jordy Benedict, the idealistic son of Rock Hudson who confronts Jimmy's Jett Rink at the banquet scene of *Giant.* He was one of the few living emblems of Jimmy's screen career. Natalie Wood had drowned in a water-logged coat in the cold midnight waters off Catalina. Sal Mineo had been stabbed to death in the dark parking lot of his seedy apartment. Nick Adams had ended his own life with an overdose of barbiturates. Albert Dekker had besmirched his naked body with lipsticked obscenities and hung himself in his shower. Ed Platt, the sympathetic detective of *Rebel,* was gone, as was William Hopper, who had played Judy's dad in the same film. Death had claimed George Stevens and Nicholas Ray.

There was a reception following the screening, but Stan and Gloria were intimidated by the jostling crowd surrounding Hopper. If his film career had been less than spectacular, Hopper had achieved the status of a cult hero for the offbeat integrity of his rebel persona. The peak of his career had been his portrayal of the drug-dealing Vietnam era biker in *Easy Rider,* which he had also co-directed. That film had obtained for him the clout to exercise his own cinematic visions as a serious film-maker until they proved incoherent. But Hopper himself, in sports coat and slacks, seemed to move through the generations remarkably unscarred and consistent in his avowal that the shining beacon of his artistic and personal life had been James Dean.

Stan was fearing that his timidity had ruined his chance to touch Hopper when the actor suddenly and grandly invited all present to board two school buses for a speedway on the other side of town where he promised that he would fold himself up under a chair wired with six sticks of dynamite and then blow it up.

Stan and Gloria ran for a seat on the bus, though it was after midnight. The bus got lost, but they did not miss the main event. The chair disintegrated in a cloud of fire from which Hopper emerged unscathed (and visibly relieved) to hug his stunt adviser. Dusty and shaken, the star suddenly seemed vulnerable. Stan decided to make his move.

He was relieved that Hopper was cordial, though there was an unnerving wildness in the icy blue of the eyes set in the pale and translucent skin of the lupine face. In hushed and disconnected sentences, Hopper obliged the intense Stan with a few remarks about James Dean. 'You know,' he said, 'I think if Jimmy had lived, he and I would have run Hollywood.' Then he excused himself.

Afterwards, Stan and Gloria hurried back to the Sheraton Inn where Hopper was staying. Stan had read that Hopper liked to 'party'. Perhaps he would make another appearance. But as the night wore on, there was no party and no Dennis Hopper. Though the hour was late, Stan wrote a letter to the actor and thanked him for his time, mentioning that Gloria worked in an office near this hotel, and invited him to call and further discuss his career before he left town.

One morning a couple of days later, Gloria's office phone rang as she was typing. It was Dennis Hopper. His voice was hesitant. He remembered meeting her. Hopper said he had autographed a poster for her, and that if she would come up to his room he would like to present it to her. No mention was made of Stan.

Gloria took the lift up to his floor and knocked on the door of 2026, Hopper's bedroom suite. He smiled when he saw her. But he wasn't dressed. As she stepped into the room she saw he wore only a robe, and his brown hair was tousled.

The curtains were drawn and the room was dark. The stereo blared rock music. Her eyes adjusted to the light and she made out the star's lady friend asleep under the rumpled covers of the bed. Gloria was suddenly uncomfortable with the warm smell of the room and the intimacy of the tableau she had entered. And Hopper was locking *and* chaining the door. He was mumbling something but she couldn't understand him over the din of the guitars. He offered her some smoke, then giggled nervously. He wasn't sure where they were coming from, the young husband with the intense questions about Jimmy Dean, and then that note which closed with an invitation to call his wife at the office.

Gloria was uneasy. It was as if Stan's obsession with film and nostalgia and James Dean was coalescing with reality into a dimension that was part of both but wholly neither. Hopper had said at the speedway that it was amazing: the Sheraton Inn reminded him of the grand hotel in *Giant*. He said that once in the middle of the night he had gone downstairs to visit the grand ballroom and it had been the same as in the movie. The art deco elevators, the panelling, even the pool, were just like the Warner Brothers' sets twenty-seven years earlier.

Now here was Gloria with a grownup Jordy Benedict in one of the Emperador suites high above Portland. Only now Jordy was forty five years old, with darting blue eyes and a self-conscious giggle, completely oblivious of the chick out cold under the sheets a few feet away, nervously puffing a cigarette and hoping he was equal to whatever scene was going to shape up. The tension was increasing.

'So you saw *Easy Rider*?' he asked.

Gloria said she had seen it several times.

Hopper said, 'You know, if this hotel reminds me of *Giant* you kinda remind me of Carroll Baker.'

Carroll Baker had been the slightly wanton sex kitten of *Giant*. The remark was at once a compliment, a slight, and an invitation. Gloria wanted to leave. She stood up and headed for the door. A bewildered Hopper came up beside her and squinted through the peephole. 'Coast is clear!' he announced. He unchained the door. Gloria hurried out, clutching in her hand Stan's poster personally autographed by Hopper.

Stan was unrelenting in pressing her for details and nuances of everything Hopper had done and said. He searched for key words and was irritated that the stereo had been so loud. He was shocked and thrilled. He was compelled to write a careful account of Gloria's encounter, disassembling and reconstituting events in perspective. Though he sarcastically called his subject 'Hopper' or 'Mr Hopper' in the beginning of the account, he suddenly became 'Dennis' as Stan relived the scene in the bedroom suite.

The retelling served to put Hopper in his place. He was a drug-addled, washed-up has-been pathetically looking for an ego boost. Stan copyrighted the story and it appeared in a subsequent newsletter.

In Fairmount, Indiana, Jimmy Dean's family finally signed a contract to license the marketing of the likeness of the long-dead boy. His homogenized image is reproduced on authorized coffee mugs and commemorative plates, official calendars and greeting cards, while a line of hats, leather jackets, red windbreakers, boots and western wear all bear his name. As strangely and suddenly as it had disappeared, the James Dean headstone was found one night resting incongruously on the stump of a tree beside a country road. It was spotted by a farmer who wrapped it in a blanket to preserve any fingerprints and hauled the 200-pound marker to the Fairmount police station. They turned it over to Dean's cousin, Marcus Winslow Junior, whom Jimmy used to pull in a wagon. Markie thought about storing it for a while longer to give the crazies something to think about; maybe they would stop carving away at it. But by the end of the month he had returned it to Jimmy's unquiet grave and cemented it again to its base.

Within four weeks it was gone.

At the intersection of Highways 41 and 46 in California, cars with strange licence plates will pull over and fevered people sporting buttons declaring JAMES DEAN LIVES! or BACK FROM THE DEAD AND BIGGER THAN EVER! will jump out and dart fleetingly across the rushing traffic to stand in nimble pirouette in the middle of the highway where James Dean died and was assumed into legend. The rain has wept rusty tears across his image on the plaque on the old phone pole to the west.

At Cholame up the road, an older Japanese man in a business suit, accompanied by an interpreter, is sometimes seen to pull up at the restaurant in an expensive rented car. He walks to the cenotaph and inspects the light poles and guard rails for damage from careless motorists. He orders any necessary repairs. Before he gets back in the car and returns to Japan, he stands for a moment in silent contemplation of the two large tablets he has recently installed and which dwarf and shelter a small footnote of his love: a tiny fallen sparrow of bronze.

Sources

BOOKS

Herndon, Venable, *James Dean, A Short Life*, Doubleday & Co., New York 1974.

Martinetti, Ronald, *The James Dean Story*, Pinnacle Books, New York, 1975.

McCambridge, Mercedes, *The Quality of Mercy*, Times Books, New York 1981.

Schatt, Roy, *James Dean: A Portrait*, Sidgwick & Jackson, London, 1982.

Von Frankenburg, Richard, *Porsche: The Man and his Cars*, Bentley, Massachusetts, 1969.

MAGAZINE ARTICLES

Bendel, Hansjoerg, 'The Spyder Type 550', *Road and Track*, January 1956.

'Dean of the One-Shotters', *Time*, March 1956.

Goodman, Ezra, 'Delirium Over Dead Star', *Life*, 24 September 1956.

Meltsir, Aljean, 'James Dean – His Life and Loves', *Motion Picture*, September 1956.

Mitgang, Herbert, 'The Strange James Dean Death Cult', *Coronet*, November 1956.

Nolan, William F., 'His Love Destroyed Him', *Modern Screen*, February 1957.

Nurmi, Maila, 'The Ghost of James Dean', *Borderline*, January 1964.

Raskin, Lee, 'Little Bastard: The Search for James Dean's Spyder', *Porsche Panorama*, July 1984.

'Wind and Rain at Bakersfield', *Road and Track*, July 1955.

Roth, Sanford, 'The Assignment I'll Never Forget: James

Dean', *Popular Photography*, July 1962.
Weutherich, Rolf, 'Death Drive', *Modern Screen*, October 1957.

NEWSPAPER ARTICLES

Breen, Ed, 'He Wasn't Perfect', *Chronicle-Tribune Magazine*, Marion, Indiana, 28 September 1975.
Miller, Jerry, 'Cameras, Chroniclers and Crazies', *Chronicle-Tribune*, Marion, Indiana, 1 October 1980.
Miller, Jerry, 'For Them, James Dean Won't Die', *Chronicle-Tribune*, Marion, Indiana, 1 October 1980.
Miller, Jerry, 'Stone is Missing, but Spirit Remains', *Chronicle-Tribune*, Marion, Indiana, 16 April 1983.

17740-1 CRAFTS, KATHY & HAUTHER, BRENDA / How To Beat the System: The Student's Guide to Good Grades / $3.95
17219-1 CUMMINGS, E.E. / 100 Selected Poems / $5.50
17987-0 DURAS, MARGUERITE / Four Novels: The Square; 10:30 on a Summer Night; The Afternoon of Mr. Andesmas; Moderato Cantabile / $9.95
17246-9 DURRENMATT, FRIEDRICH / The Physicists / $6.95
17327-9 FANON, FRANZ / The Wretched of the Earth / $6.95
62073-9 GARWOOD, DARRELL / Under Cover: Thirty-five Years of CIA Deception / $3.95
17390-2 GENET, JEAN / The Maids and Deathwatch: Two Plays / $8.95
17903-X GENET, JEAN / Our Lady of the Flowers / $3.95
62247-2 GERVASI, TOM / America's War Machine: Arsenal of Democracy III / $14.95
17662-6 GERVASI, TOM / Arsenal of Democracy II / $12.95
62345-2 GETTLEMAN, MARVIN, et.al. eds. / El Salvador: Central America in the New Cold War / $12.95
62277-4 GETTLEMAN, MARVIN, et.al., eds. / Vietnam and America: A Documented History / $11.95
17994-3 GIBBS, LOIS MARIE / Love Canal: My Story / $6.95
17648-0 GIRODIAS, MAURICE, ed. / The Olympia Reader / $5.95
17967-9 GOMBROWICZ, WITOLD / Three Novels: Ferdydurke, Pornografia and Cosmos / $12.50
17764-9 GOVER, ROBERT / One Hundred Dollar Misunderstanding / $2.95
62490-4 GUITAR PLAYER MAGAZINE / The Guitar Player Book (Revised and Updated Edition) $11.95
17124-1 HARRIS, FRANK / My Life and Loves / $9.95
17936-6 HARWOOD, RONALD / The Dresser / $5.95
17409-7 HERNTON, CALVIN / Sex and Racism in America / $3.95
17125-X HOCHHUTH, ROLF / The Deputy / $7.95
62115-8 HOLMES, BURTON / The Olympian Games in Athens / $6.95
17075-X INGE, WILLIAM / Four Plays (Come Back, Little Sheba; Picnic; Bus Stop; The Dark at the Top of the Stairs) / $7.95
17209-4 IONESCO, EUGENE / Four Plays (The Bald Soprano, The Lesson, The Chairs, and Jack or The Submission) / $6.95
17226-4 IONESCO, EUGENE / Rhinoceros and Other Plays / $5.95
62123-9 JOHNSON, CHARLES / Oxherding Tale / $6.95
17287-6 KEROUAC, JACK / Mexico City Blues / $7.95
17952-8 KEROUAC, JACK / The Subterraneans / $3.50
62424-6 LAWRENCE, D.H. / Lady Chatterley's Lover / $3.95
17178-0 LESTER, JULIUS / Black Folktales / $4.95
17114-4 MALCOLM X (Breitman., ed.) / Malcolm X Speaks / $6.95
17016-4 MAMET, DAVID / American Buffalo / $5.95
62049-6 MAMET, DAVID / Glengarry Glenn Ross / $6.95

62371-1 MILLER, HENRY / Sexus / $9.95
62375-4 MILLER, HENRY / Tropic of Cancer / $7.95
62053-4 MROZEK, SLAWOMIR / The Elephant / $6.95
62301-1 NAISON, MARK / Communists in Harlem During the Depression / $9.95
13035-6 NERUDA, PABLO / Five Decades: Poems 1925-1970. Bilingual ed. / $14.50
62243-X NICOSIA, GERALD / Memory Babe: A Critical Biography of Jack Kerouac / $11.95
17092-X ODETS, CLIFFORD / Six Plays (Waiting for Lefty, Awake and Sing, Golden Boy, Rocket to the Moon, Till the Day I Die, Paradise Lost) / $7.95
17650-2 OE, KENZABURO / A Personal Matter / $6.95
17002-4 OE, KENZABURO / Teach Us To Outgrow Our Madness / $4.95
17992-7 PAZ, OCTAVIO / The Labyrinth of Solitude / $9.95
17084-9 PINTER, HAROLD / Betrayal / $6.95
17232-9 PINTER, HAROLD / The Birthday Party & The Room / $6.95
17251-5 PINTER, HAROLD / The Homecoming / $5.95
17761-4 PINTER, HAROLD / Old Times / $6.95
17539-5 POMERANCE, BERNARD / The Elephant Man / $5.95
17658-8 REAGE, PAULINE / The Story of O, Part II; Return to the Chateau / $3.95
62169-7 RECHY, JOHN / City of Night / $4.50
62171-9 RECHY, JOHN / Numbers / $8.95
13017-8 ROBBE-GRILLET, ALAIN / Djinn (and La Maison de Rendez-Vous) / $8.95
13017-8 ROBBE-GRILLET, ALAIN / The Voyeur / $8.95
62001-1 ROSSET, BARNEY and JORDAN, FRED / Evergreen Review No. 98 / $5.95
62498-X ROSSET, PETER and VANDERMEER, JOHN / The Nicaragua Reader / $9.95
13012-7 SADE, MARQUIS DE / The 120 Days of Sodom and Other Writings / $14.95
62045-3 SAVONNA, JEANNETTE L. / Jean Genet / $8.95
62495-5 SCHEFFLER, LINDA / Help Thy Neighbor / $7.95
62438-6 SCHNEEBAUM, TOBIAS / Keep the River on Your Right / $12.50
62009-7 SEGALL, J. PETER / Deduct This Book: How Not to Pay Taxes While Ronald Reagan is President / $6.95
17467-4 SELBY, HUBERT / Last Exit to Brooklyn / $3.95
62040-2 SETO, JUDITH ROBERTS / The Young Actor's Workbook / $8.95
17963-3 SHANK, THEODORE / American Alternative Theater / $12.50
17948-X SHAWN, WALLACE, and GREGORY, ANDRE / My Dinner with Andre / $6.95
62496-3 SIEGAL, FREDERICK, M.D., and MARTA / Aids: The Medical Mystery / $7.95

17887-4 SINGH, KHUSHWANT / Train to Pakistan / $4.50

62446-7 SLOMAN, LARRY / Reefer Madness: Marijuana in America / $8.95

17797-5 SNOW, EDGAR / Red Star Over China / $9.95

17923-4 STEINER, CLAUDE / Healing Alcoholism / $6.95

17866-1 STOPPARD, TOM / Jumpers / $4.95

13033-X STOPPARD, TOM / Rosencrantz and Guildenstern Are Dead / $4.95

17884-X STOPPARD, TOM / Travesties / $3.95

17230-2 SUZUKI, D.T. / Introduction to Zen Buddhism / $11.95

17224-8 SUZUKI, D.T. / Manual of Zen Buddhism / $7.95

17599-9 THELWELL, MICHAEL / The Harder They Come: A Novel about Jamaica / $7.95

13020-8 TOOLE, JOHN KENNEDY / A Confederacy of Dunces / $6.95

62168-9 TUTOLA, AMOS / The Palm-Wine Drunkard / $4.50

62189-1 UNGERER, TOMI / Far Out Isn't Far Enough (Illus.) / $12.95

17211-6 WALEY, ARTHUR / Monkey / $8.95

17207-8 WALEY, ARTHUR / The Way and Its Power: A Study of the Tao Te Ching and Its Place in Chinese Thought / $9.95

17418-6 WATTS, ALAN W. / The Spirit of Zen / $6.95